Work It Out

Clues for Solving
People Problems at Work

Sandra Krebs Hirsh

with Jane A.G. Kise

Davies-Black Publishing
Palo Alto, California

Published by Davies-Black Publishing, a division of CPP, Inc., 3803 East Bayshore Road, Palo Alto, CA 94303; 800-624-1765.

Special discounts on bulk quantities of Davies-Black books are available to corporations, professional associations, and other organizations. For details, contact the Director of Book Marketing and Sales at Davies-Black Publishing, 650-691-9123; fax 650-623-9271.

Myers-Briggs Type Indicator , MBTI, Davies-Black and colophon are registered trademarks of CPP, Inc.

Visit the Davies-Black Publishing web site at www.daviesblack.com.

The chapter opener cartoons by Sally Stockbridge are the property of Sandra Krebs Hirsh and Ken Green. The cartoons in chapter 1 by John Bush are the property of Sandra Krebs Hirsh. The cartoons are available by writing to Sandra Hirsh Consulting, 5000 Nob Hill Drive, Minneapolis, MN 55439.

06 05 04   14 13 12 11 10 9
Printed in the United States of America

Library of Congress Cataloging-in-Publication Data
Hirsh, Sandra Krebs
  Work it out : clues for solving people problems at work / Sandra Krebs
Hirsh with Jane A. G. Kise. — 1st ed.
   p. cm.
  Includes index.
  ISBN 0-89106-088-X
  1. Conflict management. 2. Employees—Psychology. 3. Communication in
management. 4. Interpersonal communication.
  I. Kise, Jane A. G. II. Title.
  HD42.H57 1996
  650.1'3—dc20

                      96-21540

FIRST EDITION
First printing 1996

Praise for
Work It Out

"*Work It Out* is a must read for anyone serious about understanding the creative tension among psychological types. It is idea-rich, entertaining, and immediately helpful, a book that will surely have universal appeal and positively impact organizational productivity."

—Michael Laseter
Organizational Effectiveness Specialist, 3M Company

"Organizations are made up of people, and therefore anything that will contribute to the better functioning of that core resource will have a powerful impact on that organization's bottom line. *Work It Out* is a must read for anyone who wants to make a difference with co-workers, team members, direct reports, and, yes, even bosses."

—Richard J. Chagnon
Group Senior Vice President, Right Associates

"*Work It Out* helps us understand different personality styles in the work environment, so we can move to a higher level of effective communication and create better teams. I highly recommend it!"

—Robbin Brown
District Team Leader, Target Stores

"Far more teams fail because of personality differences than skill deficiencies. I highly recommend *Work It Out* as a key to creating successful teams."

—Irma McIntosh Coleman
Assistant Commissioner, Minnesota Department Of Children, Families, and Learning

"Whether you're a consultant, manager, team member, or an individual contributor, *Work It Out* offers a clear understanding of how personality differences play out in the world of work, with practical suggestions for overcoming these differences to obtain enhanced performance. I highly recommend this book to all those interested in harnessing the power of differences for their organization or their team."

—Steven D. McArthur
Director of Consulting Services, Tennessee Associates International

"The critical capability in today's organizations is the ability to develop partnerships with people. *Work It Out* can help people understand others, honor their differences, and use that understanding to help people develop themselves."

—Susan H. Gebelein
Senior Vice President, Personnel Decisions Inc.,
and author of *Successful Manager's Handbook*

"*Work It Out* is a valuable guide to understanding and working with different types of people. Insightful, practical, and fun, *Work It Out* is a necessary tool in today's work environment for maximizing individual and group effectiveness."

—Duncan McDougall
Director of Strategic Development, The Evangelical Lutheran Good Samaritan Society

"*Work It Out*'s practical insights and conversational writing style let you understand and connect better with the personality types you're teamed with and can make your work life both more pleasant and productive."

—William Rudelius
Professor of Marketing, University of Minnesota

"The real challenge in today's workplace is to achieve a better and more profound understanding of oneself and others and to look upon differences as an enriching source for building teams rather than an almost sure cause for unproductive conflict. *Work It Out* makes this challenge stunningly easy."

—Domien Van Gool
CEO and Founder, BUSINESSWISE International

"*Work It Out* guides us through all the people problems encountered at work—conflicts, misunderstandings, problematic attitudes—weaving stories that demonstrate the use and application of personality type to find clues to and solutions to differences in the workplace."

—Danielle Poirier
Training Director, Team and Management Consultant, Psychometrics Canada

Work It Out

To our husbands and children
who witnessed the two of us hard at work
and who added their enthusiasm to the projects

Contents

Acknowledgments

Sandra would like to acknowledge the following: Leigh and Maureen Bailey, Nicky Bredeson, Susan Brock, John Buchanan, John Bush, Sandra Davis, Ken Green, Sally Stockbridge, and Barbara Tuckner, her colleagues who have shared their type insights over the years; Naomi Quenk, who gave her careful attention to Chapter 7, "The Case of the Lurking Inferior Function"; and all the people represented in this book who were participants in solving the mysteries of working together.

I'm neat!

I'm flexible!

Teaming With Type

Can It Make a Difference for You?

Type Key

If you understand your own style, you can work more effectively with others.

Our second team meeting was worse than the first. Mark kept all his ideas to himself—and then passed them to me in writing two days later, after I'd finalized my plans. Susan took issue with my perfectly logical methodology, saying I'd ignored the needs of the support staff. And Jenna wanted more information on three of the four action items!

I was looking forward to working with Peter, but now I'm not so sure. He just leaps to conclusions—I can't follow his train of thought.

Our workstyles are so complementary; Carolyn addresses all of the details I overlook. And yet, I wish she would be more creative, more forward-thinking. Then we would really be a team!

Individuals are more than just sets of skills, knowledge, and competencies; there is something intangible that brings order, excitement, and unique nuances to each one of us. That intangible is our personality, our bundle of preferences for how we are energized, how we take in information, how we make decisions, and how we choose to relate to the world.

Personality type theory brings a framework to the complex—and sometimes chaotic—interactions between people in the world of work. I am seldom asked to consult with a workplace that is "one big happy family"! Psychological type helps me recognize the clues to the mysteries of missing harmony, spot the underlying causes of lost opportunities, and take the "whodunit" out of the atmosphere of troubled teams, leading to more productive relationships. While one can spend years (as I have!) learning all the nuances and intricacies of each personality type, there are also key factors that can reduce the myriad of clues to a framework of preferences, bringing new levels of understanding to the players involved.

For me, finding those key factors in each new organization with which I work can be like solving a mystery, with the theory of personality type serving as my detective's tool kit. I search for clues that point the way to the personality differences. In each of the case studies in this book, I'll highlight the clues to which I pay attention as we go.

I have seen teams blossom tremendously as the leaders go beyond the simple knowledge of the competencies of the team members to the more complex understanding of their personality types. Generally, treating all members of a team as if they are the same is like trying to herd cats: Not only are the results doubtful, but most team members resent trying to fit a single mold. Understanding people's types allows you to tap into their strengths, discover how you work best together, and minimize unnecessary conflict. Type frequently can be helpful in predicting both the strengths and developmental needs of each personality type, yet provides a positive language for discussion and understanding.

Type Theory

You may seek direct help to determine your personality type by taking the *Myers-Briggs Type Indicator*®(MBTI®) personality inventory. Isabel Myers and her mother, Katharine Briggs, were long-time observers of human differences. Katharine Briggs developed her own four-part framework to study human diversity; however, she found Carl Jung's work *Psychological Types* more complete. Isabel Myers constructed an "indicator" so that Jung's theory could be more widely understood and its theories made more practical. Your human resources department or local community college most likely has the MBTI in stock because it's the most highly used psychological instrument. Or, you can get more information about the MBTI by calling its publisher, Consulting Psychologists Press, at 800-624-1765.

If you find these concepts of type theory intriguing—complementary styles, better problem solving because all factors have been considered, mutual usefulness (effectiveness) of opposites—then let's start by determining the styles most characteristic of yourself and then of others. But before reviewing the clues, I want to be sure you have a clear understanding of the idea of preferences. You will find that you may use aspects of both styles in each of the personality preferences we are about to discuss, but one will be a *preference,* even if it's only *slightly* more preferred.

An analogy may help cement the ideas of this theory of personality preferences developed by Carl Jung. Just as there are in the psyche, there are many sets of two in the physical body. Generally, when there are two in a set (hands, eyes, ears, etc.) one has preference over the other; for example, one eye is for focus while the other is for peripheral vision. The eye preferred for focus varies in people. Some of us use our left eye, others our right. There is no right or wrong here—just difference. In order to view the stars through a telescope, however, it will be important to know which eye you can rely on to do the job.

Let's give you a chance to experience this concept of physical preference. In the spaces below, write your name, address, and phone number with your *nonpreferred* hand. For extra challenge, you can use the second hand of a watch to time yourself. When you are finished, note the quality of your output.

_____

_____

How did it feel? Most people will say it felt awkward, clumsy, uncomfortable, even unnatural. Others mention that it took time and concentration and that the output looks like childhood penmanship.

Now let's see what happens when you write your name, address, and phone number in the spaces below with your *preferred* hand. Notice the clock if you want the extra challenge, and proceed.

_____

_____

Most people say this experience is comfortable, easy, and flowing—it feels natural. There's even a flair, a distinctiveness that differentiates one's name (one's signature) from that of others. "It's me!" many exclaim. This type of physical preference is mirrored by psychological preferences. The source of these preferences is unknown, although evidence is mounting that one's psychological preferences are as innate as one's preference for an eye to focus, or a foot to step forward with, at any given time. While we believe one's psychological preferences are innate, they are not immutable. Factors such as one's parents, family, educational experience, and functional training may affect the expression of one's true nature.

Now go back and look at your handwriting samples. Where is the quality higher? Which took less time? What would happen to your learning and performance if you were to work for the next six months with your nonpreferred hand? As you started this task, it would be frustrating and slow. You might want to give up and reach for your pen with your preferred hand—"home sweet home." That's how it can feel psychologically—tiring and frustrating when we use our nonpreferred psychological preferences all the time at our work.

To add to these outcomes, one may also feel a loss of self-esteem, which is a very important commodity at work. Ask yourself if you would like to work for or with or manage someone with low self-esteem and its cost becomes readily apparent. There are, however, some tasks for each of us that don't come naturally. What's more, when I get stuck with such an assignment, I'm usually sitting next to someone who *instinctively* does it right from the start! Too much of this sort of comparison and I'm exhausted and discouraged. How much better to find work and a lifestyle that support using one's strengths and preferences—where one can do what comes naturally.

Now on to the clues to understanding your unique style and that of others. Think about what you do most easily, comfortably, and naturally, and turn off ideas of what you *should* say as you respond to the clues.

Clues for Extraversion (E) and Introversion (I)— The Source of Energy

People differ in how they draw energy to themselves. Some of us prefer to work with people and things, welcoming interactions with others and the outer environment. People in this group, known as those with a preference for Extraversion, prefer to do their thinking aloud in the company of others. Mix Extraverts on a team with Introverts who tend to enjoy working alone or with one or two other individuals, and watch the misunderstandings. One group claims, "I can't concentrate!" while the other complains, "I can't tell what they are thinking!" Through understanding, each can give the other space to operate as they do best. Think about yourself. Which of the following do you tend to do?

EXTRAVERSION

➤ Talk it out

➤ Extend into your environment by reaching out to others

➤ Act first, think later

➤ Like variety and action

➤ Prefer to talk face-to-face

➤ Frequently hear that you're not available because you're out and about

INTROVERSION

➤ Think it through

➤ Defend against your environment by stepping back, sometimes by avoiding others

➤ Think first, act later

➤ Like concentration and reflection

➤ Prefer to use memos, e-mail, and other written forms of communication

➤ Frequently hear that even though you are present, others see you as difficult to read or perhaps remote and hard to know

These clues are just that, clues. As you read chapter 2, you will see an example of Extraversion and Introversion at work. Which clues seem most like you? Extraversion or Introversion?

Clues for Sensing (S) and Intuition (N)— Gathering Information

Next, let's look at what you pay attention to in the competing world of mass (and some may say over-) communication. Each of us has developed a preference for how we like to take in and process information. Sensing individuals seek information that can be verified by the five senses. They

like things to be accurate, detailed, factual, and practical. Think of how different this is from people with a preference for Intuition: gathering information by using insights, associations, relationships, and connections. While the first group concentrates on current reality, the second group is dreaming about what could be.

Those who focus on the specifics are called Sensors. Those who focus on the big picture are called Intuitives. Which of the following do you tend to do?

SENSING	**INTUITION**
➤ Avoid fabrications and generalities regarding things	➤ Overlook details, lose focus when things are too "spelled out"
➤ Value accuracy and precision	➤ Value insights and analogies
➤ Relish the present	➤ Anticipate the future
➤ Let the facts pile up to find the trends	➤ Generalize from one fact or happening to larger meanings
➤ Let experience be your guide	➤ Let imagination and ideas be your guide
➤ Want to know the practical applications or results	➤ Want to know additional uses or possible innovations

Which do you prefer, Sensing or Intuition? Remember, you can gain more awareness about your patterns by reading chapter 3, which deals with the relationship between Sensing and Intuition at work.

Both groups have much to offer each other. Where would new ideas be without the practical foundations to implement them? Where would quality production be without forward-looking products to meet new demands? Yet these differences in how we perceive all too frequently lead to conflict, not synergy.

Clues for Thinking (T) and Feeling (F)— How We Make Decisions

After gathering information, as we all do by either Sensing or Intuition, we need a way to organize that information, to draw some rational conclusions about it, or to put it into categories. We prefer to do this in one of two ways—either through Thinking or Feeling. These are our decision-making processes. But people differ dramatically on what they view as a *rational* decision-making process. Perhaps you've heard conversations like this: "I *think* mine is a perfectly logical solution." "Well, I don't *feel* that way at all!"

Some of us are Thinkers, preferring an analytical, objective, and linear approach to decision making. Thinkers like to weigh the pros and cons of each alternative and find flaws in advance.

An equally rational but diametrically opposed process is used by those with a preference for Feeling. Feelers consider the impact of a decision on themselves, on others within their immediate environment and organization, and on their deeply held values. They proceed after subjectively studying motivations and the nature of people.

Several clues as well as the case study in chapter 4 can tell you which is most like you. When you are trying to make a decision, do you:

THINKING	**FEELING**
➤ Weigh the pros and cons	➤ Sort through your values
➤ Want to be logical	➤ Want to have a harmonious outcome
➤ Seek to find the truth, influenced by objective reasoning	➤ Seek to find the most important, influenced by personal information

➤ Concern yourself with the underlying principles behind a decision

➤ Concern yourself with the impact the decision may have on people

➤ Tend toward skepticism and controversy

➤ Tend toward acceptance and tolerance

➤ Care that flaws are discovered, sharing them with others in an effort to "care for" them

➤ Prefer not to critique others but rather to find an appreciative comment

It doesn't take much imagination to think of possible conflicts between Thinkers and Feelers working together on issues such as downsizing, promotions, or even space utilization. But businesses suffer when they run solely on Thinking or solely on Feeling—both styles are needed for effectiveness (Thinking) and collegiality or trust (Feeling).

Clues for Judging (J) and Perceiving (P)— How We Choose to Live

Finally, we differ on how we prefer to live: according to plan or open to the moment. Those with a preference for Judging tend to plan their work and work their plan. They enjoy having matters settled and like to make decisions quickly. Equally valid is the preference for Perceiving, individuals who enjoy the process of gathering information more than the process of coming to a conclusion. They are likely to be flexible and respond in the moment as a situation warrants. Check through these clues. Do you tend to:

JUDGING

➤ Plan your work and work your plan

➤ Schedule out your time, settling dates and arrangements

➤ Make decisions quickly, putting a stop to seeking new information

➤ Find surprises or interruptions an annoyance

➤ Want to have things settled in advance

➤ Focus on tasks and timetables

PERCEIVING

➤ Solve problems as they arise

➤ Leave scheduling options open as long as possible

➤ Enjoy considering new information, putting off final decisions

➤ Find surprises or interruptions a welcome distraction

➤ Want to face a few challenges with spontaneity

➤ Focus on processes and options

Assign an employee who has already decided which marketing strategy is best to work for a manager who wants to keep *both* marketing strategies open and watch the frustration level rise. Yet consider how they can create balance: The Judging types tend to ensure that deadlines are met and the Perceiving types tend to lend flexibility where it is needed. To learn more about this preference, read chapter 5.

What patterns seem most like you? Do you prefer Extraversion or Introversion? Sensing or Intuition? Thinking or Feeling? Judging or Perceiving? Remember, if you have trouble deciding, think about the experience in writing using both hands. Choose the preference where you feel most natural, act without much thought, experience it as easy, and do so quickly. Forget what might be required of you by family or work or the task you need to do—at least for now. You *are* able to use both, just as you could write with both hands, but for most of us, one will be preferred. So, are the clues leading you to believe that you prefer E or I, S or N, T or F, J or P? Write your chosen letters below:

———————   ———————   ———————   ———————

The eight different preferences lead to sixteen personality types. You may be wondering if trying to solve such a complex mystery is worth the bother. Well, if gaining insights into the personality types of your team members or co-workers sounds overwhelming, the following overview of what you can do with those insights may give you cause to go on.

➤ *Identify and reduce sources of conflict.* For example, if one person prefers to talk about everything out loud (Extraversion) and the other one likes peace and space alone to reflect (Introversion), they can negotiate about their public and private space.

➤ *Recognize strengths and blind spots of teams.* Knowing what a team habitually prefers and, as importantly, habitually overlooks, can help that team strategize to be more effective. For example, a group dominated by Intuitors may learn to develop checklists to ensure that facts and details, the province of Sensing, are not overlooked.

➤ *Clarify the fit between managers and their direct reports.* For example, when a manager with a preference for Thinking (who may tend to give praise only after a task is completed or exceeded) manages another with a preference for Feeling (who prefers to receive praise from the *start* of a project), problems can arise. Understanding each other can lead them to manage their different perspectives on praise and recognition productively.

➤ *Get value from diversity.* Leaving the most important for last, type theory emphasizes the positive contributions of each preference. Teaming a Judger who prefers to plan everything with a Perceiver who enjoys spontaneity can ensure that a plan is in place *and* that implementing the plan will be enjoyable.

We all know it would be absurd to form an investigative team made entirely of forensics experts or cryptologists; however, in business the tendency is often to choose teammates who view issues from perspectives that are similar to ours. Type theory values diversity.

The Type Table

Let's build a type table with all sixteen types on it. Isabel Myers and others, in putting this table together, also gave us some mnemonics to remember the placement of the sixteen types. So if you are

➤ An Extravert—E's like to move around, so they are at the *foot* of the table
➤ An Introvert—I's like time to think, so they are at the *head* of the table

Introversion
Extraversion

➤ A Sensor—S's like "left brain" activities (careful use of facts), so they are at the *left*
➤ An Intuitor—N's like "right brain" activities (meanings and hunches), so they are at the *right*

Sensing	Intuition

➤ A Thinker—T's like to stand apart from their decisions and be objective, so they are on the *outside* columns of the table

➤ A Feeler—F's like to please and consider others in their decisions, so they are *next* to each other in the *middle*

Thinking	Feeling	Feeling	Thinking

➤ A Judger—J's like structure and order, so they are in the *top and bottom* rows, providing structure for the table

➤ A Perceptive—P's like flexibility and adaptability, so they are in the *middle* rows of the table, just *enjoying* it.

Judging
Perceiving
Perceiving
Judging

This gives the table its structure; can you find the box for your type in this type table?

ISTJ	ISFJ	INFJ	INTJ
ISTP	ISFP	INFP	INTP
ESTP	ESFP	ENFP	ENTP
ESTJ	ESFJ	ENFJ	ENTJ

The Type Descriptions

Now that you've found your place on the table, let's tell you some more clues about the particular combination of preferences you have—your psychological type. This information is presented in Type Chart 1.

If you've been undecided until now, does the chart help? If not, ask a spouse, friend, or colleague to read the clues for each pair of preferences (Extraversion–Introversion, etc.) and to look at the chart to find the type that describes you best.

The Four-Part Framework

Now you can take the many possible clues and come up with lots of possible scenarios. And guess what—type-writers (no pun intended) do just that! One of the key aspects of psychological type is the combination of the Sensing or Intuition preference with the Thinking or Feeling preference. These possible combinations, ST, SF, NF, and NT, are called the *functions* because they say so much about how we function in life.[1] You will see an example of this in chapter 6 on the four-function framework. These pairings are useful in looking at communication patterns, organizational cultures, and teamwork. Here are some clues to determine your functional type:

	ST	SF	NF	NT
Are you most likely described as	Practical and logical	Sympathetic and friendly	Enthusiastic and insightful	Logical and ingenious
Is the work you prefer to do	Tangible and useful	Social and personal	Creative and people-oriented	Theoretical and complex

Here are the positions of the four-function framework on the type table:

ST	SF	NF	NT
ISTJ	ISFJ	INFJ	INTJ
ISTP	ISFP	INFP	INTP
ESTP	ESFP	ENFP	ENTP
ESTJ	ESFJ	ENFJ	ENTJ

Type Chart 1

ISTJ	ISFJ	INFJ	INTJ
• Leads by bringing order and efficiency to meetings and tasks • Influences by using logical arguments backed by specifics and realism • Focus is on facts, details, and results	• Leads by encouraging others in tasks that suit them best • Influences by ensuring that information is accurate, things are organized • Focus is on setting priorities based on the needs of people	• Leads by encouraging others to cooperate in working toward a vision • Influences by being creative and dedicated • Focus is on creative insight and strong values	• Leads by setting the course to make an idea become reality • Influences by intellectual depth and dedication • Focus is on designing systems, changing the status quo
ISTP	**ISFP**	**INFP**	**INTP**
• Leads by quietly setting an example • Influences, when asked, by having all the needed information ready • Focus is on finding the logical ways to get things done	• Leads by encouraging others to cooperate • Influences by example, helping others pursue their ideals • Focus is on the practical care of people	• Leads by promoting harmonious teams where each person is valued • Influences by highlighting common ideas and new possibilities • Focus is group consensus and shared values	• Leads by convincing others of the merit and logic of their ideals • Influences by providing in-depth knowledge and analysis • Focus is on logical, intellectual insights to problems
ESTP	**ESFP**	**ENFP**	**ENTP**
• Leads by finding the most efficient way to work together • Influences by establishing logical processes, pursuing them with enthusiasm • Focus is on action, taking care of problems as they arise	• Leads by encouraging the contributions of others • Influences by enthusiasm and enjoyment of the tasks at hand • Focus is on creating an upbeat atmosphere for people	• Leads by creating a vision, helping people see their potential • Influences by listening to and incorporating the ideas of others • Focus is on exploring all the possibilities	• Leads by developing novel strategies for new enterprises • Influences by going the extra mile • Focus is on innovative models, conquering challenges
ESTJ	**ESFJ**	**ENFJ**	**ENTJ**
• Leads by planning, providing direction, and assigning responsibilities • Influences by modeling the standards and commitment they expect from others • Focus is on structuring tasks so goals are met	• Leads by paying attention to the needs of others and making sure they feel important • Influences by being conscientious and hard-working • Focus is on getting things organized so that people's personal needs are met	• Leads by facilitating, helping others plan and cooperate to meet goals • Influences by clarifying processes by which goals can be met • Focus is on encouraging others in building consensus	• Leads by presenting a vision, then energizing and directing others to meet it • Influences by objectively analyzing ideas, setting goals • Focus is on making decisions

The Dominant Function

Now that you've gotten this far, let's really challenge you. One of the biggest mysteries of psychological type is what hierarchy our two middle letters (S or N and T or F) take in our lives. One of these four functions, S, N, T, or F, is developed earliest in our lives and takes charge of who we are. It's called our *dominant,* like a dominant force. It uses the other three letters in its support. We rely on our dominant function the most, so the type of work we do should reflect this foremost function. If our work does not reflect its use, then we should give our dominant function its way in our personal life. Furthermore, our dominant function is our greatest gift in solving problems.

Some characteristics of the dominant functions are:[2]

SENSING DOMINANTS
It has to make sense—
Stability

➤ Point out pertinent facts, especially those from their past experience

➤ Have the right thing in the right place at the right time; keep the essentials on hand by adopting realistic schedules and time frames

INTUITIVE DOMINANTS
It has to appeal to the
imagination—Change

➤ Recognize new avenues and possibilities and develop ingenious insights

➤ Conjure up plans for future contingencies with a spirit of optimism

THINKING DOMINANTS
It has to be logical—
Effectiveness

➤ Analyze a situation's or person's strengths and weaknesses and point out flaws in advance

➤ Move from past to present to future in an objective, straightforward way

FEELING DOMINANTS
It has to consider people's
aspirations—Integrity

➤ Anticipate the needs of those involved and how they feel

➤ Monitor and hold the organization and team to its values while encouraging everyone's contribution

Here are a few clues about how our dominant function works on problem solving:[3]

SENSING

➤ How is the problem best defined? What exactly are the facts?

➤ What costs are incurred— financial, emotional, and so on?

INTUITION

➤ How does this problem relate to the ways or patterns through which similar problems are solved?

➤ What interpretations can be made from the information or lack thereof?

THINKING

➤ What are the pros and cons and interesting alternatives? Why are they so?

➤ What is the relationship of cause to effect?

FEELING

➤ What are people's feelings concerning this, and can different views be accommodated?

➤ How does this affect me and the people I care about? How much does the outcome matter?

If you want to identify your dominant function and the rest of your hierarchy, use Type Chart 2. It has the same type table structure we have discussed—I's at the head, E's at the foot, and so on—and shows the hierarchy for the sixteen types.

Now, the dominant function is balanced by the second function on your list. It's called your *auxiliary* function. If your dominant wants to get information (either through Sensing or Intuition), your auxiliary will want to organize that information (through Thinking or Feeling) and vice versa: If your dominant is Thinking or Feeling, then your auxiliary will want to add information, either Sensing or Intuition, to your decisions. The auxiliary usually develops when a person is in adolescence or early adulthood.

We don't know as much about your third function, which is the preference opposite to your auxiliary. It usually develops in adulthood. If your auxiliary is Sensing, then your third function will be Intuition, and vice versa; and if your auxiliary is Thinking, then your third function will be Feeling, and vice versa. The third function is not as large a part of your conscious mental activity as your dominant and auxiliary. It's more elusive—getting mysterious, no?

Type Chart 2

ISTJ	ISFJ	INFJ	INTJ
1. Sensing	1. Sensing	1. Intuition	1. Intuition
2. Thinking	2. Feeling	2. Feeling	2. Thinking
3. Feeling	3. Thinking	3. Thinking	3. Feeling
4. Intuition	4. Intuition	4. Sensing	4. Sensing
ISTP	**ISFP**	**INFP**	**INTP**
1. Thinking	1. Feeling	1. Feeling	1. Thinking
2. Sensing	2. Sensing	2. Intuition	2. Intuition
3. Intuition	3. Intuition	3. Sensing	3. Sensing
4. Feeling	4. Thinking	4. Thinking	4. Feeling
ESTP	**ESFP**	**ENFP**	**ENTP**
1. Sensing	1. Sensing	1. Intuition	1. Intuition
2. Thinking	2. Feeling	2. Feeling	2. Thinking
3. Feeling	3. Thinking	3. Thinking	3. Feeling
4. Intuition	4. Intuition	4. Sensing	4. Sensing
ESTJ	**ESFJ**	**ENFJ**	**ENTJ**
1. Thinking	1. Feeling	1. Feeling	1. Thinking
2. Sensing	2. Sensing	2. Intuition	2. Intuition
3. Intuition	3. Intuition	3. Sensing	3. Sensing
4. Feeling	4. Thinking	4. Thinking	4. Feeling

The Inferior Function

Even more mysterious to all of us is our fourth function—the one that is least preferred. When you are functioning normally, it's pretty much hidden from you—unconscious. It is with this function that mistakes often occur because we haven't been able or didn't make a conscious effort to tap its gifts. However, in midlife and beyond, many of us find the fourth function begins to claim our attention, though still a small part. At midlife or beyond:

SENSORS, who naturally know and appreciate the here and now . . .	Begin to seek out new and untried futures
INTUITORS, who do best at envisioning the future . . .	Begin to enjoy the here and now, paying attention, perhaps for the first time, to what *is*
THINKERS, who keep logic and objectivity at the forefront . . .	Begin to focus on values, relationships with people, and service to others
FEELERS, who know best what matters to people . . .	Begin to look for intellectual or scholarly pursuits

However, when we are tired, anxious, or under stress *or* when we've been too one-sided in our type, acting as an overwhelming ISTP, for example, then we may experience some internal self-correcting to counteract this one-sidedness. Then the fourth function, now feeling very much like the *inferior* function it is, emerges. And emerge it does! We don't act like our usual selves but like a caricature of our opposite type—from ISTP to ENFJ but with a vengeance (a bad "type" day).

Thus, for a Sensing dominant person (ISTJ, ISFJ, ESTP, and ESFP), the usually inferior Intuition becomes predominant. When this happens, the Sensors tune into insights or future possibilities—all of which look bad or are filled with doom. The Intuition dominant person (INTJ, INFJ, ENTP, and ENFP) now sees the details but can become obsessed with those details.

The other two dominant functions don't escape from the inferior function, either. The Thinking dominants (ISTP, INTP, ESTJ, and ENTJ) become maudlin Feelers—overly emotional and self-pitying when their inferior function takes over. And finally, the Feeling dominants (ISFP, INFP, ESFJ, and ENFJ) become tyrannical Thinkers—cold, calculating, and domineering to an extreme as they critique others. Quite a mystery! So the next time people say, "What's gotten into you?" or "You're not acting like yourself!" pause and reflect on whether you've been out of balance either by being too much of your type—the overwhelming ISTP, for example—or by giving way suddenly to your fourth function.

Leadership and Psychological Type— A Word to the Wise

In the world of business leadership, four types seem to emerge worldwide. These are the four types who like to take charge: ISTJ, INTJ, ESTJ, and ENTJ. Each of these four types (check the table above) have Feeling as their third or fourth function. What gets overlooked in these business set-tings, then, are the gifts of Feeling: values, interpersonal relationships, and concern for people and their needs and wants. Instead, the focus can easily become an unbalanced pursuit of the product at any cost to people or the environment. You can see that when we ignore just one of these four functions (S, N, T, or F), we're in danger of making *big* mistakes.

If you want to avoid those *big* mistakes, look at your type's order of pref-erences and do your darnedest to factor in each preference in a thorough and systematic way when you are facing a major decision or a critical prob-lem. Realize that your dominant and auxiliary functions will come easily (you *preferred* them) and that the third and especially the fourth functions will be less natural but well worth the effort when you view the results.

How This Book Can Help

If you are in search of more on the *theory* of type, check the appendixes and the list of additional resources, because the rest of the book is a hands-on guide to practical *applications*, stories to help demystify type.

The next six chapters present case studies of companies that improved performance by growing in their understanding of personality type. The cases represent a wide array of businesses: growing companies, small con-sulting firms, large manufacturing firms, and partnerships. All the names and industries have been disguised (to protect the innocent—and me, too!) and in all cases are composites of two or more organizations. But the plot, the motives, the "smoking gun" of what actually happened is there—many times, it's the "same old thing" in team-building work.

In each case, there are guides to help you choose the characters with whom you identify most closely, that is, who have personality types similar to yours. Although the scenario and the problems may not be an exact match for your situation, as we present the interventions and the team-building or coaching techniques that guided their process, you will see applications for your personal and work life. Each chapter includes a Type Takeaway: specific clues to implement the general principles in your situation.

To get the most out of this book:

➤ Figure out your own type.
➤ Choose the characters most closely identified with you or someone you know.
➤ Consider how you would react: What aspects would cause you most concern?

➤ Use the Type Takeaway section to apply the principles to yourself and your team or organization. How could these understandings bring about better teamwork? Better understanding? Better interpersonal relationships and better productivity and fun?

And as you read, remember:

➤ Psychological type isn't a box others put you into but rather a way to understand your preferences and those of others.

➤ Psychological type doesn't explain everything. Within each of the sixteen personality types is an infinite variety of personalities, each unique and valuable. No two ISFPs are *exactly* alike—there's still lots of room for individuals.

➤ Type alone cannot solve all of your organization's problems. However, it can lead to a deeper understanding of the value of each team member and provide a logical model for why people do and say the things they do.

➤ No one type is better than another—each one has its unique combination of assets and—without some effort—its blind spots.

➤ Psychological type should not be used for selecting your work, life partner, or teammates because it looks at natural preferences, not abilities.

So, let's put on our detective hats, grab those magnifying glasses, and get busy investigating how you can work with type!

The Case of the Communication Conundrum

The Extraversion–Introversion Dimension

Type Key

If you know why you drive others up a wall, perhaps you can help them down.

Have you ever wondered why someone on your team couldn't keep quiet or why another one wouldn't speak up? This chapter uses as an illustration a team that had, as most offices do, people with a preference for Extraversion and people with a preference for Introversion. This means they are energized in different ways for the tasks at hand—one group (those with a preference for Extraversion) wants to talk things out while the other (those with a preference for Introversion) wants to reflect in private first. The Extraverts want to explore ideas through conversation, processing new information as they go, and the Introverts don't really want to voice their opinions until they thoroughly understand their own position. Put them on a team together and it is easy for one group to misinterpret the other's motives or behaviors.

Adding to the confusion, people in the United States seem to have a love affair with Extraversion, starting with our perceptions of children. Some teachers reward rapid responses to their questions, often favoring those who participate actively, and may even think that those who *don't* speak up are slow learners. Many parents worry less about their gregarious children than they do about their quiet, perhaps shy children. Work relationships often follow suit. If someone is quietly sitting at his or her desk (doing "thinking work"), others may ask, "Is that person working?"

Office space arrangements often reflect Extraversion or Introversion. Think of a stockbroker or realty office (these tend to be more Extraverted than Introverted) with their constant phoning and interaction as opposed to a university professor's or scientist's office (these tend to be more Introverted than Extraverted) where full walls, doors, and Do Not Disturb signs defend the occupants against the outer world.

Bookstores often have more titles about how to speak up and be noticed than about how to be quiet and think. Dale Carnegie's *How to Win Friends and Influence People* is an enduring bestseller. In contrast, books on solitude, reflection, or journal writing don't generally fly off the shelves. People tend to be more concerned with how *others* view them than with how *they* view themselves. Even though the data on frequency of the E–I preferences in the United States indicate that these two preferences are evenly distributed, Extraverted energy makes us take notice.

Extraverts are often rewarded for being "go-getters," action-oriented, energetic, enthusiastic people who are willing to voice their opinions, while in some ways the culture seems to penalize the Introvert's way of being—you may not be noticed if you choose to think before you speak, select your words carefully, prefer to work with ideas and things in peace and quiet, or study a matter in depth rather than broadly. These cultural biases can further heighten misunderstandings between Extraverts and Introverts.

Type Story: Commerce Bank, N. A.

Cast of Characters

Luis, Head of Operation Commerce Call	E S T P
Systems Design Subteam	6 Introverts and 1 Extravert
Marketing Subteam	1 Introvert and 6 Extraverts

At Commerce Bank, the misunderstandings were halting a team in its tracks. Commerce Bank had set up a special task force to design and implement a telephone banking system that would allow consumer banking customers to conduct almost all transactions and receive information without using teller or bank officer services. Because the project needed both superior technological design and persuasive marketing to succeed, the best and the brightest had been pulled from many areas of the corporation to work together to successfully launch within twelve months Operation Commerce Call. Teamwork between the technical and marketing people was crucial to meeting the deadline. The general feeling was that more market share could be gained if the product were introduced sooner, before the other major banks in town had similar systems in place.

I received a call from the vice president of new product development for Commerce Bank. "Our new product SWAT team is in trouble. The Marketing people cannot get the information they need out of our Systems people. The designers don't seem to understand the fact that if they don't communicate both their needs and achievements, Marketing won't know what it is they are about to sell. Right now, the Systems people feel sorry for themselves, thinking that the senior managers only cater to the needs of Marketing. Well, we know what Marketing needs—they *tell* us."

I asked her to describe the Systems team and she said, "They are typical 'Midwest nice' and don't like to toot their own horn. The head of Commerce Call is fed up with Systems' lack of communication. You know, Luis was selected to head this project because he is smart, energetic, and he's been in Consumer Banking, Marketing, and was in Systems at another bank when they developed their first phone transfer system. I handpicked him because he handles facts and details so well and he has good communication skills; I thought he could win over the Systems managers. I also wanted a risktaker and promoter who could keep this project on track— but Luis is floundering a bit as he tries to get them to act. What do you suggest?"

"Have you talked to Luis and the Systems people about the importance of communicating as their work progresses?"

"The problem actually goes a bit deeper, which is why I'd like your coaching. The Systems managers *are* impressive—but their communication style is unimpressive. Their presentations are so lackluster that senior management misjudges what they really have to offer and the level of resources they need to finish the project. They say they don't want to be like the 'overconfident Marketing loudmouths,' but this is one project where the two sides have to talk. Otherwise either Marketing will sell something that can't actually be designed or Systems will build something our customers won't want to use."

We decided that I would hold meetings with each side of the team—Marketing and Systems. (You know a team is in trouble when the sides are already chosen!) I also set up a private meeting with Luis.

Type Clue

It sounded to me as if Commerce Bank had an Extraversion–Introversion conundrum. Marketing positions are often filled by Extraverts who enjoy the challenge of promoting their products. Many technical areas are populated by Introverts who have an in-depth knowledge of their area and enjoy thinking through their ideas on their own. The fact that Luis wanted to see action hinted to me that he had a preference for Extraversion. Luis's action orientation, if pushed too hard on Systems, could cause the Introverts to begin a quiet insurrection.

Before meeting with Luis, I read his résumé, which was very impressive, showing his quick climb to the top of another financial firm before coming to Commerce Bank. Several projects for which he had served as cross-functional leader were listed. He seemed a perfect fit for the job at hand. I also reviewed his MBTI results, and when we met he confirmed his preferences for ESTP. I expected him to appear energetic, direct, and willing to talk and take charge. He didn't disappoint me in this regard. However, he was also a bit nervous as our meeting began, almost as if preoccupied.

After introductions, I asked him to tell me about himself and this project. Luis said, "You know, I handpicked nearly everyone on the team and we have a guarantee from the executive committee that this project has priority for company resources, so it's a great assignment. I like to approach new products such as Commerce Call directly by finding out the specifics—let's see what the customers want, here's what Commerce Bank is capable of doing, and then let's get going. I do my best work when I can think out loud and engage others in the process. I told this team that while the task at hand may seem like an outrageous goal, it only makes it all the more fun to meet it and beat it.

"The Marketing team is on the same wavelength with me. They present their findings to me at our regular meetings—I'd rather *hear* a report than read a report. That way we can interact about the details right away. With their continual status updates, I know right where they're at in determining the needs of our end users. Some of our consumer bankers say we'll never get our conservative customers to lessen their dependence on our teller lines, but that's the kind of challenge I like—all the data I have shows this is the way banking will be done in the future. And we're making great progress. Marketing has already held several customer focus groups. These gave us lots of data for determining the kind of system that will get used."

Type Clue

Luis moved about in his career seeking breadth rather than depth. He seemed to understand the Marketing team members (generally Marketing is more Extraverted) better than the Systems team members (generally more Introverted) and placed value on Marketing's visible, quick start on the project. He also liked face-to-face conversations and meetings; this is quite characteristic of Extraverts—something I well understand because I also prefer to talk out my ideas and find that interaction with others improves the quality of these ideas.

Luis continued, "But as I mention systems . . . Ah, the Systems folks are a different story."

"Tell me about your relationship with the Systems people," I said.

"Well, if I manage to get them away from their offices for team meetings, I have to almost force them to participate. They don't share enough information to suit me. When Marketing states a customer need, I want Systems' reaction. Instead, I end up continually hounding them for their ideas."

"Don't they speak up?"

"Heck, no," he said. " I know they must be thinking about something, but I rarely get any of them to talk. Sometimes one of them will challenge me— but I want *lots* of challenge and discussion in order to find out what works and what doesn't work with this new product. Marketing comes to the meetings ready to accomplish something, but Systems . . . Systems just sits there. Well, that's not true either. At the meetings, they just follow my lead even when I go off on a tangent. If the tangent's to the left, they look left. If it's to the right, they look right. I think if I said, 'Stand up,' they'd stand and stay standing until I told them to sit down! Why don't they challenge me and Marketing more; ask us why we're doing things the way we are? Questions bring out better ideas."

Luis mused, "I wonder what could possibly be going on in their heads. When there's so much going on with this project, how can they help but talk about it? I almost have to force them to attend team meetings and then they sit there in their own worlds. And they're ready to leave before

I've finished talking through everything! Once I almost locked the doors to make them stay until they'd heard me through and given me feedback."

Type Clue

Luis was clearly on a roll about Systems, not realizing just how differently Extraverts and Introverts operate. Now I knew where to focus. Often, if Introverts have not had time to mull over a new idea, they are hesitant to voice their thoughts about it. To others, it may seem as if they have no opinions, but in reality they are in the process of formulating the right thing to say, which they tend to share only when they believe they are ready ("No idea before its time . . .").

"What would happen if you gave specific topics for Systems to prepare in advance of the meetings? That way they'd be ready to go."

"I've tried! When I give Systems an assignment, it feels like it falls into a deep, dark hole. I follow up and they are definitely working at their desks quietly by themselves, but I don't know what they are working *on*."

"Do you ask Systems for progress reports like Marketing provides?"

"Oh, I do all right, and they often say, 'Well this is what I just finished and I'll get back to you on the rest.' Then they send me a memo or e-mail about their progress."

Type Clue

A typical problem among Introverts and Extraverts is their differing preferred communication styles. Introverts like to see their thoughts in writing where each point can be checked for clarity. Luis found this frustrated his brainstorming style.

"What's wrong with that?" I asked.

"Well, I don't like memos and e-mail. We work right across the hall from each other. If they'd come in and talk to me, we could interact about what they're currently working on. I'm certainly not going to e-mail my questions back to them! I like to communicate face-to-face; passing memos drives me up the wall. You know, each person in Systems acts like a one-man band."

"Why do you say that?"

"Well, they're all like Lone Rangers who each want to solve their own technical problems independently. We are supposed to be a *team,* not fourteen individuals working by themselves in their own space and place! If we don't hear from each other, the pieces of Commerce Call will never fit together."

I asked Luis if he knew anything about the psychological type of the people on the team.

"I know everyone had an individual MBTI interpretation before. People were told to save their results because we might use them in the future. It seems to me that many of the people I chose for Systems were more on the Introverted side—certainly more Introverted than I am. I suppose there's a potential mismatch in styles here."

"Could be," I said, trying not to smile. "Would you like to have any input to my team-building approach?"

"I think you should still work with the Marketing and Systems groups separately, using the MBTI as data. I remember that in the past the MBTI gave us words we could use to work through problems."

I suggested, "Once I've met with the two groups, we could then hold a full team meeting. Both groups can ask questions of the other and discuss what each side needs to do to work better with you and to get Commerce Call online. Then everyone from both camps can say what they need to know and do to work better with each other."

"Sounds like a good idea to me. I guess I *could* push that e-mail button on my PC and let everyone know our plans," he said with a grin.

Luis decided to start the process *without delay,* so he polled the team and within a few days he called me with each person's MBTI results.

Type Clue

Once they've decided a course of action, ESTPs *act.*

The type preferences of the Commerce Call team were distributed as follows:

SYSTEMS—7 PEOPLE

➤ ISTJ (1)

➤ INFJ (1)

➤ INTJ (3)

➤ INTP (1)

➤ ENTP (1)

MARKETING—7 PEOPLE

➤ INFJ (1)

➤ ESTP (Luis)

➤ ESTJ (2)

➤ ENFJ (2)

➤ ENTJ (1)

Systems: six Introverts and one Extravert. Marketing: six Extraverts and one Introvert. The split on the Extraversion–Introversion dimension was as obvious as I had suspected. I decided to start first with the Marketing team. I was fairly certain that they would for the most part echo Luis's sentiments about the team and I thought Systems might be more comfortable speaking up if they knew they were having the last say.

The Marketing session proved to be a lot of fun. Joking and verbal quips flew back and forth. That everyone enjoyed each other's company was demonstrated by their humor, often at one another's expense. They also were very obviously excited about the progress they had made on Commerce Call and for the most part were pleased to be a part of the project. They voiced the same concerns Luis had about not being sure of the progress Systems had made. We talked about their relationship with Luis. Before the meeting ended, they generated two lists for me: one about what Marketing needed from Systems and the other listing what Systems needed to know about Marketing. The first was their blueprint for discussion if Commerce Call were to be launched successfully:

➤ You are doing too much preliminary work—we want to see some action!
➤ We want immediate responses from Systems. We need time to create an image in the end user's mind of what Commerce Call will mean both as a time-saver and security device. Until we know what Systems can produce, we can't start the campaign. And none of us wants to be caught overselling the product because we didn't have the specs in advance.
➤ We'd like to dialogue about the most crucial aspects of this product from both the technical and the customer sides so we appear more knowledgeable in our marketing and sales efforts—and so we don't crash the Gantt chart.
➤ We need to get to know you better both personally and professionally.

The list of what Marketing wanted Systems to know about them:

➤ We want to discuss the customers' ideas with you as soon as possible so we can better develop Commerce Call.
➤ We like interruptions—they fuel our creativity. Come over and talk anytime we're here. Because we're often out with customers, though, please understand that being away from our desks is a major part of our job.
➤ Remember that what you hear us say is usually not our last word on things—we're only talking to find out what we think. Give us your reactions as soon as possible so we can rethink—out loud of course!
➤ We've got our eyes on the end result. Let's find a way to have fun as a team getting there.

When I met with the Systems team the following day the meeting had a decidedly different feel to it. The session was not as noisy as Marketing's was. The Systems team's quiet camaraderie and shared humor was a contrast to the marketers' almost superficial joviality.

Type Clue

Extraverts often enjoy working on a team, seeing it as a social environment where being with the group satisfies the Extraverts' needs to belong and to express themselves. Even when on teams, Introverts prefer to "own" their piece of the project, working on it alone or occasionally with input from another. Introverts enjoy team meetings if they are infrequent. They like to know the purpose of the meeting in advance so they can come prepared. When these conditions are met, Introverts view meetings as a chance to pool knowledge with their colleagues.

When I asked the Systems team what kind of work environment allowed them to be most productive, after a short pause one of them said, "Well, not this one! If they'd get rid of the paging system and the canned music that goes on and off all day, maybe a person could think! The constant interruptions and lousy music over the intercom make it very hard for me to concentrate."

Another person nodded, "It can be hard to find a quiet place to work. You know, because we're just a temporary cross-functional team, we weren't given a designated part of the building. Three people share office space with me and our desks actually butt up one to the other. Phones ring constantly—they've put us in the customer service area because Marketing does so much customer contact work. What a zoo it is around here."

"This technology is so new," said the first, "that I need fewer distractions in order to read and absorb all of the information. Luis may want answers, but first I need to understand our limitations for myself."

Type Clue

Aha, I thought, the characteristic Introverted desire for in-depth study of the subject at hand. They like quiet for concentration and are less productive without privacy—four desks together!

I interjected, "It would be hard for me to concentrate, too! If these problems could be addressed, what else would you say it's like to be a member of this team?"

"The project itself is a fun challenge, but I'm not sure that forming a team with Marketing is the best way to meet our goals. They're on such a different wavelength that I think we'd be better off just having our managers talk, not all this team stuff."

"Why are they hard to interact with?"

The person sitting next to her said softly, "The kickoff day?"

"Oh yeah," the other went on. "We spent a whole day together to start the Commerce Call project and Marketing brown-nosed the entire time with the executive team. Since we Systems people were all pulled from different divisions of the bank, we looked at this as an opportunity to learn about each other, so we ate *together*. Then we teamed up with each other for golf, finding out our specialties and such."

Type Clue

This sounded like typical Introverted behavior. The Commerce Call team was brought together to get started on the task of developing this new product. Not wanting to waste time on social frivolities, the Systems team members began their work of finding out about each others' technical expertise during the "play" part of the day.

Introverts often dislike what they perceive as "apple-polishing" with senior management, viewing that behavior in many Extraverts as rather pushy. Lots of noisy talk and back-slapping can make Introverts uncomfortable. The intermingling and small talk that are appropriate at corporate gatherings feel unnatural to many Introverts.

"What did Marketing do?" I asked.

"*They* raced for spots at the senior manager tables, played golf with the corporate executives—they practically tap-danced to get noticed."

"And they haven't stopped," added another. "We hear loud and clear when they've met a goal or come up with another idea. But the plan is seldom there as to how they're going to accomplish things other than by telling us what they want *us* to do. It is hard for me to team with them because they don't think about all the bases to be covered or think through all the alternatives. Shouldn't people's work stand on its own merits, rather than be advertised to everyone and everybody?"

"So you really find it difficult to work with Marketing. It sounds like you find them to be a different breed from you," I commented.

Others nodded in agreement. "We talked this over before meeting with you and I guess our biggest fear is that Marketing's tactics will produce a flash-in-the-pan product. Commerce Call will cost millions of dollars. What if it quickly becomes obsolete because Marketing stayed with its deal-maker mode?"

"What do you mean by *deal-maker mode*?"

"Their questions to us are, 'Can you do this, can you make the system do that?' as they hear what consumers will use. We can answer those questions easily to help them wheel and deal while selling Commerce Call, but those aren't the questions that matter. The tough question that we need to focus on is: 'If we make the system this way, will it give the customers what they want two years from now?' That's why we on the Systems side are moving more slowly. Marketing seems to have a fundamental misunderstanding of our role here—for us, it's about a system that's on target now and has the potential to serve Commerce Bank for years to come."

Type Clue

Extraverts generally want to take action and in this case, the Marketing team was being encouraged to act by the tight deadlines for the project. No wonder the Introverts were feeling tension because of their natural tendency to "Think-Act-Think and Think Some More" versus the Extravert's method of "Act-Think-Act."

I asked, "Have you tried to talk to them about this?" I looked directly at one of the team members who had not yet spoken, hoping to encourage her participation (how "E" of me!).

"We were talking about that before you arrived," she said. "We just about have a presentation set to go on our systems prototype. You know," she became more animated, "Commerce Call is just the start of a technology that will make banking by phone as easy as ordering pizza. With our automation systems, customers will, of course, be able to transfer funds and check balances, but also take out loans and open CDs—and that's just the beginning. If we set the groundwork, soon if a customer signals to be transferred to a personal banker, the banker's system will pull up the customer's file automatically, showing current account activity and past loans, etcetera. The banker will be able to answer questions at the drop of a hat. Marketing doesn't grasp that we're aiming for the Cadillac here, not the Edsel."

Type Clue

Her answer is a classic Introverted response, well thought out yet revealing the excitement that those in Systems truly had for Commerce Call. Extraverts are often surprised at the depth of commitment and understanding that Introverts show and how much Introverts *do* have to say when they finally have a chance to speak up.

"Marketing seems so action-oriented that I would imagine it is hard for them to think past the project's deadline, given the visibility Commerce Call has," I commented as I turned on the overhead projector. "Here is a list of what Marketing wants to tell you about themselves. As you read it over, think about your reaction to it. Then let's discuss that and make a similar one to hand to them."

There were a few chuckles as they read Marketing's items. I began, "I shared with you that all but one of the Marketing team members have a preference for Extraversion and all but one of you have a preference for Introversion, which can definitely place some barriers between you. Much of what is listed here is almost like a textbook description of Extraversion. They need to process out loud. Often the fun of a project is in working on it with others, hearing ideas grow as each person adds a viewpoint. I share their preference for Extraversion—I am energized by doing, by being involved with people. If I have an idea, you'll hear about it right away. I'll adjust it as you comment on my idea. Those of you with a preference for Introversion might find that scenario a bit draining, though, wouldn't you?"

The group seemed to concur. One spoke up, "You know, after we initially took the MBTI, I gave a lot of thought to my Extraversion–Introversion preference. I know I'm often quiet in meetings, but people respect me because what I say often moves us from stagnation to progress. I recalled many times in meetings when I listened to everyone's discussion. By the time they finished talking, I had had enough time to process my own thoughts and was able to summarize and save the day. This is how I do my best work. Luis doesn't seem to understand nor appreciate this, though."

We talked more about the differences between Introverts and Extraverts, took a break, and then moved on to preparing a list of what the Systems team wanted the Marketing team to know about them.

One woman spoke up. "For me at least, I need to go deeply into the developmental issues. I can't give the broad picture of Commerce Call until I understand my part of it in depth."

Another nodded. "And when I'm working on an idea, not simply staring into space as they might think if they happen to see me, interruptions can send me back to square one. I suppose my behavior might seem rude if I brush Marketing off, but concentration is key to my work."

We came up with the following list before moving on:

➤ We *are* really excited about Commerce Call, even if we seldom cheer out loud about it.

➤ It goes against our nature to think on our feet—if we can't think things through we'd rather not give an answer right then.

➤ We communicate more clearly when we write things down.

➤ We do our best work independently. Maybe we seem to not want your input, but in truth we want it as we start and then again when we are finished, not *during* our thought process.

The one Extraverted Systems team member spoke up. "It's no surprise that I can see both sides here, but we've been ignoring the fact that Marketing can't read our minds. *We* know that we'll be able to meet the Commerce Call deadlines and *we* understand the customer-driven nature of the product, but we've been remiss in letting Marketing in on our thoughts and process. When we get so intent on completing our own parts of Commerce Call, we tend to forget to give others information along the way unless they ask for it."

I then put up an overhead of the list of what Marketing said they needed from Systems. I remarked, "Sounds like you've read their list in advance. Any thoughts?"

"Well, their second point about telling them immediately—immediate isn't in our vocabulary for this project, but I guess I understand their needs better now," one said with a smile.

"Well, perhaps your only immediate response is to give them a schedule for when you'll be getting back to them. Let's make your list of what you need from Marketing before we move on."

Because many of the Systems people had thought this through in advance, making notes to themselves as well as discussing it together, we quickly came up with the following list of Systems needs for Commerce Call:

➤ If you give us time, we'll have the bugs worked out of things and be better able to tell you what we can deliver and when.

➤ In some ways we're a step ahead of your thinking. We want to work with you to have you understand how Commerce Call might tie to later products. Perhaps you can even help us persuade senior management to slow down if we need to develop another technology alongside Commerce Call that will promote the long-term good of the bank.

➤ We tend not to toot our own horns—but we are contributing. Take a look at what we've written, our best form of communication, to see what we've done and where we're at.

"But writing all this stuff down doesn't help the Commerce Call team if the Extraverts demand responses on the spot!" commented a team member.

"And you wouldn't be able to function as well if you tried to meet their demands in *their* fashion, would you?" I asked. "We made these lists to meet the first goal for the process: understanding what Marketing needs and what you need. Now let's use the lists to find tools for each of you to use to team together to keep Commerce Call on track. First off, what might be some ways that you could meet their needs for immediate feedback?"

"What about a project board placed in a spot where Marketing could see it without interrupting anyone? If we consistently update it with notes on our progress, they might feel more connected."

"And I don't mind meeting for discussion," said another, "if they inform us of the topics to be discussed ahead of time; maybe a few hours before if not the day before. I hope that can be 'immediate' enough."

Another team member said, "I'd still like an off-limits area—kind of a war room where we can concentrate without interruptions."

"First, though," spoke up the sole Extravert, "it's time we presented our ideas formally. We need to give them our in-depth plan for Commerce Call, with each of us presenting the advantages and possible limitations of the systems we're involved with. Certainly by now we've dug deeply enough to think on our feet as they ask for clarification."

"That's easy for you to say," said the person sitting next to her. "Since it's your idea, why don't you give the whole thing? You like to get up in front of everyone." Other heads nodded in agreement.

"You know, one of the reasons I was called in," I said, "was to coach you in being more persuasive verbally. Luis knows your abilities well and has full confidence that Commerce Call will be technically superior, but because you have the corner on technical expertise, he wants you to be responsible for more of the presentation to senior management. He thinks you're best able to field any questions, particularly technical ones. And before you give your presentation, I'll coach you through a practice session. Many aspects of presentations are simply skills to be learned and some of the best presenters I know have a preference for Introversion. If standing in front of a group isn't natural for you, and I'm well aware that many people would rather die than give a speech, you can still become more comfortable by learning the basics."

This idea was greeted with cautious enthusiasm and we agreed to gather the next week to polish their Operation Commerce Call preview. We actually videotaped each presenter as I coached them on the following: organizing information from the audience's perspective, presenting a positive, self-confident image, using humor, projecting one's voice, using gestures including good use of eye contact, handling hostile questions, and in general showing their underlying enthusiasm to others. The Systems team left with a practiced presentation about Commerce Call that they all felt appropriate for their communication style and for the technical information they needed to sell to senior management.

Later, I met again with Luis. I showed him the comments Systems and Marketing made about him:

MARKETING	**SYSTEMS**
On the Positive	*On the Positive*

➤ He's great—he has lots of energy.	➤ He's got a good handle on what needs to happen.
➤ He's easy to work with because he tells us what's going on with him.	➤ We know he's sold on Commerce Call.
➤ He's responsive.	➤ He has senior management's ear.
➤ He's direct with us—he says what's on his mind.	
➤ He makes Commerce Call fun.	
➤ He represents us well to senior management.	

On the Negative	*On the Negative*
➤ Sometimes it's hard to get a word in edgewise.	➤ When he doesn't seem to understand, it's often because he hasn't read his memos or e-mail.
➤ He can be pretty impulsive.	➤ He doesn't know what we need to work effectively.
➤ He sometimes overcommits us because he didn't bother to check with us before he responded to a request.	➤ He talks before he listens and wants us to talk before we think.
➤ He needs to think about how he responds to our requests for resources.	➤ He needs to think about how he responds to our requests for resources.
	➤ When we're thinking, he goes overboard in pushing us to respond immediately.

We reviewed the needs of those with a preference for Introversion and Luis resolved to incorporate the feedback into his leadership style. He said, "It clears the air to understand those Introverts across the way. You know, a word to the wise is sufficient."

I then showed him the lists each group had developed for the other group and asked for his feedback on the suggestions Systems had made for improving communication. He replied, "This still isn't really my style, but I can see their viewpoint. I think the meeting with Systems and Marketing can help open things up."

The next meeting of the Commerce Call team was a combined meeting. Prior to the session, both Systems and Marketing received a copy of the lists that the other group had generated. Luis kicked off the session by stating his goal: to increase communication and understanding among all players on the team, himself included. After he finished, I led a discussion of the suggestions of each subteam.

Feelings on both sides seemed fairly positive as the meeting continued. I commented, "You know, psychological preferences are just that, preferences. They do not always equal your behavior because when it is important for you to do so, you can all act outside your comfort zone. When the Systems team presents their ideas to senior management, you will see a group of Introverts who can use verbal communication to their advantage and do it very effectively. And those with a preference for Extraversion can stop to reflect, difficult as that may be, and go deeper into the subject matter, when they understand why that will be of benefit to themselves and to the team. Are there any questions you want to ask to clarify Extraversion and Introversion or how it operates within this team?"

To no one's surprise, an Extravert from Marketing spoke first. "So what do you expect from us while you're busy thinking? I mean, if I don't get a response, I generally keep talking, figuring you need more information from me before you can answer. Otherwise I repeat my question even louder, thinking that you may not have heard me."

"I never thought of it that way," spoke up a Systems analyst. "Your comment helps me realize how important thinking out loud can be for you and how necessary letting you in on my process can be. I'd still rather know the question in advance, though, so I can have time to think."

"And what do you do," asked another Marketing manager, "when you reach a goal? You think we overdo the celebration, but we'd like to know when to pat you on the back—softly at least."

"That's a good point," said another person from Systems. "We tend to focus so much on our work, absorbed in our own little successes, that we don't let anyone else in on our progress. Speaking for myself as an Introvert, I don't need or even like a parade or celebration when I've succeeded. Sharing my success with a few people who really know what effort went into the project is sufficient. But for starters, Marketing can join us for pizza when we successfully test the security coding."

"Any questions from those who prefer Introversion?" I asked.

"Well, do you ever wish you had thought things through before voicing your ideas?"

One of the Marketing reps laughed. "Sort of. You know, I sometimes wish that I could retract a statement from midair because I realize, but only after I've said it, that it was a dumb thing to say. Sometimes, just as I might interpret your quietness as a lack of ideas, people who meet me for the first time think I never keep my mouth shut. Really though, I'm a thoughtful kind of guy, my thoughts are just expressed quickly and more loudly than yours."

"Any others?" I asked to keep things moving.

Someone else from Systems stated, "I think it's easier for you to tell us to speak up than it is for us to tell you to be quiet. Any suggestions?"

Luis spoke. "Just tell me, 'Go away'—but also give me an idea of when you can get back to me with an answer or what issues you've thought of that prevent you from giving me an answer right then. Just clue me in to where you are. I may still hound you, so don't worry about telling me more than once. Each side has to give a little."

Once these questions and several others were discussed, we moved on to generating the following commitment list that focused on the Extraversion–Introversion differences on this team.

Commerce Call Team Communication Prescription

➤ Each team member needs to acknowledge when they are thinking about an issue as opposed to when they have no answer to give on an issue.

➤ Team members will give each other time to think before responding.

➤ Team meeting agendas and other information will be sent out in advance.

➤ Both Systems and Marketing will list their critical events. The entire team will celebrate reaching those goals together. However, the team member or subteam that accomplishes the goal(s) gets to choose how to be recognized for their achievement. [For more on the different ways people prefer to receive recognition and praise, see chapter 4 about Thinking and Feeling preferences.]

➤ Representatives from both Systems and Marketing will work together to make a project board to ensure that all will understand the current status on each aspect of Commerce Call.

➤ Everyone will work to mitigate the effects of what is already an environment filled with interruptions.

Luis agreed to explore whether partitions could be used to block off Systems's area in order to provide them with a separated space divided into individual cubicles. He also said he would lobby senior management to disconnect the intercom from the Commerce Call team area. Even though their office space would still be noisy, the group agreed that these steps would be beneficial to all—both Extraverts and Introverts.

Later that week, Systems previewed their senior management presentation with Marketing. Some of the presenters did better than others, but I could see an overall improvement as evidenced by the way Marketing's ears perked up as the information was relayed. Systems finished with a list of response items for Marketing to handle. Then the questions flew back and forth, demonstrating how well Systems people could dialogue when they were prepared to do so.

When discussion finished, Luis stood up. "This is exactly what senior management needs to hear: You've convinced me today that Commerce Call is not only under control but will be up and running online on schedule. Give the same presentation Wednesday when we meet with senior management and you'll get any additional resources you need, I'm sure."

When I checked back on Commerce Call a month or so later, I was delighted to see that the team had managed to work their differences into an almost playful framework. The music was off, the partitions were up, meeting agendas went out in advance, and the project board was prominently displayed outside Luis's office. Because Luis preferred face-to-face oral communication, he did reserve the right to ask questions of anyone posting progress notes. The Systems team learned to be ready.

Marketing almost made a joke of writing out ideas and then tiptoeing them to the appropriate desk in Systems. Frequently, Systems responded immediately with at least an "It depends and I'll get back to you in an hour" response, rather than the deep, dark hole of the past.

Meeting agendas helped a great deal, but Marketing had to fight the impulse to hound Systems before the meeting time. However, Systems learned to use the interruptions, now far fewer in number, to determine if and when they needed more input from Marketing at various stages in their thought process.

All in all, the Introverts and Extraverts of the Commerce Call team had learned to translate their needs into terms the other could understand, even if they still spoke different languages. The Commerce Call team found a balance between keeping quiet and speaking up.

TYPE TAKEAWAY

Because the differences between Extraverts and Introverts often affect productivity directly (each style can keep the other style from doing their jobs effectively), working toward compromise and understanding benefits everyone.

Type Solvers to Try

When you suspect an Extraversion–Introversion problem, try these ideas.

☑ Prior to the meeting, have the following questions (so that the Introverts can come prepared to respond!) on hand:

➤ What positive contributions does your Extraversion/Introversion make?

➤ What does the other style contribute?

➤ What do you value about your style?

➤ What do you value about the other style?

➤ What do you, your team/company/organization do that honors the Extraverted style? The Introverted style?

☑ At the meeting, divide into two groups according to preferences on the Extraversion–Introversion dimension. Allow each group to present its answers to the above questions.

☑ After each presentation, allow time for questions and discussion. Brainstorm first in Extraversion and Introversion groups, then together, about possible ways to improve your work environment to fit the needs of both preferences.

The following table summarizes the natural styles of each preference and may be beneficial for discussion.

It is more natural for Extraverts to:	It is more natural for Introverts to:
➤ Give spontaneous presentations	➤ Give presentations that are in-depth and planned in advance
➤ Network with other departments and outsiders	➤ Network with a few people who share the same interests
➤ Promote their ideas and products to outsiders, new customers, or strangers	➤ Promote their ideas and products to well-established customers or through one-on-one sales

➤ Enjoy door-to-door or cold-call sales

➤ Prefer long-term sales arrangements (for example, multiple-year construction contracts)

Extraverts, to be more effective, yes, you need to be out and about, but . . .

Introverts, to be more effective, yes, you need time for yourself, but . . .

➤ Introspect.

➤ Speak up earlier in the process when you have a good idea.

➤ Keep a journal or use another technique to consider ideas in more depth.

➤ Make sure to connect with those who will promote or fund your ideas.

➤ Schedule time-outs for yourself, away from constant activity.

➤ Drive the long route home to give yourself time to reflect on the day.

➤ Lobby for opportunities to think through ideas in a collaborative environment.

➤ Lobby for workspace that is considerate of your need to work without interruption.

➤ Yes, you need to go to another meeting, but you can also practice Introversion. See the list below.

➤ Yes, you need time for yourself, but you can also practice Extraversion. See the list below.

For personal development, consider the following.

If your preference is for Extraversion, you can practice Introversion:

☑ Count to ten when feeling especially action-driven, enthusiastic, or enamored with an idea. Reflect to see if your ideas are all you think they might be.

☑ Practice holding your tongue for periods of time at meetings. Do so especially if you're the boss! (One Extravert in desperate need of toning down even placed a cough drop in his mouth as a reminder to shut up!)

☑ Keep a journal, reflect, meditate, pray silently, sit or walk alone in nature—practice the contemplative arts.

☑ Take an area that needs your thorough understanding and dig in; get steep and deep with the information.

☑ Let the other person speak first, then listen, then listen again.

☑ Slow down your actions; before starting a task, ask yourself, Have I deeply thought this through?

If your preference is for Introversion, you can practice Extraversion:

☑ Join and become actively involved in a professional, business, or trade association with people who share a similar interest.

☑ If you think someone can help you formulate an idea or get an idea into action, ask him or her for assistance, even if you're not sure of the merits of doing so.

☑ Open up with at least one other trusted person at work and share what's going on in your mind.

☑ If you think you've limited your interests too severely, try adding something new periodically—a course or a concept to study or a new leisure activity, preferably one that involves other people.

☑ Have lunch with one new business contact per week to increase your networking circle and to add breadth to your relationships.

☑ Try getting out and about at work—keep the office door open at times and leave the security of the walls that surround you, if only periodically.

When You're One or Few Amongst the Many[4]

When you have a preference for Introversion and your teammates have a preference for Extraversion, consider:

☑ Arriving at work early to take advantage of quiet time

☑ Intentionally seeking out private reflective time—commute the long way home

☑ Planning private breaks throughout the day to collect your thoughts

☑ In meetings, voicing even partially thought-through perspectives

When you have a preference for Extraversion and your teammates have a preference for Introversion, consider:

☑ Networking with others outside your team

☑ Asking others to voice their ideas

☑ Paying attention to the written word

☑ Allowing others to think about your idea before they provide feedback—count to three—or ten!

The Case of the Expansion–Minded Executive

The Sensing–Intuition Dimension

> ## Type Key
> Perceiving is noticing both the forest and the trees.

What is success? We all have our own definitions, don't we?

Given that Sensors are interested in what is tangible or practical, they might measure success by criteria such as:

➤ Establishing a proven track record
➤ Providing customer satisfaction as indicated by repeat business or tangible positive feedback
➤ Showing a profit—financial rewards
➤ Attracting additional investors
➤ Setting product standards or project results that can be replicated over and over

When Stan Maslack decided to start a restaurant, he began with what he knew: He could make a better roast beef sandwich than any restaurant around. He purchased a local corner bar and began serving hot roast beef sandwiches prepared with his secret overnight marinade.

Within three years, even on the coldest days Minnesota can produce, customers waited in line down the block for a plateful of beef that could probably serve three—except that one's willpower often disappeared at the first bite. He achieved his own definition of success by serving the same sandwiches for over thirty years, creating a loyal customer following and a mystique around those famous sandwiches.

My educated guess is that Stan was a Sensor. Although not even many Sensors would stick to a single sandwich for so many years, Stan clearly demonstrated the attributes of Sensors. In essence, he created a successful, standardized product and flourished according to the criteria listed above. Other Sensors might expand upon a proven product or replicate a prosperous restaurant in another location or find ways to franchise their business experience—doing it cheaper, friendlier, or faster.

In contrast, the chefs who create first-of-its-kind offerings, like those who saw the market for vegetarian cuisine or pizza eaten out of a cardboard box, were probably Intuitors, interested in gambling on possibilities. They probably wouldn't stick with a single sandwich for thirty years, but they would add to the menu and redecorate, or leave the restaurant business for an entirely new venture or career.

Intuitors, who are more interested in insights and possibilities, might measure success by criteria such as:

➤ Being recognized for ingenuity or creativity
➤ Adding value, creating new jobs, having a positive impact on the local economy
➤ Breaking out of the mold
➤ Triumphing against the odds
➤ Coming up with a new product or service

Both Sensing and Intuition are needed for long-term success in almost any business endeavor (roast beef sandwiches may be one of the rare exceptions!). However, the natural domain for Sensing tends to be in organizations that focus on standardization, replication, efficiency, and cost-benefit enhancement. People with a preference for Sensing gravitate toward fields such as construction, production, banking, manufacturing, and medicine, where exactitude and precision are held in the highest regard.

Intuitive arenas tend to provide a domain for invention, ingenuity, and doing things differently, such as arts organizations, entertainment, public relations and advertising, research and development, and publishing. These fields place a premium on novelty, long-term perspective, departure from the norm, and new concepts or insights. For example, an advertising agency would not survive if it replicated or even reproduced ever so slightly its previous work or the work of other agencies. People who are the most successful in advertising are those who challenge the status quo, at times creating something entirely new and distinctive. This role of advertisers is very different from the role of a pilot, for example, who is expected to follow proven procedures.

Many new firms are started by Intuitors who have a dream. These organizational founders often have an uncanny ability to perceive an opening, a niche, or a product to meet a need that wasn't recognized before. Frequently, Intuitors know "intuitively" that for their idea to succeed, it must be backed up by sound accounting practices, business planning, and the ability to consistently produce a product or service on time—the gifts of the Sensors.

Other business organizations are started by Sensors who find a way to do things cheaper, quicker, and more easily, to which they perceive the need to add Intuitor insight for new markets or developments. Both types of organizations, if they are wise, look at things from the perspectives of their opposite yet complementary preference.

In the following case study, we will see an organization started by a visionary (Intuitor) who had enough sense to know that he needed an efficient manager to organize his dreams, without even knowing his partner was a Sensor. As you read through the case, observe what happens when either Sensing or Intuition is given too much weight. Visions do need to meet up with current realities.

Type Clue

Although people may not know their psychological type, they are often drawn to those who augment their style when they're trying to run a business. This is true not only for Sensing and Intuition but for the other preferences and the sixteen types as well.

Put the two ways of perceiving (Sensing and Intuition) together in a start-up company and listen to how they view the path the company is taking. The Intuitors see the *potential,* perhaps already brainstorming the next products or markets, while the Sensors see the *current situation,* concentrating on improving procedures, efficiency, financial systems, and whatever else is needed to establish that proven track record.

Type Story: Alpha Omega Systems (AΩ)

Cast of Characters

Darin, Founder and President	**E N** F P
Blaire, Executive Vice President Seminar and Training Coordinator	**I S T J**
Steve, Controller	**I S T J**
Keith, Consultant	**E S** F P
Shea, Consultant	**I N** F P

Alpha Omega Systems (AΩ) was a start-up company committed to providing full-service approaches in the field of human resources training for small companies. They offered assessment, team building, problem solving, strategic thinking and planning, customized materials, and program design. In its mission statement, AΩ proclaimed, "We provide opportunities for the growth of organizational learning by sharing knowledge and practice through consulting and training services. We strive to be a dominant force for creating value for organizations transitioning into the next century."

Type Clue

Note the future orientation, the broad statements where much is possible, and the lack of specifics—can you even tell what they do? This is characteristic of the way an Intuitor might perceive his or her "mission"—limitless possibilities and few boundaries.

Darin, one of the founding partners of AΩ, had been working on his training ideas for two years prior to starting the company. Described by those who had worked for him as a man on a mission, he spoke with a religious fervor about the need for companies to develop the potential of their human resources. He was convinced that giving smaller companies access to the types of training, team building, and planning that were common at large organizations could have a tremendous impact on the lives of their workers.

Darin envisioned a team of experts who were well known from their publications and speaking platforms. From this consortium, he developed

AΩ's consulting products and hired most of AΩ's key players. AΩ consisted of a dozen young, highly talented individuals and, as a firm, was known for its keen entrepreneurial approach.

Typically, I receive a call because the client has an acute sense that things are not going well—perhaps schedules are being shredded or people just don't seem to be getting along. However, many times the issue presented is only a symptom of the real issue. In this case, what had been a team unified around a common organizational mission became a team that was starting to come apart. Darin called out of concern about conflicts between him and his partner, Blaire, and between the partners and the staff. "We need to put aside our interpersonal differences and get this company on the move again."

He continued, "Sandra, the major issues in my new company have to do with communication and trust. We need to be on board for the same common goals as we prepare to go national—we're getting ready to open offices in Boston and Phoenix. But I'm not sure that this will go smoothly because of all the contention in the office. I think the MBTI might help us out. Would you facilitate an MBTI session for us?"

Type Clue

Intuitors, especially Intuitors with Feeling, are hampered in their ability to be effective when conflict exists or communication is awry.

Making a judgment based on the urgent tone of his voice, and his immediate mention of conflicts with his partner, I said, "Perhaps rather than just introducing type concepts, we should consider a team-building approach. I could interview each of the team players and gather information that could be used along with the MBTI. This allows me to tailor a problem-resolution and action-planning session to the needs of your office."

"You're probably right," he said. "When can we start? I guess I should tell you what happened at our staff meeting this morning, since that's what triggered my call to you."

This is what he relayed:

The staff meeting had started amiably enough as Darin gave his views on their decision-making process, "Everyone here is a quality player and we need everyone's input to move forward. In front of you is a list of items we need to find consensus on as we explore the next phase of AΩ's development: a new office in Boston and then one in Phoenix."

Blaire, the other founding partner, quickly scanned the agenda as Darin went on. "Darin," she interrupted, "you didn't tell me that you were ready to discuss opening more offices—you barely mentioned it to me in passing last week. And what's this here about designing a seminar on incentive programs? I thought we'd agreed not to add new products in the near future—not until we standardize the ones we have and get our travel schedules under control."

Darin seemed rather defensive as he answered, "I have several clients in mind for which this seminar would be perfect; they'd buy it right now if we were ready. I know we need to clarify our internal procedures, but we can't stagnate, either."

Keith, one of AΩ's consultants, laughed rather bitterly. "We're hardly in danger of stagnation. With all that we're involved in right now, not one of us has put in less than sixty hours a week all fall. New clients, new services, new everything—everything except new ways to handle the expanding system needs, client records, course development procedures—in essence, what we need to keep the business going."

Blaire tried to speak more calmly, "Darin's right. If we don't have the demanded services in place, even our most satisfied customers will look elsewhere. However, let's not add helter-skelter. I'm not sure how this incentive seminar idea fits our mission."

Darin leaned forward. "It creates opportunities for excellence for our customers; that's our mission, isn't it?"

"As you yourself stated, we need more consensus on that mission. Excellence in what context? We aren't out to make them all better at everything from basket-weaving to opera, are we?"

Some in the room stirred, uncomfortable at the partners' lack of harmony. Steve, AΩ's controller, who seldom spoke up in meetings, finally broke the silence, "But where's *our* excellence? I keep my own work up-to-date, but I spent all morning covering for someone here who neglected to get quotes for their new course notebooks, leading me to be late on estimating the course costs for our biggest account. And I hate to miss deadlines when I've given my word. So therefore, I want concrete policies; I want to know where my responsibilities start and stop; and an organizational chart showing who does what would be nice, while I'm asking. I know I'm sounding adamant, but let's stop this pie-in-the-sky expansion stuff until we are grounded locally and know what it is we are about."

"I do know what we're about and the details are up to the rest of you," Darin shot back. "I'm not a directive leader. I'm about people, ideas, relationships, and marketing—the less I'm caught in the details of running this office, the more we can move ahead.

"Listen, we're helping companies meet the future—this is a great place to be. I want us to work together efficiently, in harmony, and not waste our time on the small stuff."

"But we don't seem to be in agreement anymore," said Shea, the other consultant. "I think we've lost our way. We aren't getting along as well as we used to. And efficiency? Everything is so tentative that we're constantly reinventing the wheel. If you want to attain your mission, Darin, clarify it. Limit the possibilities so we can get ready to meet a few of them, not stay open for anything we might fall into."

Darin drew a deep breath. "Let's reel this discussion in and get back to the subject at hand. Remember where AΩ started? Consensus decision making. Teamwork. A group with a common mission, ready to move on . . . so let's go back to work and revisit this later when we can be more civil, because it appears to me that the productive part of this meeting is over."

Blaire pulled Darin aside after the meeting. "You know, there's a lot of truth in what we discussed this morning. We're on the cutting edge of our field; our customers choose us because we're the best, but can we keep it up? Keith almost lost a client last week because of a billing misunderstanding. It never would have happened if I could have looked at pricing policies—which aren't written down anywhere. With our size, one major goof could close us down. It's not logical to keep expanding at the possible risk of losing all we have gained."

Darin replied, "I've got the procedures underway. I said I'd turn them over to you as soon as I had them roughed out for my end of the business. And from where I sit, expansion is vital to our future."

"But we're *both* supposed to be in charge, aren't we? You partnered with me because I could bring reality and the clear light of day to your dreams. I can't do that if you race on to the next task before we've neatly boxed in the current one."

Darin didn't answer.

After hearing his description of the meeting, I knew I had my work cut out for me. I suggested that I could begin the next week as I was available then.

I began my interview process with Darin and he confirmed his preferences for ENFP on the MBTI personality inventory. As we talked, he seemed nervous, almost confrontational. He reiterated how much he had contributed to the organization and how his previous training experience and his master of business administration (MBA) degree in marketing made him well suited to run much of the business. "I've kept responsibility for a lot of the networking, marketing, and course development. I'm a marketeer, and while Blaire also has an MBA, hers is in operations.

Documenting what I do is not my favorite part of the day, but I eventually get it done. From what other people say, you'd think I ignore it all."

Type Clue

As a fellow ENFP, I was acutely aware that Darin might be taking personally even the slightest critical feedback about his attention to detail. This often happens when Intuitors are under stress. Generally, Intuitors don't enjoy the administrative detail Darin shouldered, even when they *do* have an MBA degree.

Darin went on, "You know, our mission is to prepare companies for the *future*. That future keeps changing, so how can we slow down? Our customers know how on-target our training is—why, I could call almost any one of them and get them to sign up for the incentives course I proposed last week as our next development. These companies are hungry for what we have to offer—and I am tired of Blaire and the rest of the crew saying we aren't ready to launch any more training seminars, let alone open up a Boston office. Before we'd be able to do that, Blaire would want the whole thing planned right down to whether we should buy or lease the copy machine there! Time is too short for all of that—I just know there's a need in Boston. I don't need a cost justification study to prove it."

"What is it like to work with Blaire?" I asked.

Type Clue

Although I had not yet talked with Blaire, her reported preferences were for ISTJ, the exact opposite of Darin. Blaire wanted procedures in place while Darin wanted to move on to the next exciting venture. Sounds like a Sensing versus Intuition conflict. I wanted to know more . . .

"Blaire is one of the most efficient, reliable people I have ever met, which is why I invited her to partner with me here at AΩ. But lately . . . lately, she and I have been tripping over each other. She has a form for everything and wants everything planned, requisitioned, documented, and signed. She even keeps track of how many pens we each use!"

Type Clue

Ah, the gifts of an ISTJ—organizing, managing details, having things in the right place at the right time. ENFPs like Darin admire these abilities and then find themselves frustrated when they are caught in the midst of the red tape that these abilities sometimes create! The little-used Thinking preference of the ENFP may recognize the necessity of these requests, but they feel like a restraint on the Intuitor's creativity, which is too ready for the next venture to be bothered with details!

Darin went on, "I was really trying to go along with Blaire's methods because I *do* know I need someone to keep me organized, but last week when she tried to put a stop to the new incentive seminar idea and balked at expanding to Boston, that was the last straw. That's why I called you. I need your help to get this place moving again."

"I'll be talking to Blaire later today," I said, "but I'm not surprised that this is one of the trouble spots for AΩ. I share your preferences for ENFP and we tend to lead through our enthusiasm rather than through concrete agendas and plans."

Type Clue

This was a nice way to say that Intuitors can ignore the facts altogether as we originate new ideas! Perhaps what was needed here was a concrete strategic plan, but I needed to talk to everyone first.

Darin and I talked further about his frustrations with the company's slowdown in developing the next stage of growth and then it was time for me to meet with Blaire.

Blaire was right on time, carrying a legal tablet. I later learned it had a list of the points she wanted to be sure to cover. As we began, she confirmed her preferences for ISTJ.

"How do you view your role here at AΩ?" I asked her.

"I consider myself the realist in the office, the one who makes sure we keep track of the essentials of our business. I've no doubt that AΩ is here

---

Type Clue

Being a dominant Intuitor, if I'm involved in any administrative matter, I want a dominant Sensor on *my* side, checking all the details. Blaire seemed true to type, making sure she was prepared to cover each point during our meeting.

---

to stay—Darin and the consultants consistently deliver what our customers want. I've worked with Darin before, so I was quite certain that anything he started would succeed. When he asked me to come in as a partner, I found the decision to join an easy one. I thought our work division was along the right lines—I implement and schedule our training network and he dreams up our courses and similar products.

"And our division of labor has worked pretty well, at least up until a few months ago. Now I sense that Darin resents the responsibility I feel to ensure that we stay on the same track that has given us so much success. Our customers deserve to know that the consulting services we provide will consistently be of the same high quality. I'm having trouble keeping up on the procedures side with Darin's pace of creating new seminars and consulting packages. Last week, he mentioned opening a new office! Well, we can't do that until our structure is in place here and is ready to be copied elsewhere. We can hardly manage this office, let alone one in Boston!

"You know, we have the best line of seminars around, our customers tell us how useful they are, and we're at capacity. Who needs more than that?"

Type Clue

Sensors are attracted to proven track records, so Blaire's willingness to partner with Darin made sense. Sensors tend to find success in knowing that they have established rules and procedures that lead to reliability. Suggestions for radical change, such as opening new offices, can cause them to become almost inflexible in the pursuit of their duty—yet an Intuitor like Darin *lives* to envision radical change!

"I am finding it very difficult to talk with Darin about these matters. He is becoming more defensive and even less planful, from my point of view. I tried to relieve him of some of the administrative burden he carries, dislikes, and avoids to the detriment of my responsibility for schedules and deadlines. We'd be better off moving all of the documentation of seminar procedures to my area, but I can't get him to make a decision on it. He seems to avoid conflict at all costs. I call it his 'democratic paralysis.' He wants to be democratic and consider my opinions, but he doesn't want to fight with me over it, so he won't discuss it!"

"What else bothers you about Darin?" I asked. I wanted to uncover any other areas of conflict.

"Well, I don't really care for his mission statement. It's too general. We actually help people develop practical, job-related skills and it doesn't even mention that."

Type Clue

Hmmm. Darin mentioned assisting companies with long-term development; Blaire mentioned teaching practical skills. There's quite a difference between the two . . .

"Frankly, every day he seems to have a new idea for the business, and it's beginning to frighten me. We are barely honoring our commitments right now. In my opinion, we are in danger of overextending ourselves and falling flat on our face—especially if we move now to establish a Boston branch, and he's even thinking of a Phoenix office, too!"

Type Clue

ISTJs can be counted on to honor every commitment that makes sense, be on time for almost every meeting that is appropriate, and follow through on just about every promise they make. For Blaire, Darin's expansion mode was beginning to endanger her ability to follow through. Most ISTJs work to set up contingencies for any possible threat to missing a commitment. Perhaps it was with good reason, then, that Blaire was finally digging in her heels.

"Tell me how you feel about Darin's ideas. Do they seem sound or a bit crazy, or what?" I queried.

"I can't help but admire his originality and vision, but recently Darin is all vision and no common sense." Blaire looked at the notes she had prepared.

"His vision of the future keeps shifting, leaving me and the staff with nothing certain to prepare for. The fact is, our consultants are booked solid for the foreseeable future with AΩ's current seminars and products. Last month we had to hire two freelancers whose quality we couldn't for certain vouch for, and our overtime bill for the support staff is incredible!"

"What one thing would you work toward if you could?" I asked, thinking of a possible strategic planning process.

"Everyone is trying to keep their work up-to-date, but it seems as if we're losing the battle, and it's costly to AΩ, too. I want a concrete business plan, not all of this grandiose dreaming about how we can take our show all over the country. None of this national stuff until we are well grounded locally—until we can pay our expenses, find a training schedule we are comfortable with that doesn't require hiring freelancers and overloading support staff, and figure out how to make decisions together."

Blaire and I discussed her current projects a bit longer before it was time for me to meet with Steve, AΩ's controller. Actually, Steve was waiting outside the conference room door, literally pacing up and down. As he came in he said, "I'm sorry, but there's so much to do on my desk right now that I had hoped to start a bit early. Will this take as long as scheduled?"

"I'll do what I can," I said, and we quickly worked through type theory and confirmed his inventory results as ISTJ. Then we moved on to the interview questions.

Type Clue

Steve seemed rather stressed, almost as if he feared losing track of all of those tasks awaiting him while spending time thinking about the larger issues facing AΩ. Sometimes Sensors react more to the situation at hand than to the future implications. When they're extremely stressed, they may see the future as their enemy, especially when change coupled with major uncertainties looms.

"What is it like to be the controller for AΩ?" I asked.

"Most of the time it's like rowing a boat up a waterfall," he said without a trace of humor in his voice. "Darin knows just enough about finance to be dangerous. He has to have his hands in everything and sometimes keeps me from doing what he hired me to do."

"Can you think of a specific example?" I asked, hoping to gather more information on the root of the problem.

"That's easy. About a month ago, I said that AΩ needed a concrete financial plan, with targets for revenue growth, expense control, and the like. Darin immediately said that as president that was his responsibility and he would complete the first draft. He wanted to make sure it captured the essence of his mission, I think, but there's no way he should be drawing it up. In the first place, he doesn't have time. Secondly, he's *not* trained in finance—that's why he hired me. And thirdly, controllers are supposed to *control* the finances of a business! Why else would I be here?

"We need a financial plan that we can hang our hats on, one that will help us determine objectively whether and how fast and how far we can expand. How Darin could even mention a new office, let alone one on the opposite end of the map, without a financial plan, I can't understand. Any financial plan designed by him would probably assume away the fact that we need more capital before we can open a new office.

"I'm also concerned about the profit-sharing system he proposed recently. It is so general that I'm not sure if we could administer it consistently, especially as we open more offices."

Type Clue

Steve, the Sensor, wanted a fact-based financial plan and a profit-sharing system that was replicable from location to location. He knew that he could rely on his knowledge of financial planning gleaned from his experience at other businesses. He probably also wanted to make sure a realistic approach was taken in projecting the financial picture of the company. A plan created by an Intuitor like Darin could indeed assume away the facts.

"When we first started out," Steve continued, "Darin accepted the fact that expenses needed to be monitored closely. He worked with me on budgets and listened to my cash flow concerns. But with our bit of success, all of that has gone by the wayside. He says I'm too hung up on every penny. I say he's spending every penny we have! After those kinds of exchanges, we tend to avoid each other for as long as a week. He just doesn't realize that a truly successful business builds on a solid financial foundation before it expands! My being pragmatic just produces conflict with him.

"I also think we need clearer lines of authority and responsibility. How can we expand to Boston without a definitive organizational chart that assigns responsibility for each area of the business?"

Type Clue

Sounds as if in the face of uncertainty, Steve was doing his best to let Darin know the facts of the situation, much like Blaire, the other Sensor. But Darin was so caught up in AΩ's potential that he had no time for facts—a frequent foible for Intuitors. It was time to talk to the other Intuitor in the office, Shea, to round out the picture of the conflict there.

Shea, one of AΩ's two key consultants, was next on my interview list. As she came in, she smiled warmly. After some pleasantries, she said, "This seems like such a good idea—working with an outsider to help us get back to cooperating again."

Shea confirmed her reported preferences for INFP. As she read her type description, she said, "This makes a lot of sense in light of my reactions to all the changes in the past month. I like working here because we offer something that is of real value to our customers. Usually, we have a lot of fun together, too. But we're losing our camaraderie. I'm not sure whether it's because Darin is trying to do too much, or because others can't see through the clutter of day-to-day matters to the wide-open opportunities that are out there for us. I empathize with Blaire's desire for better procedures—often I get stuck on the correct process for dealing with a customer, wondering if I'm doing it the right way. But I also agree with Darin that those new opportunities beckon. It's always exciting to move on to get the next seminar or product ready. I didn't realize until *now* how bothered I was by their conflict."

Type Clue

Shea's Intuition was perhaps being tempered by her Feeling function that allowed her to step into the shoes of another. She was thus able to respect Blaire's position. But note that her heart was still with Darin's position, wanting to move on to the next step or to try out new ideas. Still, her dominant Feeling process acted as a bit of a reality check on her focus on the future. She was excited about possibilities for AΩ but was better able than Darin to understand the concerns of Blaire and Steve. (See the section "The Dominant Function" in chapter 1 for more on the dominant function in each type.)

"What's it like to work here?" I asked her, as I had the others.

"From my standpoint, Darin has created the perfect team of people to make AΩ a success. Darin has the ideas and the contacts, Blaire and Steve know how to run the business side, and Keith and I are great with clients, if I may say so myself. Darin gives me free rein to adjust my work as I see fit and I appreciate that flexibility."

Type Clue

It was good to hear something positive about Darin—ENFPs generally have a knack for putting the right people together on a team and guessing correctly the contributions each person will make.

Shea continued, "I tend to find the hit-or-miss use of procedures somewhat frustrating, though. Not that I want my hands tied to keep me from changing things, but I'd like to see the ground rules so I can know easily when I'm on track.

Type Clue

INFPs like Shea tend toward perfectionism. Having a "few ground rules" can keep them from falling into the trap of not completing something out of fear that they left out an essential item and their results will not be perfect.

"This business about having a Boston and even a Phoenix office opened a can of worms. Until that, I think all of us at AΩ were enough in agreement about our goals that we worked together naturally. Even if there were an occasional dispute about how to perfect a new course or even about who used too many flip chart pages, we were generally in synch. Now, however, we're really split apart. Have you heard about our last meeting? Darin caught the rest of us off guard, I guess."

I acknowledged learning about that meeting. Shea told me a bit more about it from her viewpoint before we continued to talk about the team.

"Keith and I are a great team when it comes to designing AΩ seminars. Usually I think of a framework and he knows just how we can get there. We have a lot of fun together at this stage in the process. When we're presenting to our clients, however, we often tailor the seminars to our own unique styles, but I think that's best for everyone. Usually, Keith stays with presenting our bread-and-butter seminars while I work the bugs out of the new designs—I do that best when I think about the needs and even the faces of a specific client."

Type Clue

It sounded like Keith (a reported ESFP) and Shea understood each other's strengths. Shea, the INFP, came up with the ideas, while Keith, the ESFP, knew how to implement Shea's ideas and deliver the course. Maybe Shea and Keith's way of working together could serve as a model for the rest of the office?

"What would you like to see AΩ develop from my team-building work here?" I asked in conclusion.

"I want a direction for new course development. That's really my favorite work activity, but I don't want to waste time on ideas the others don't want to use or customers won't buy." Shea gave me some more ideas about her needs before our time was up.

Keith was last on my interview list. While he confirmed his ESFP preferences, he was hesitant about the Judging–Perceiving dimension. "Maybe it's just because I'm so scheduled in my job here that I feel more Judging right now. I know I have to be that way from nine to five—or actually from seven to six with the amount of work we've had recently!"

"That sounds kind of grim. What is it like for you to work at AΩ?" I asked.

"As far as my responsibilities go, things couldn't be better. Shea is a great partner and we share enthusiasm for what we do. I spend most of my time up in front of people, helping them learn about what they need to improve and how to develop the skills to do so. Half the time all I need to do is get people in my courses talking to each other. AΩ's training designs give them plenty of time and a common language to finalize their own action plans."

Type Clue

Keith as a Sensor liked to focus on current realities; thus his work with clients was very fulfilling. ESFPs in particular like to facilitate productive conversations among people and enjoy helping others work out their differences.

"You know, I really like everyone in the office here and wish I could help them get over whatever is causing all the recent disharmony."

I asked, "What is most needed from your point of view?"

"That's easy," he replied. "We've got to get the immediate crisis of opening a Boston office solved—Darin and Blaire are great leaders, just different. I can see both their perspectives on Boston. Blaire doesn't want to rush ahead and Darin doesn't want to miss out on developing a new office, but there has to be common ground for making sure whatever we do is effective and well planned. I'd hate to be without either Blaire's or Darin's point of view."

After my brief meeting with Keith, the interview process was concluded. As I looked through my notes before meeting again with Darin, I felt strongly that a plan was just what AΩ needed to determine the feasibility of opening a Boston office and to help solve some of the internal conflict. AΩ required a strategic plan that:

➤ Could be created and signed off on by all five of the key players
➤ Contained the mission Darin needed with the realistic steps on how to get there included for Blaire and Steve
➤ Outlined the assumptions underlying the plan so that the Sensors could see how the Intuitors took their leaps of faith
➤ Set goals for the necessary foundational matters needed for expansion so that Darin could see what others thought needed to be done

I summarized the interviews with Darin and outlined the planning process I proposed they use. "The vision comes from you as the president— and that's set," I stated. "There may be some value in letting your team rework the mission statement so they buy into it. But I highly recommend that you work as a team through the next steps of the planning process. Let the team help you set the goals for the next three to five years. Not only will you have a richer product, but all of you will understand where those goals came from and how you thought they could be met."

Darin was thoughtful. "I don't know how I feel about a five-year plan. Things change too rapidly in this type of front-runner business."

"In a good plan, the goals are general enough to be long-lasting, yet specific enough that they are measurable. The objectives—the things you commit to doing during a year—are the explicit part of a good plan. And the objectives are modified as you complete some and adjust others through a systematic review process to meet changing needs.

"Shea said it best when she complimented you for pulling together such a complementary team. AΩ works because you are all so different. This type of plan can help you work better within those differences. While you may feel that planning could box you in and close off some of your options, I think you'll see, once we're into the process, how it will help and maybe even open some new doors."

Darin agreed to the process, saying, "While I may feel a bit tied down, it would be nice to have more than the mission statement to point to when I *know* an idea needs action. The downside will be, Blaire will be able to point to the plan, too, when she wants more red tape."

I laughed. "I try to think of red tape as a healthy restraint to my enthusiasm. Occasionally it *does* catch me before I charge over a cliff! But let's start the process and see where it takes us. I think you'll be pleased."

We scheduled a half-day session to set goals for AΩ. I called Blaire to make the arrangements, asking her to find an off-site meeting location so that interruptions could be minimized. Blaire commented, "I'll believe it when I see it—Darin committing in writing to what he's going to do, that is."

Type Clue

There is no doubt that teams work better together when they have a common picture of the future. In most cases, a good planning process will first set the broad-reaching goals that tend to capture the needs of the Intuitors. Then the realistic subgoals, objectives, and specific steps that back up the goals allow the Sensors to believe that the plan is feasible.

I opened the planning session with a description of the Sensing and Intuition preferences. "These preferences guide what you pay attention to. The Intuitor connects an idea with a future trend . . . and leaves the Sensors wondering how in the world the facts can be brought to bear. The Sensors want to use their past experiences to approach a solution, and the Intuitor wants to try something new. When I talked with each of you, similar issues crept into our conversations, as you may recall.

"Sensors and Intuitors often have trouble working together because they really see the world differently. Sensors see 'what is' and Intuitors see 'what if.' Let me use this picture as an illustration." I showed an overhead of a simple country scene with a few trees and a boy at play outside his home. "Darin and Shea, you work together to describe what you see. The rest of you can do the same in your group." After a minute or so I turned off the projector.

"Let's start with the Sensors. What did you notice about the picture?"

Keith gave their report. "We saw a boy with a wagon. Inside the wagon there were three balls and a pail. A woman was standing to the side of the house. There were seven trees in the yard and six clouds in the sky. The boy had blond hair and was wearing a blue sailor suit."

I asked Shea and Darin, whose preferences were for Intuition, to report. Shea looked a bit surprised as she asked, "Are you sure there was a woman in the picture?"

I said, "I'll show it again after you've given your report."

Darin began, "Well, given the costuming and the rustic style of the building, we thought that the picture might be of England, perhaps even Winston Churchill or the Duke of Windsor as a child in the late nineteenth century. I didn't notice how many trees there were, but the grass seemed to be losing its greenness, so perhaps the scene was of a late summer day."

Blaire interrupted, "There's nothing in that picture that lets you know for sure the scene is in England—or the time of year. And certainly you can't tell the identity of the boy!"

"Well, no," said Shea, "but only a rich child—or the child of an artist—would have been painted." Then she asked with some suspicion, "But how did you count the clouds? Weren't the clouds behind the trees?"

"Only one was partly behind a tree," answered Steve, "and you could see the outline through the leaves."

I turned on the projector. "Let's look again. There *are* two people, seven trees, and six clouds," I pointed out. "Intuitors, can you see how well the Sensors find exactly what is there? But Sensors, what may be interesting to you is that this portrait *was* made in England in the 1890s and portrays one of the princes. All of you correctly discerned what was there, but look how differently you viewed this simple picture. Notice that those of you with a preference for Sensing and those of you with a preference for Intuition did not pay attention to the same information even in the same picture—and both ways of viewing were right! Think of the implications for AΩ of how each of you looks for information in a different manner—you have not just a picture but a whole business in which to find misunderstandings!"

Darin said, "Now you know that I really can't see the trees for the forest! When I talk about AΩ's mission, I need those of you who can see the trees to fill in the details." The group chuckled a bit and talked about the exercise before we moved on.

I put up an overhead that summarized the immediate needs to bring AΩ back on track that each had given me in his or her interview:

➤ Darin: New offices (Boston, possibly Phoenix) and products to meet the ever-changing needs of AΩ's customers
➤ Blaire: A business plan, with policies and procedures in place to support it
➤ Steve: A financial plan

➤ Shea: Agreement on new course development
➤ Keith: Cooperating as a team, building on the strengths of AΩ's diversity

"As we look at these, are there any to be eliminated? You're all shaking your heads, No! But it wouldn't surprise me if the Sensors want more clarification on what Darin and Shea have in mind or if the Intuitors want to know how financial and business plans are going to affect their ability to adapt the business to new needs.

"We're going to work together on bridging those differences, actually practice presenting your ideas for AΩ in the language of those with the opposite preference. Why doesn't each group pick a single goal from the five listed here and work to justify it to the other group. While you do, keep in mind the differences the picture of the little boy so aptly demonstrated.

"Darin and Shea, you'll almost need to pretend you are reporters, because the Sensors want to know 'who, what, where, when, why, and how.' The further you can take the details, in specific steps, the better. Sensors want to hear how any conclusions you draw are grounded in facts. If you don't, they'll be sure to ask, 'What about this or that (and how many trees are there)?'"

Darin smiled, "If I tell you how many offices I *really* envision, I think I'll have to find a new team."

Others rolled their eyes, and Blaire responded, "Now wait a minute. I didn't say we can't expand. I just want to know how we're going to provide *perfect* service while we do. Give me the 'who, what, where, why, when, and how,' and I'll start the process!"

"I think you're catching on," I said. "While the Intuitors are busy being reporters, you Sensors are going to be daydreamers. Forget about the details for the next few minutes and look at one of your goals in Intuition language: How does this relate to the mission statement, what is the main point that all the facts support, and how does it open up new pathways for future growth or service? Intuitors will accept what they affectionately call your red tape if you can articulate why it is necessary. I'll float between the groups to answer any questions and translate your ideas if you need help."

The groups formed amidst joking and high spirits, a change from the contentious meeting a few weeks before. Both sides spent considerable time getting at the essence of what the other side needed, but stuck to the task as if they saw the benefits it offered. Shea presented for the Intuitors.

"We chose the topic of a new office. Over the past six months, our business on the East Coast has tripled, causing a 35 percent increase in travel time and expense for our consultants. With nine established clients in the Boston area, we would open our first remote site there. Darin has contacted three of his Massachusetts associates and has several candidates to become AΩ consultants based in the Boston area. The new office would also employ an office manager and a training associate. Keith or I would train alongside any new consultant until he or she felt competent alone. The office at first would replicate the seminars we already present. All new seminars would still be developed here. No new offices would be considered until Boston is up and running smoothly and this office has determined the procedures necessary to adequately manage a remote site.

"Because of the eventual reduction in travel time and temporary help for our current location, the new office would reach the breakeven point by holding four to six seminars each month. We currently hold three to five per month within a commuting distance of Boston."

Type Clue

Note that while Shea added many facts to her presentation, they were in no particular order and many facts were of a general nature. The answers to the "who, what, and where" questions were mixed together.

Steve asked, "When will you work with me on concrete projections?"

Darin replied, "My doodle pad is full of ideas that I'd better turn over to you. Let's meet next Monday."

Blaire asked, "Do I get to determine when the procedures are adequate?—because the two of you haven't spelled out what *adequate* means."

Darin said, "All you have to do is justify your procedures to me . . . which I think you get a practice stab at now."

Steve presented for the Sensors. "Looking at our list, we decided that the business plan was the most urgent matter. First, our main point is that a business plan will allow us to set expectations. Note that I said expectations rather than limits," he said with a wink. "With a sound business plan in place, we will know just what the financials need to look like before we can open a new office. We'll be able to ascertain which training sessions meet our profitability standards. And perhaps best of all, we can better administer a profit-sharing plan based on meeting or exceeding our common expectations.

"Secondly, I want to show how business plans tie in with our mission statement. Part of excellence is knowing with certainty before we make promises that we have the resources to follow through. Planning our financial future, then tracking our progress, will let us have that type of certainty.

"Thirdly, addressing the issue of red tape: We will agree together on the amount of detail the financial plan will include. For example, out of interest in determining the actual cost of each seminar we do, I may *want* to keep track of each client represented by your long-distance phone bills, but I understand that you would not enjoy filling out the kind of usage forms this would require. We can dialogue about just what line items are most important for our business to track—maybe just one line for office supplies rather than one for each kind of pen you use?"

Shea joked, "And no line for times when I change my mind about the handouts for a given seminar?"

Type Clue

Note how orderly Steve's presentation was (remember, his preferences were for ISTJ). Even when speaking to meet the style of Intuitors, he followed the exercise instructions explicitly—something Intuitors generally have trouble doing.

The meeting continued as the group worked to formulate their desires for AΩ into a set of five goals. Many of the ideas they added fit neatly as subgoals to those on the original list.

At a subsequent meeting, after everyone had had a chance to think about their own information needs, we met again to set the objectives for the next year. The team quickly realized the benefit of assigning responsibility for some items to *both* a Sensor and an Intuitor. In the end, their list of objectives met the most urgent needs of both sides:

➤ Develop a three-year financial plan for AΩ. Set profitability goals and growth benchmarks. Assess how profit sharing might be tied to success. (Steve, Darin)
➤ Design a customer survey process to detail their most urgent product needs. (Blaire, Shea)
➤ Determine policies for seminar development: what needs to be standardized and how initial sessions should be evaluated. (Blaire, Keith)
➤ Conduct a future team-building session to gain more knowledge of the strengths of each team member. (Keith and an outside consultant)
➤ Explore and develop projections for the possibility of a Boston office. (Darin, Steve, Keith)

➤ Document pricing policies and standards. (Blaire, Darin)
➤ Evaluate the need for another full-time consultant at this office. (Shea, Steve)
➤ Systematically track AΩ's competitors to keep the edge sharp. (Shea, Keith)

Having these action items on paper did indeed help communication at AΩ. When I returned a few months later for the team-building session Keith arranged, I found several signs of progress. There was a financial plan, which Darin actually used in his decision-making process. He found the plan helpful in gaining Blaire's and Steve's support. On the flip side, with the numbers in place, Blaire found it easier to discuss the expansion plans now that the whats and hows were spelled out more clearly. No new consultants had been hired, but the team had agreed that if they achieved a 15 percent increase in their business, another training consultant would be needed. This surety eased the minds of Shea and Keith.

Blaire admitted that Darin's "just trust me" attitude had been toned down to suit her and Darin admitted that Blaire seldom admonished him with "Get real!" Did it take hard work? Yes. Was it worth it? Well, it was for AΩ!

TYPE TAKEAWAY

Whether your office is filled with Intuitors (in which case, who's paying attention to the current situation?), or Sensors (in which case, who's considering the new possibilities?), or a mixture of the two preferences, there is much to be gained from honoring the strengths of both sides.

Type Solvers to Try

When you suspect a Sensing–Intuition problem, try these ideas.

To work through a specific problem such as reconfiguring your office space, launching a new product, or setting up new communications systems, use the following lists:[5]

☑   Sensors want specific answers to questions such as:

- ➤ How is the problem best defined?
- ➤ What are the current ramifications?
- ➤ What goals are we working toward?
- ➤ How can time lines be established and what are the intermediate objectives?
- ➤ What costs are incurred—financial, emotional, and other?

☑   Intuitors want not-so-specific answers to questions such as:

- ➤ What are the common threads?
- ➤ What other alternatives exist?
- ➤ What is the relationship of the part to the system?
- ➤ What are the opportunities for growth?
- ➤ What are our hunches about this issue?

To improve communication, consider having the Sensors give presentations (or prepare written information) for the Intuitors and vice versa. Use these lists to meet the needs of the other group:[6]

☑ For the Sensors:

- ➤ Point out the pertinent facts.
- ➤ Relate ideas to past experience.
- ➤ Make note of what needs attention.
- ➤ Have the right thing in the right place at the right time; keep the essentials on hand.
- ➤ Adopt realistic schedules and time frames.
- ➤ Remember, for the Sensors, it has to make sense!

☑ For the Intuitors:

- ➤ Recognize new avenues and possibilities.
- ➤ Develop ingenious insights.
- ➤ Predict future outcomes.
- ➤ Conjure up plans for future contingencies.
- ➤ Supply enthusiasm, zest, and a spirit of optimism.
- ➤ Remember, for the Intuitors, it has to appeal to the imagination!

For personal development, consider the following.

If your preference is for Sensing, you can practice Intuition:

☑ Do an executive summary (one or two pages) with all the trends or patterns your data suggest.

☑ Try some creative thinking such as brainstorming (be sure to follow all the rules!). Use metaphors or analogies and think about how this problem can be related to your other areas of expertise.

☑ Take a literature, art, or music class that focuses on motives, relationships, or themes. Or ask yourself, What does this book, painting, song really mean—how does it reflect its larger culture? Additionally, look at your organization's annual report or advertising brochures. Ask what hidden or subtle messages the customer might glean from the pages.

☑ Consider, What's meaningful about my work? Where do I want to be ten years from now and how will I get there?

☑ Take a class in strategic thinking or long-range planning.

☑ Find out what creative functions (advertising, art, communications) exist in your organization. Sit in on one of their meetings—what in their processes can you use in your work?

If your preference is for Intuition, you can practice Sensing:

☑ Take stock with your five senses periodically. What do you see (be sure to see the scene as it truly is), what do you hear (not what it reminds you of, but what is it?), what do you smell (pungent, floral, spice . . .), what's the taste of your food (salt, sweet, bitter, sour . . .), what are you touching right now (hard/soft, smooth/rough, cold/warm . . .)? Remind yourself to enjoy things as they are!

☑ Remember not to kid yourself—this *is* reality.

☑ Stay in the present—what's actually happening right now?

☑ Ask yourself, Of all my perceptions, which ones can be verified (measured, timed, corroborated)? What would an impartial other say?

☑ Practice relaying direct, concrete facts.

☑ Use precise, exact, or specific language in a report that you think may not merit this kind of detailed information.

When You're One or Few Amongst the Many

When you have a preference for Intuition and your teammates have a preference for Sensing, consider:

☑ Practicing step-by-step presentation of information

☑ Providing specific examples of vital information

☑ Honoring organizational values tied to experience and tradition

☑ Reading the fine print and getting the facts straight

When you have a preference for Sensing and your teammates have a preference for Intuition, consider:

☑ Getting involved in projects that require long-range or future thinking

☑ Practicing brainstorming with the rest of the team

☑ Preparing yourself for roundabout discussions

☑ Going beyond specifics—try asking about the patterns, meanings, and themes

I'm just back from that training session. . . .
Let's try closing with a group hug.

To Think, Perchance to Feel—
That Is the Mystery

The Thinking–Feeling Dimension

Type Key

Looking at an issue from all sides leads to good decisions.

As Charles Dickens wrote in *A Tale of Two Cities,* "It was the best of times, it was the worst of times. . . ." It is the best of times for Thinkers —current psychological type research indicates that the Thinking preference for decision making is much more common than the Feeling decision-making style in business culture, both in the United States and worldwide.

This emphasis on Thinking can make this the worst of times for Feelers. Writers such as Carl Jung have suggested that the Thinking decision-making style has been the primary intellectual and culture-shaping force in the Western world since the Renaissance. The Thinking decision-making style emphasizes principles, logic, objectivity, and scientific reasoning. People with a preference for Thinking tend to put priority on the task first and on people next. The role of Thinking in most organizations is to question, find flaws, make corrections, solve problems, and seek improvement in general.

So what does the world of Thinkers look like? Many professions found in almost every organization—accounting, business administration, engineering, finance, legal—are overwhelmingly populated by those who prefer Thinking. Many functional areas—administration, compensation and benefits, construction, health and safety, manufacturing, marketing, production, quality control, government, military, physical sciences—tend to rely on Thinking.

The learning environments that produce our scientists, engineers, accountants, and business managers support the Thinking decision-making style. They are trained in rigorous intellectual debate with its analytical reasoning, challenges to one's knowledge, and a prove-disprove style. Examining and critiquing the work of others including experts, teachers, and fellow classmates is standard practice as the way to find truth. Continual training in this learning style, added to Thinkers' natural predisposition, encourages Thinkers to stand firm against any opposition while learning to support their own viewpoints with proper logical evidence.

In academic preparation for many of the occupations listed above, it is atypical to study other models of problem solving and decision making. The Feeling style is generally found in the fine arts, liberal arts, humanities, and social sciences, where the emphasis is on methods that take into account the needs, wants, and aspirations of the people who will be affected. These approaches might look for areas of agreement as one searches out values and motivations. This way of solving problems and looking for acceptance is the Feeling decision-making style.

Because Thinking is so dominant in the industrial world, unwittingly the industrial culture tends to support those with a preference for Thinking. Many Thinkers are therefore surprised to learn that there is another equally valuable way of making *rational* decisions, that of Feeling. The Feeling style includes considering the impact of one's decisions on others, on one's organization, and on those about whom one cares. Feelers will use themselves as "litmus paper" to assess subjectively by putting themselves into a situation or in others' shoes. By considering how the other person might *feel*, they make discoveries about the impact of that situation's variables on themselves and their values, just as litmus paper can determine the acidity of a solution. Using their own response to the situation, Feelers are often able to determine what is meaningful and important for people. Feelers generally can forecast how others will respond to a set of circumstances and what factors will win over others' hearts as well as minds.

In organizational life, Feelers are often found in areas where the "softer side" of management prevails or where an accurate understanding of the impact on people is crucial. Some of these functional areas are advertising, human resources (especially human resource development), customer service, community or customer relations, and in organizations whose mission is people or where quality is values-driven (community and social service organizations, museums, religious institutions, schools, and so on). Feelers are often in fields such as journalism, publishing, entertainment, and public relations.

Feelers frequently choose academic coursework in the arts, fine arts, humanities, and social sciences. In this coursework, they are trained to understand the motivations and character of people and groups. They often design cooperative and collegial learning environments where the focus is on empathic and careful handling of each other as learners as well as exploring the subject matter to determine what is of value and importance to people.

Workplace experiences can feel like "the worst of times" to Feelers because they feel pressed to prove to others whether they, their position, or their problem-solving style add any value to organization life. The benefits that the Feeling decision-making style brings to organizations have long been discounted in the whole of the business world.

Analysis of business teams worldwide indicates that Feelers are definitely in the minority—rarely reaching more than 20 percent of any given management team except in some specific Feeling domains such as human services or human resource development. Because the gifts of the Feeling function are absent, ignored, overpowered, or devalued in most business organizations, the warmth and harmony Feelers bring may be absent as well.

So it is the best of times for Thinkers because they will:

➤ Fit easily into the higher academic and business world
➤ Find their decision-making style matches that of others with whom they work
➤ Be supported by an industrial culture that emphasizes an objective, logical approach to decisions
➤ Be, by nature, prepared to solve problems in a detached and impersonal way

It is the worst of times for Feelers because they find their decision-making style and opinions are:

➤ Discounted and often not trusted in the business world
➤ Misunderstood because Thinkers have often had little exposure to the merits of the Feeling way of making decisions
➤ Thought of as "emotional" even though Jung and others clearly describe feeling as a *rational* decision-making process
➤ Considered soft, touchy-feely, and unbusinesslike

However, paradoxically it is also the worst of times for business teams with a predominant preference for Thinking because their blind spot can be so great. Thinkers often lack awareness of the impact their decision may have on their team, their organization, their community, or even on themselves! The long-term implications of their decisions may not become apparent until it is too late, when the damage has been done. In analyzing situations where poor decisions were made, writers who understand the concepts of Jungian psychological type recount instances where the special perspectives of the Feeling function were ignored. "Buyer beware," "You're being paid to do this," "Everyone is looking out for number 1," and "Clobber the competition" can be examples of Thinking run amok in organizational life. Notice that there is no need to consider other people if the rules of the business game call for everyone to look out for themselves. Think of the problems this poses for Feelers, who want to look out for others!

Thus, ignoring the unique gifts of the Feeling decision-making process (values orientation and impact on people) can be a risk-laden way to do business. Thinkers and their organizations are often bewildered when they encounter the strength of the unleashed Feeling function because few things in their training or background allow them to even know what hit them.

However, now may be the best of times for Feelers. If Feelers get any education in the Thinking ways of business or exposure to the business world to add to their innate people-centered disposition, they may gain an advantage over one-sided Thinking colleagues. If they can find a way to articulate and bring their Feeling values-based approach to business issues and decisions made by teams to which they belong, their Feeling insight can add a needed perspective and perhaps everyone will be better served. However, because Feelers prize harmony and want to get along well with others, they may hesitate to raise their Feeling voice above a whisper, not wishing to ruffle feathers.

Before going on to our case studies, which illustrate the best and worst of each decision-making style, let's consider the way each preference handles the important team tool of employee recognition or praise. The very word *recognition* is more aligned with the Thinking preference, and the words *praise* or *appreciation* are more clearly aligned with the Feeling preference.

Throughout the years in classes and in team-building sessions where I've used psychological type, I often ask people to tell me about their style for giving recognition or appreciation to their employees and to each other for work that is well done. Uniformly, Thinkers say that recognition should occur when job standards are achieved, or in many cases *exceeded*. Many times those with a preference for Thinking will say, "When we pay a specific amount to people to do a job, included in that pay is an indication of a principle—we pay what the job is worth, or more if the performance is stellar or if the market demands it of us." For example, one member of a large county hospital's board, which was in a labor dispute with its nursing organization, stated, "Of course we appreciate the nurses. We pay them *above* the market! What more do they want?" The nurses responded that while they appreciated the money, they also wanted personal acknowledgment and direct feedback for their efforts from the very start.

Thinkers, on the other hand, may be suspicious if they are paid more than the market or given recognition or appreciation before a task is accomplished, believing that anything that seems illogical or that predates their accomplishment might be a "ploy" representing an ulterior motive on the part of the giver. "Why would someone praise me if I haven't met the standard or if I'm just starting the task?" they ask. The Feeling way of giving recognition and appreciation, therefore, may hinder Thinkers rather than motivate them.

Feelers often state that they give praise and appreciation (rather than recognition) to individuals who are just beginning a task, continuing the praise and appreciation throughout the work cycle until the task is completed. Feelers managed by Thinkers often say they feel undervalued and unappreciated because, while they've given their all to a project, they have yet to receive any positive feedback! They may also comment that when they have exceeded the expectations or requirements of the task, they want to hear a word of praise. Feelers in a Thinking organization rarely receive the kind of appreciation that motivates them.

Thinking and Feeling teams and organizations can both become so unbalanced that the situation can waver between comical and pathetic to anyone who knows about psychological type. The two stories you are about to read are true; only the names and locations have been changed, à la *Dragnet*.

Type Story: Software Technology, Inc. (STI)

Cast of Characters

Tony, Founder, Inventor, and CEO	INTP
Roger, Executive Vice President	ENFJ

Software Technology specialized in software products that linked computers worldwide. Tony, the founder and the inventor of STI's premier software, was uniformly described as brilliant. Prior to starting STI, Tony worked in research and development at IBM and taught mathematics at an Ivy League university. As chief executive officer (CEO), he hired only the best and the brightest for his senior management team. Most of the team members were previously employed by blue chip organizations where their innovative work had gained industrywide recognition—they were giants in their fields.

Tony's inventiveness was so advanced and ingenious that the STI product lines had been the industry leaders for more than a decade. Tony had a clear preference for Thinking and lived by logic. He loved mysteries and technical books as well as the computers with which he worked. His life reflected the principles he had set for himself at an early age—choosing a path of rigor, challenge, and inquiry. Tony's inner thought process and decisive style were responsible for the genius that surrounded the workings of STI.

Unfortunately, working for Tony was seldom pleasant; even his closest colleagues were intimidated by his harsh style. Tony was unaware of the impact he had on his colleagues or STI's employees. The senior executive team of STI was filled with fear, anxiety, and negative energy. People didn't know what to expect from Tony from one day to the next. Tony's executive vice president, Roger, asked me to work with Tony. Roger had been brought in eighteen months earlier by the board of directors as a balance to Tony and most employees recognized his positive influence. He was also well trained in current management and leadership theory. He was fairly certain that a deliberate outside intervention, designed to assess Tony and make suggestions, was needed to change Tony's fear and intimidation style of management to one that could engage people's hearts as well as their minds.

Over the phone, Roger relayed to me, "Tony just doesn't have a clue as to what his behavior does to people. My résumé is as high-powered as they come in this industry, and he makes *me* nervous. Several of our key people are grumbling about leaving STI and we need help before our top ranks are dealt any serious blows." I asked Roger if he had discussed contacting me with Tony. "Oh yeah," he replied, "Tony said, 'If you need someone to hold your hand, go ahead and call her.'"

In my introductory meeting, I found out just how imposing Tony was; well over six feet tall, he looked every bit the tough manager he was. Tony said to me, "I know not everyone likes my style, but frankly, my style pushed STI to the top. People can adjust to how I am. Maybe morale has dipped a bit, but I certainly don't keep them chained here, unable to leave. Good people are hard to find, I know, but it seems that many of them like our compensation and benefits package and want the reflected glory that comes from working with me," and he chuckled.

Type Clue

The life of the mind is important to INTPs. The outside world is less important—especially illogical (people) parts of that outside world. Many INTPs shine in academic endeavors because of this ability to focus. However, in their quest for intellectual truth, they may neglect to pay attention to their impact on people.

I smiled. "From what I hear, your staff finds the projects they work on very exciting. There's no doubt you've made STI what it is today and they know you deserve the credit, but there are probably some key people that you would have trouble replacing, given that you already hired the best away from your competition. I suggest some data-gathering to see what the facts are and whether people have a basis for their complaints. I can interview everyone on your senior staff. In analyzing their responses, we may find that some changes are called for, either in your leadership style or in organizational practices."

Tony agreed to my proposed process but was somewhat skeptical about its merits. I sensed he was defensive about how many fingers might end up pointing at him. He was perceptive enough to know his style was causing him and others problems and that he was fortunate not to have incurred any serious damage for STI yet.

I decided to formally interview members of the management team and other selected employees. In these sessions, I gathered an amazing list of complaints against Tony's management style. While his team was well aware of his technical genius, many team members stated that they remained with STI only because of the pay they were getting and the incredible products the organization developed. Dealing with Tony was such a major issue, however, that several people thought he might need a psychiatric evaluation! To illustrate just how far to one side Tony's style had moved, here is a summarization of interview comments:

➤ He disrupts most of our meetings with questions that put us on the spot. When someone can't answer, or doesn't answer to his satisfaction, he goes into a tirade, accusing that person of being dumb. The rest of us sit there placing bets on which one of us will be the next target of his scorn.

➤ We have a rating scale for the Tony Factor—on a scale of one to ten, we assess how biting and brutal Tony's criticism and mood are for the day. Our grapevine keeps everyone well informed on the Tony Factor all day long.

➤ Tony manages like a screaming banshee. I spend more of my time figuring out how to keep him from attacking me and my ideas than I do at my work. If I and the others spent as much time working on our system designs as we do on analyzing Tony's behavior, we would be light-years ahead on our projects.

➤ He expects us to match his eighteen-hour days in pursuit of the Holy Grail. No matter how many hours we put in, Tony doesn't acknowledge our efforts. His reply to our complaints is, "I am as hard on myself as I am on you. You know one reason why I hired you is because you are the best. You are paid way above market rates; you have a great financial package; and I can't fathom why you need to hear any more thanks than that!"

➤ Tony is Marketing's worst enemy. We're embarrassed almost every time he meets with customers. His arrogant, abrasive attitude turns them off. Many customers leave the meetings feeling upset or stunned at his treatment of them—not the way to run customer meetings!

Type Clue

To say I was somewhat anxious when I met with Tony to report the interview results on his style was an understatement. I was aware that I would have to be extremely objective in my presentation if I didn't want to personally experience the Tony Factor and further exacerbate the problems at STI. I thought perhaps if I got to know the man behind the STI founder-inventor-scientist, I could determine the best strategy to give Tony the feedback so that he would benefit from it.

We chatted for a while and I asked Tony if he would share something about his background with me. In listening to him, I found that Tony had a fairly one-sided childhood, ideal for creating a Thinker with the flaws of Tony's magnitude. His birth parents were killed during the Holocaust. His adoptive father was internationally recognized and had a name familiar to most people. Tony's adoptive father wanted to make sure that Tony's mind reached its full potential. As early as he could, his father focused the dinnertime discussions on debates over scientific or mathematical topics and concepts. Tony was grilled nightly on his school work and was taught to challenge every assumption and find the weaknesses in every idea. He came to regard challenging people as normal. These characteristics as well as his obsession with work led to the breakup of his first marriage.

He said to me, "Life hurts. Mine has been filled with many personal losses and my solace has been in my work. Because my work is so fulfilling, I find that I'm hard on those who don't put in the hours that I do. I have low tolerance for people who take up my time with questions that seem irrelevant to me—I have too much on my mind regarding the technical process that gets our products out there. But . . . I suppose I may be making a few enemies along the way and I realize I need some help to improve staff morale, so let's cut to the chase. What did they have to say about me?"

Type Clue

Thinking types often manage emotional distress by thrusting themselves into areas where their natural Thinking style is emphasized. From childhood on, Tony's training in handling his emotions and dealing with others was haphazard compared to the training his Thinking preference received. No wonder he retreated to his work rather than become more involved with others.

"Well," I began, "your management team is concerned about you personally. They also feel hindered in their ability to do their best technical work because they feel that so much time needs to be spent managing you. They put a great deal of energy into forecasting how you may respond, anticipating your questions, and defending their ideas to you. I asked several individuals to estimate how much time was spent on these issues."

"What was their answer?" Tony asked.

"Well, up to 25 or 30 percent goes into safeguarding themselves from possible confrontations with you."

Type Clue

Because Thinkers habitually look for the flaws in any situation, I knew Tony would be curious about the critical reactions of others to him. I wanted something objective and reasonable regarding Tony's leadership style for him to realize how serious the problem was.

Tony said, "You're kidding . . . Wow, I guess I'd better listen. Twenty-five to thirty percent of their time . . . Well, go on, because I want to know the complete picture. What else do they have to say about me? And when you've done that, you and I better figure out what strategy to take on this."

Tony and I continued to discuss the rest of the data from his senior management team.

"I'm aware I lack some people skills," Tony responded. "You know, I haven't allowed myself to get close to other people, nor do I spend much time analyzing personal relationships and how I affect others. I want to make some changes in my personal relationships as well as my work relationships or they may interfere in accomplishing my personal goals."

Type Clue

Tony could use his flaw-finding radar on himself, too, and was beginning to see what the problems were with his leadership style.

Personal and family relationships are not aspects of team building or the work I do, but Tony did tell me that he was in marriage counseling as well as individual therapy with two of his teenage children. He had looked at therapy and the study of emotional health as a dilettante thing to do. He also found it hard to respect the "soft" point of view and accepting style that the therapist used. "Yet," he said, "it seems to be bringing some good results—at least my wife and kids think so."

"Consider whether or not that soft side might be something you've really defended yourself against over your lifetime," I said. "Now that you know something about personality type, incorporating some of your Feeling side might bring noticeable results—a potential gold mine for yourself and your family in addition to STI."

Tony thought this was an interesting consideration and agreed to spend some time becoming more "user friendly" with his management team.

We further explored the benefits of Tony incorporating into his personal style concern for the impact of his ways on others and of beginning to publicly acknowledge their expertise. I added that I knew a few Thinkers who counted to ten before making criticisms of the ideas of others. "Perhaps," I suggested, "if you listen long enough you will find valuable information and options in their proposals that make sense to you.

"You say you've hired only the best—you can trust them to run their own areas, calling you in for those special times when your overall vision is necessary. Putting more trust and faith in the people who have stayed with you will leave you free to pursue those areas that you most enjoy."

We decided that prior to any team-building session, instead of doing a group interpretation of the MBTI inventory I would work with each key player individually. Tony requested that I give them information on his MBTI type profile and a little bit about how his private life may have intensified his Thinking style.

Tony and I agreed that in the time between the individual interpretations and the actual team-building session, I would sit in on several top staff meetings to coach him. At these meetings, managers gave updates on their specific areas. In many cases, their information was very positive for the company. I suggested to Tony that if I heard something that deserved at least a "thank you" or an "I appreciate the effort you've put in on this task," I would raise a red pen as a signal for him to make an appropriate compliment.

He liked the idea and suggested that we try it out. The positive results were very evident, helping Tony put recognition into his logical formulation of working with people. "If I give appropriate acknowledgment and appreciation, then I may create an atmosphere that increases our productivity," was how he stated it.

Type Clue

When Thinkers add the human element to their logical outlook and see the results, the effect is often tangible enough to give them permanent incentive to keep trying. This may give them an extra edge in their business and personal dealings.

Because I had met with each person prior to the team-building session, discussing Tony's history and acknowledging their comments about his style, fear and trepidation about the upcoming session was reduced. I advised Tony that this would be his biggest opportunity to build a more responsive and less apprehensive team. We held a practice session so that I could send him some of the worst barbs and comments about his style and allow him to practice listening without responding in a negative or emotionally hostile way. And because Tony was the able person that he was, he managed the practice well.

On the actual team-building day, we reviewed everyone's psychological type, emphasizing what each person needed to contribute most effectively to a climate of trust and openness as well as what each person needed to keep in mind as this climate was being established. Tony's list was one of the longest. Each person also mentioned how, in the intervening time, Tony had done something positive. Some people had to search hard, but there were enough comments to confirm that Tony was already beginning to change his leadership style. The team developed a code of conduct and professionalism for STI as it moved forward. It included:[7]

➤ Acknowledge initially what is right about an idea before offering a valid critique.
➤ Respect each person, attacking only the problem being discussed.

➤ Use language that is positive, upbeat, and emotionally neutral.

➤ Count to ten if a critical thought or word comes to mind.

➤ Follow the Golden Rule with each other as well as with customers and vendors.

➤ Acknowledge each other's effort to meet or exceed goals.

➤ Develop a trial run system to test new ideas in advance of taking them to Tony.

➤ Have an STI social gathering each quarter to get to know each other better. (Suggestions for this included golf, a pizza party, a day at the local stock car racetrack, attending a baseball game.)

It is now several years into my working with Tony and STI. While he still has his "rough edges," he also recognizes that it is easier to catch flies with sugar than with vinegar. He is still working on his personal therapy with his family and acknowledges that the carryover of this therapy into his business life has been quite helpful. He continues to follow the STI code of conduct and professionalism established by his executive team and periodically asks for and *listens* to feedback about his leadership style from his colleagues and other STI employees. He has found some value in being open to areas that he previously thought were soft. Roger serves as his mentor on the Feeling side of the business and they lunch together at least weekly. Tony and Roger have developed into an excellent team, combining technical expertise with people skills.

Type Story: Lynstarr Corporation

Cast of Characters

Malcolm, Executive Vice President
of Corporate Communications   ESFJ

Tony's lack of an informed Feeling process certainly caused problems, but no worse than the problems caused by others who rely too completely on Feeling, seldom considering what the Thinking preference may add to a situation. For example, there was Malcolm, the bright, young executive vice president of Corporate Communications for Lynstarr Corporation, a large manufacturing company.

My call came from René, the CEO. René, who had been a client of mine, was initially pleased with his selection of Malcolm. He told me that Malcolm had impeccable credentials: an advanced degree in business and communications from a top-notch school, prominence in several community service organizations, and involvement in the right professional associations. He was currently president of the local chapter of the International Association of Business Communicators. Furthermore, in his previous position as corporate communications director for a similar manufacturing company, Malcolm had adeptly steered it through a major product-tampering scare.

Because I had completed a team-building process with René's staff just at the time of Malcolm's hiring, I knew that his confirmed type was ESFJ.

René told me, "Malcolm inherited a group of individuals that could hardly be characterized as a team. They each had separate areas of responsibility and they all felt overworked. They had a long way to go to function as a team.

"When Malcolm first started, I received a lot of good feedback about his friendliness and his habit of visiting the factory floor, talking with each person in a way that made them feel like an important part of Lynstarr, but I am disturbed by recent rumors. I know in my dealings with him he tends to back off from his requests, seemingly more concerned with not ruffling feathers than with fighting for more resources for his department—which I concur they need! He seems to be a people-pleaser, especially toward me. You know, everyone likes him as a person, but his 'let's be one big happy family' style gets in the way of his effectiveness."

René sent me a packet of information, including a copy of Malcolm's formal statement of mission to his communications team. Here's an excerpt from that memo:

"The Corporate Communications function is more than window dressing for Lynstarr. We have an important calling. In the past, your mission was task-oriented: keep the senior managers happy; write the corporate newsletters, annual reports, and departmental brochures; and field any media inquiries. Under my leadership, your mission will be people-oriented: In our publications, we will strive to highlight the individual contributions of Lynstarr employees, spotlight Lynstarr's numerous community endeavors, and show that a profitable manufacturing company can have a heart. We will champion the people part of Lynstarr's business, making sure that good communication flows throughout all levels of the organization as well as to all its stakeholders.

"To do that, we need to be a united team, working together toward this common goal. With today's uncertain environment of lawsuits and the watchfulness of the press, finding a balance between legal and economic sensibility is tough. Yet we want to show a workplace where diversity of opinion, environmental friendliness, and high productivity coexist—this is our challenge and our opportunity. Lynstarr can gain a competitive advantage by presenting itself as a preferred place of employment for talented people who are enthusiastic about their work and are ready to offer excellent performance.

I look forward to learning more about each one of you and the role you will play on our team."

Type Clue

Let's give our best for truth, justice, and the American way! ESFJs often lead by communicating a sense of tradition or value for the tasks at hand. They want their actions to be consistent with the needs they see in their followers and those whom they serve.

They also place a high value on harmony. Notice Malcolm's emphasis on friendliness and teamwork—but beware, Feelers. Read on to see the dangers of harmony at all costs.

Malcolm's initial communications with other departments informed them that Corporate Communications would respond to Lynstarr's people-oriented information needs and would serve as a direct link between the various business units and the external environment. He asked for their suggestions for improving communications and promoting Lynstarr to its various constituencies. He also argued for and won a communications technology center to give employees access to all the latest technological developments.

High flyers like Malcolm foster high expectations. People were initially enthusiastic over Malcolm's style, partly because of the deep need Lynstarr had for the types of change he promised. But when Malcolm failed to increase his staff after guaranteeing he would gain approval to hire an additional three communications specialists, and when he made several promises to senior management that placed a heavy strain on his team, harmony in Corporate Communications seemed to vaporize almost overnight. Eight months into his tenure, the department was anything but the united team its mission statement delineated. Instead, Corporate Communications had become a hotbed of back stabbing, favoritism, one-upmanship, and under-the-table communication (the cobbler's children have no shoes?).

My first meeting with Malcolm was very pleasant. He reluctantly acknowledged that there was conflict in his department and that things weren't going well for him as a member of the senior management team. He said, "I'm really glad I joined Lynstarr, with its emphasis on its employees, but these first few months have been rougher than I anticipated. René warned me that I inherited a team of rugged individualists, but given my previous experience, I didn't foresee having this much trouble establishing a department characterized by good working relationships. I'm a bit worried that I'm part of the problem. I guess I'd like some feedback on my leadership style from those with whom I work most closely.

"In my former job, I came up through the ranks and knew everyone so well—I handpicked my managers and we clicked from the start. Also, I guess I didn't realize how lucky I was having Jeff, the general counsel, as a mentor who advocated for me and was always available as a sounding board for the logical thing to do in a crisis. I came here at Jeff's urging, the benefits of a larger company and all."

Type Clue

ESFJs like Malcolm tend to put their heart into finding the good in every situation, and Malcolm was searching for the most positive aspects of his move to Lynstarr. However, he seemed to be struggling with some of the larger issues in his role as Corporate Communications Executive Vice President—an advocate for his team as well as for Lynstarr.

Although Feelers want to change in any way they can to create harmony, it can be tough for them to listen to feedback objectively, without becoming defensive. It was my job to deliver that feedback in a constructive manner.

After talking with Malcolm, I decided to begin my process by asking everyone on the team to respond in writing to some simple questions:

1. What does the leadership of the department do best?
2. What one change would you make if you could simply wave a magic wand and make that change happen?
3. What would make Lynstarr's Corporate Communications a more collaborative department?

Almost all of the resulting comments were directed at Malcolm. This is not surprising because of his visibility as a leader and the impact his style had on the team. In those written comments, there were several positive statements about Malcolm. Team members noted that he had:

➤ A warm personality and a good sense of humor
➤ Excellent academic and practical understanding of current corporate communication philosophies, trends, and technology
➤ A "service mentality"

> ## Type Clue
>
> The warm and practical approach to people and problems that ESFJs, in particular, favor can create a harmonious work environment, but read on.

However, the negative feedback for Malcolm far outweighed the positive. Comments included:

➤ Malcolm is not a strong leader; he seems unable to use his power to make things happen. When we come up with ideas to significantly improve our systems, he won't push them through. If we are to meet our goals, Corporate Communications must be more proactive.

➤ Malcolm acts like a parent, trying to fix our quarrels rather than making us work things out ourselves. Because of this, some team members have become tattletales, running to him instead of dealing with the person with whom they are having problems.

➤ Malcolm avoids rather than manages conflict. He takes the easy way out by playing favorites. He seems to regard the opinions of two of his direct reports more highly than anyone else's. These two people are the ones who think and act most like him, so in soliciting their input he generally gets the answers he wants.

➤ He does not communicate to us with strong, clear messages. He rambles on, giving a ten-dollar response to a two-bit question.

> ## Type Clue
>
> Many Feelers are accused of being talkative when in part they are trying to make acquaintances into good friends. These are not idle conversations but data-gathering sessions with what matters most—people.
>
> They also may be accused of favoritism when they simply prefer to work with like-minded spirits. Whereas a Thinker might logically pick the most suitable associate to assist him or her on a task, a Feeler might make that decision based on the ensuing relationship as they go about the project.

➤ Malcolm isn't willing to "toot his own horn" nor that of the department to the line vice presidents. As a result, we are understaffed and underfunded.

➤ Malcolm seems to speak out of both sides of his mouth. He announces his decisions, then backs down when someone on the executive team complains. In order to please top management, he agreed to produce a weekly rather than monthly newsletter even though he knew we struggled to find resources to produce one every four weeks. His attempts to placate antagonized both sides.

Malcolm clearly needed help. The force and direction of the comments indicated that his Feeling preference seemed to be getting in the way of his effectiveness. His decisions were made without the balance that comes from incorporating Thinking gifts of fairness, consistency, and logic. Lynstarr's manufacturing environment, which had a predominantly Thinking style, probably highlighted Malcolm's style difference even more.

Type Clue

I used my knowledge of the ESFJ type to soften the blow. Feelers often take criticism so personally that they become incapacitated. Or, they may begin to avoid situations because of negative comments or barbs. There was too much promise to allow Malcolm to become overly self-critical.

Because Malcolm knew his MBTI type (ESFJ), we discussed his type as well as the possible avenues an intervention might take. I asked him first to describe his leadership style.

"I feel my role as leader should be based on trust. I'm a mentor, a guide, and want to be a model for the people who work for me; that way I hope each of them can use their skills to the very best of their ability. I feel this will benefit Lynstarr as well. I think it's my role to represent both sides of an issue; it's part of my training and part of my style. I dislike conflict and can generally see the merit of both sides of an issue."

Type Clue

Feelers are good at just that—putting themselves in the shoes of another and understanding why people on both sides feel the way they do. However, seeing both sides was causing problems for Malcolm because he was not applying some other tools of his Feeling function to determine which side's viewpoint was more favorable to all involved or in line with the values to be served.

René had given me the results of a recent organizational climate effectiveness survey, which I now shared with Malcolm. "You know, according to this survey, your staff recognizes the value you place on relationships and creating a friendly atmosphere, but for the most part they feel a lack of team effort from the top down. Several mentioned that you tend to rely most heavily on the input of two people on the team, leaving the rest feeling second-class. In fact, many distrust your warm, friendly style, thinking suspiciously that it is a put-on to get more out of them."

Type Clue

Many of Malcolm's direct reports had a preference for Thinking. Because Malcolm's friendliness lacked a logical basis, they assumed the worst motives for it.

This was an eye-opener for Malcolm. "I don't think I play favorites. Those two people have great educational credentials and lots of Lynstarr experience and furthermore, they seem to see the world the way I do—they are kindred spirits. It's simply easier for me to work with them. I knew *some* conflict existed. I've had an inkling that a few people might be jealous of my relationship with both of them, especially Jim. Some team members seem downright hostile toward Jim because he's so talented, so they use any chance to get back at him."

Type Clue

If Feelers find a sympathetic ear in the midst of conflict, it's hard for them to avoid seeking that person out even in the face of being perceived as playing favorites. I thought we could use type data on Thinking and Feeling to help further.

Malcolm and I reviewed the results of the organizational climate survey. He was taken off guard to see that his department's score regarding the amount of warmth and support people gave each other was one of the lowest of those surveyed within Lynstarr. Communication was also given low ratings; many viewed it as lots of talk or information of little substance. Malcolm had unconsciously chosen to ignore his "feeling" that people were as frustrated with his communication style as the results of this survey indicated.

Malcolm set the report down and said, "So is there a place to begin or should I throw in the towel? I hate conflict—all I want to do is make this a great place for everyone to work."

"Conflict is probably exactly where we should begin," I said. "Because I share your preference for Feeling, I also dislike conflict! But your aversion and avoidance of friction seems to cause even more conflict within the department.

"Have you ever said one thing to one person and another thing to someone else just to hold conflict at bay? Or tried to help one person without realizing the favoritism implied? If people cannot see the rationale behind your decisions, or find that you sweep all conflict under the rug, leaving everyone to ignore the elephant—that is, conflict—in the office, they may not trust you. This seems to be what is happening currently.

"Avoiding conflict and trying to please everyone seems to lead to problems for you with senior management as well. If you want to have the type of Corporate Communications department that your mission statement delineates, you might need to ruffle a few feathers and advocate more strongly for increased financial resources and staff for the department. When your team hears that you have promised a weekly instead of monthly newsletter, but refuse to rock the boat by asking for more people or materials, they become demoralized, knowing that they cannot deliver on what *you* have promised without *their* extraordinary effort."

Malcolm sighed, "I *have* been trying to please everyone, ever since I arrived, I guess. And as I look back—and look at these surveys—I suppose I've pleased no one. What you are saying makes sense, though—how do I help myself become a rational Feeler?"

I laughed. "The Feeling preference *is* a way to make rational decisions. What you need to add to your process is a way to consider the logical consequences of each decision. And remember, sometimes you will need to detach yourself from the situation and look at it impersonally in order to make the best decision."

"What you need to tell me," he said, "is how I am supposed to do that. I realize the merits of using more objectivity, but it hasn't been a part of my style. I supposed I've learned that trying to please everyone pleases no one. I'll need to be more directly honest with people so they can learn my real intentions. When I look at the feedback, I guess I should listen to my most vocal critics because they may give me some insight into what I could do to be more effective."

"You're on the right track, Malcolm. Perhaps you could try some of the following suggestions." I gave him several ideas, including:

➤ *Focus consciously on conflict as it arises*. I suggested a course on conflict management—one that emphasizes the role of conflict in establishing good working relationships, leading to more productive decisions.

> ➤ *Delay promises until there is a chance to think through the logical con-sequences.* Were the resources currently available for Corporate Com-munications to achieve what he was promising? Or if a promise is made to one person, could it extend to others?
> ➤ *Try to remain objective about criticism and look for truth amid the thorns.*

Malcolm requested several articles that he might read and I gave him some references on leadership and taking unpopular stands. I added that René was very interested in his success at Lynstarr and had offered to mentor Malcolm, especially in the area of balanced decision making. We then agreed that at the upcoming team-building session, we would tackle Malcolm's leadership issues straight on.

Initially, the team-building session was tense, but the team relaxed as we progressed through the agenda. As I went through the differences between the Thinking and Feeling styles of decision making, I could see understanding beginning to build among the team members. Malcolm fol-lowed my talk with his perspective about his past performance. "My first impression of the Corporate Communications culture was that it was all business. If I had known more about my own type preference for Feeling and the company's Thinking culture, I would have recognized the differ-ence in our styles. In my attempts to live up to the mission I set for the department, I probably tried too hard to create a family-like environment. Actually, I got *part* of it—a dysfunctional family!

"I also became defensive and didn't take your feedback into account because it seemed that resistance and criticism was coming on so many fronts. I just dug my hole deeper and deeper.

"But I believe I have a handle now on how we can all work together. Today, I'll begin by telling you the commitments I have made to foster bet-ter teamwork and communication within our department. Then we'll work together to develop some suggestions for us as a team. Let me tell you my personal goals," he concluded as he put up the following overhead:

➤ Manage upward by advocating for sufficient team resources, especial-ly the actual financial and human resources needs, before making promises.
➤ Stop being a third party to team member disputes.
➤ Schedule a course on productive conflict management for myself and anyone on the team who feels they'd benefit.
➤ Speak the truth to my team and to senior management even if the truth might hurt.

➤ Personally pledge to close the gap between our mission and current reality.

➤ Stop readily volunteering the department to the whims of senior management just to appear "the golden boy"!

Toward the end of the session, Malcolm and the team formalized some norms for Corporate Communication that included the following:

➤ Bring any disagreement directly and solely to the source (leave Malcolm out).

➤ Before accusing anyone of ulterior motives, come up with some possible positive intentions a teammate might have.

➤ If you're feeling left out of Malcolm's orbit, advocate for time with him.

➤ Provide Malcolm with sufficient financial data for him to take in hand when requesting additional resources from senior management.

➤ Remember, you don't have to like everyone to work with them—but be civil!

As a group they all agreed to address problematic issues immediately with the other person involved. The team also decided to seek a human resources facilitator to resolve any residual bitterness among team members, and then take the department through training on conflict management and conflict resolution. Finally, the group decided to designate a process person for each meeting to make sure that all conflict was met and dealt with at the time it surfaced.

Malcolm did not change overnight, nor did anyone else in the department. Through their intentional focus on better team relationships and an understanding of their personality differences, the Corporate Communications department at Lynstarr started to communicate among themselves as well as they did with others.

TYPE TAKEAWAY

To achieve the best of times for your organization, remember that the most effective decisions are made when the impact on people is factored in along with the impact on the bottom line. Achieving a balance of Thinking and Feeling in your organization will lead to choices that are good for people and business.

Type Solvers to Try

When you suspect a Thinking–Feeling problem, try these ideas.[8]

☑ Think of a recent incident or meeting and answer the following:

➤ What does the presenter care most about regarding the topic he or she is addressing? What is most important to him or her about the topic?

➤ How is the presenter reacting to the response or lack of response? Is he or she feeling encouraged, motivated, upset, hesitant, concerned, ignored, pleased, or having other feelings?

☑ Use the following questions to see how much you've tuned in to each other. Go through the questions for each person. Remember to include yourself.

➤ What does this person care most about in his or her work? What's most important?

➤ What inspires and motivates him or her the most about work? What concerns him or her the most about work?

➤ What kind of appreciation or recognition does this person need the most? From whom? Under what circumstances?

➤ What kind of criticism or correction seems most acceptable and most effective? From whom? Under what circumstances?

➤ What kind of support and help would he or she value most from you? From others?

➤ What about *your* behavior and *your* interaction with him or her is inspiring and motivating? What is upsetting or discouraging about your behavior and your interaction?

☑ From the experiences in your last working day, try to identify answers to the following questions.

➤ What interaction(s) particularly pleased you and what led to that sense of being pleased?

➤ Whom did you particularly appreciate on that day for their work, their help, or their insight?

➤ Who or what inspired and motivated you the most that day?

➤ Who or what was most discouraging and draining that day?

☑ To activate team improvement at work, try the following techniques:

➤ When you're starting a meeting, particularly about a new project or work focus, ask people to identify what's most important to them, what they care the most about in the new effort.

➤ Engage the staff periodically about what they feel *proud* of and what they feel *sorry* about, regarding the way the work is going and the way people are treating each other.

➤ If the group tends to be critical of ideas and suggestions, initiate the rule, "Before saying anything critical, you must say two things that you like about the idea or suggestion."

➤ Get the team to discuss whom they would like to work with and how they would like to treat each other. Ask them to identify explicit interaction guidelines to which they are willing to commit themselves.

➤ Do an appreciation audit of yourself.

Are there particular individuals, projects, or tasks that deserve your appreciation?

Are you proud of the quantity and substance of the appreciation you express?

Did you express appreciation of contributions to process (such as helping resolve conflict at a meeting) as well as outcomes (such as the sales figures)?

What actions could you take to enhance the depth and breadth of your expressions of appreciation?

For personal development, consider the following.

If your preference is for Thinking, you can practice Feeling:

☑ Acknowledge your own emotions and feelings. Then generalize those emotions and feelings to others who may be in an experience similar to yours, and anticipate such feelings in others when you think of the scenario a certain decision would produce.

☑ For a week, keep track of your ratio of compliments to criticism. Judge whether the ratio is in good proportion. If not, do something to improve the balance.

☑ See if you can gain cooperation rather than enforce compliance. When working on a project, ask yourself, How can I win that person over? What's in it for them to join up with me?

☑ Spontaneously, or as close as possible to that, acknowledge with an appreciative comment or note when someone is putting a lot of energy into a task.

☑ Move outside your normal range of conversational topics to share a personal fact, detail, or insight about yourself and its underlying emotional tone.

☑ Tell someone at work what you value about him or her (resist discussing accomplishments or performance).

If your preference is for Feeling, you can practice Thinking:

☑ Practice giving simple, direct, to-the-point feedback to others. When feedback comes *your* way, be objective and use what's helpful.

☑ Ask yourself if-then and cause-effect questions such as, If I say yes to this, then what do I need to give up? What are the effects that result from these causes?

☑ Make a business decision using an objective framework that lists two to three options to be evaluated against major criteria such as cost, schedules, and ease of implementation. Give each option a score when judged against your criteria. Then select and *do* the option with the highest score.

☑ After logical consideration (using pros and cons or other approaches), take a tough-minded stance and hold firm.

☑ In business communication, especially voice mail and phone calls, practice "Keep it short, sweetheart!"

☑ Remember that to some people, business means business and, therefore, don't try to make all business relationships into friendships.

When You're One or Few Amongst the Many

When you have a preference for Thinking and your teammates have a preference for Feeling, consider:

☑ Working on projects in which alternative causes and solutions are evaluated

☑ Reminding yourself that factoring in the impact on people is the logical thing to do in decision making

☑ Softening critical remarks—find the positive, too

☑ Looking for points of agreement first

When you have a preference for Feeling and your teammates have a preference for Thinking, consider:

☑ Practicing laying out an argument logically by using *if . . . then* or by discussing the causes and effects

☑ Understanding that critical feedback is given in the spirit of improving your professionalism

☑ Bringing attention to stakeholders' concerns regarding the projects or work

☑ Using brief and concise language to express people's wants and needs.

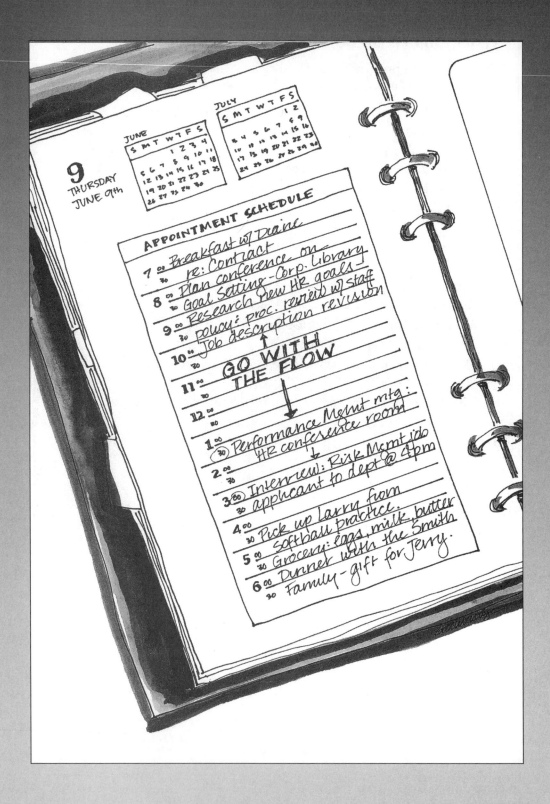

The Case of the Deadline Dilemmas

The Judging–Perceiving Dimension

> ## Type Key
> Behaviors that annoy you in others may be clues to areas for your *own* self-development.

Time—no one ever seems to have enough of it. How we use time, and our view of effectiveness and efficiency, may be colored by our preference for Judging or Perceiving. And the concepts of time for each preference can be as different as night and day. When asked to define what "on time" for the theater meant, one Judger said, "On time means you're in your seat fifteen minutes before the curtain goes up so that you can read the program notes." His Perceptive counterpart said, "As long as I arrive before the end of the first act, I'm happy!" No wonder our different ways of approaching life can cause frustration. We don't speak the same language.

Judgers tend be decisive and want to build a framework for life's happenings. They schedule their time in advance, generally with a Plan B to manage any contingencies. They enjoy getting things finished and are often single-minded in pursuit of a goal. They also like to do things in an organized way so they don't have to rework the same tasks. "Get it right the first time" is a maxim for those with a preference for Judging.

In this day of daily planners, schedules, and PERT and Gantt charts, many business teams seek to plan their work and work their plan. Most corporate cultures emphasize finding the best way to do something in the least amount of time. Academic business courses also stress the need to plan, organize, direct, and control oneself, others, and work production. Thus it is not surprising that studies of managers in business organizations find a majority of people (65 to 70 percent) with a preference for Judging.

Because they like to have a daily regimen for themselves, Judgers often attempt to systemize those around them, believing this is the most effective way to get things done. Timetables, deadlines, advance warnings to others in keeping with the motto "No Surprises," with life divided carefully between work and play—Judgers tend to create a life of stability and routine.

However, there *is* another equally valuable way to live one's life. Those with a preference for Perceiving like to adapt and experience life as it comes along. To them, "going with the flow" allows for a flexible, tolerant, open attitude about things so that life can be enjoyed in its fullness. After all, surprises, last-minute changes, detours from agendas, or sidetracking on issues often become exciting paths to new discoveries. Perceptives enjoy unexpected opportunities and don't want to miss out on anything.

People with a preference for Perceiving resist closure and imposed structure. Instead, their focus is on finding out and knowing more. They may be uncomfortable designating "the right way to do this" because they want to experience the world fully. This means there can be many right ways to live one's life or to accomplish any given task. Perceptives ably change with new, incoming information and often adjust readily to different people, environments, and ideas. Therefore, unusual things coming their way tend not to upset them. They are perhaps more able to follow their belief that life is richer because of chance and change.

Often, people find complementary business relationships or mates on this dimension—yes, *opposites do attract.* Judgers tend to appreciate the spontaneity and easy flexibility that Perceptives bring to the workplace—do they have an inkling that they may be missing out on the fun? Perceptives tend to value the structure and decisiveness that Judgers bring in tow—is it because they've had so many narrow squeaks with deadlines?

However, because these ways of approaching life are so different, the chance for conflict is high. In the business world of goal setting and strategic planning, where daily interactions are about determining how to get things done, chances are the Judgers and Perceptives will occasionally disagree with each other.

As with all of the preferences, neither Judging nor Perceiving is best in and of itself. If businesses are too intent on deadlines, they may miss late-breaking developments or trends that have an impact on their products or services. Of course, not meeting deadlines and being *too* open to last-minute changes can mean missed opportunities in the marketplace or customer dissatisfaction.

Many work and team-related issues result when the two styles choose to badger each other. How much better to respect the creative tension that exists between the Judging style that likes to plan and organize and the Perceiving style that likes to gather information and leave options open as long as possible.

Type Story: Donelle Sales Company

Cast of Characters

Dean, Sales Manager	ENTP
Gwen, Operations Manager	ISFJ

Conflict was the story between Dean and Gwen, two senior executives in the South Central district sales office of Donelle Sales Company. Donelle contracted with various manufacturers of medical devices to serve as their sales representatives. Dean, the sales manager, was one of Donelle's top salespeople, and had brought in several of the organization's biggest accounts. Gwen, the operations manager, ran one of the most efficient offices in Donelle's system. When the South Central office was established a few years back, Gwen and Dean had been chosen for their roles because of their specific gifts: Dean for his flexibility, his way of keeping abreast of market trends, and his ability to adjust quickly to customer needs; and Gwen for her ability to manage, organize, and deliver products to customers in a timely and efficient way.

However, to say there was continual friction between the two managers is an understatement. In Dean's eyes, Gwen was *too* organized, trying to impose her order on *him* as well as on the office. In Gwen's eyes, Dean was continually one step away from unintentionally derailing a sale or customer delivery because of his tendency to be late or to not follow office procedures.

The tension between Gwen and Dean was affecting the whole office when Ray, the CEO of Donelle, asked me to interview each of them as well as members of the South Central team to see if conflict resolution coaching using the *Myers-Briggs Type Indicator* might work. Ray said to me, "I don't want to lose either Gwen or Dean. They're both very valuable players on my team. I recognize that each of them has a different style and I want to use both sets of talents. If they could only work out their differences, I know they would be quite a team. However, because they are so different, they seem to be at each other's throats rather than at each other's sides as they run the South Central operation. I've seen the Myers-Briggs used before in other district offices and I know how helpful it can be in resolving workplace issues. I'd sure like your help to get Gwen and Dean back on a more cooperative track."

As a start for this assignment, I conducted separate telephone "get acquainted" sessions with Dean and Gwen. I told them about the MBTI inventory and asked them each to take it. I said we would first meet individually to discuss their MBTI results as well as go over the issues that existed between the two of them. Because they were such competent and seasoned Donelle employees, both of them seemed anxious to find a way to resolve their disputes. Their work life and teaming together had become very stressful for each of them.

During our telephone conversation, Gwen shared with me, "It's a relief to talk to someone who has dealt with these types of issues before. Just last night I thought, Dean and I need a referee to call the whistle when we start arguing about deadlines and procedures.

"Perhaps there is just bad chemistry between the two of us. We never seem to be on the same side of any procedural issue. We both agree that the customer's needs come first and that our sales will increase when we meet those needs, but we have widely different ways of accomplishing this goal. Frankly, I would love any kind of assistance you can offer so that I can better understand Dean. To be able to do all this with a neutral third party sounds really productive to me. Donelle is a great place to work—other than battling with Dean—and I truly want to resolve our issues."

When I explained my process to Dean over the phone, he said, "I really respect Gwen and her expertise. She seems to have the company and the customer's wishes foremost in her mind. But sometimes I feel like she clobbers me over the head with her schedules and procedures, as if I'm not *also* working to meet the customer's needs. I dislike doing things too far in advance because in this business, the game plan always changes.

"I would really like to be on better terms with Gwen. We spend way too much time trying to manage each other. This game playing detracts from the other things we have to do on the job—so how quickly will you be here? The sooner Gwen and I learn to work together, the better."

Type Clue

Dean's description of Gwen was of a classic Judger—efficient and organized. Gwen's description of Dean was classic, too—more flexible about meeting operating procedures and deadlines. Dean said he liked to leave things open; Gwen said she liked to nail things down. Both stated the importance of meeting customer needs, but each had a different way of meeting this goal. The Judging–Perceiving preference seemed to be the place to start my work with the two of them.

As I heard both of them expressing a similar goal, I expected that the MBTI would provide an excellent framework for discussing their different work styles. Before my meetings with them, I reviewed their reported MBTI results. It appeared that Gwen was an ISFJ and that Dean was an ENTP—exactly opposite in all four preferences. Their Judging and Perceiving processes were most noticeably different, with each having a very clear preference on this dimension.

I pulled out a series of questions that I often use with a larger team to help compare and contrast differences. I thought they would be useful for analyzing the problems between Dean and Gwen. I planned to ask these questions in separate interviews with each of them:

1. What contributions do you bring to Donelle's South Central office?
2. What actions or habits do you have that may be unsettling or irritating to the other?
3. What does the other do that annoys you?
4. What do you find valuable about each other?
5. What outcomes do you hope for as a result of this conflict resolution process?

These questions usually work well with any of the preference combinations or with entire type categories where there is conflict in a relationship. It is important to ask question four regarding value of the other person, especially following questions two and three, as a way to help rebuild any bridges that may have been torn down between the combatants.

Additionally, I arranged to gather information from several of the other team members of the South Central office to see whether the different approaches of Gwen and Dean were affecting anyone else, as I suspected they might.

My first meeting to work on the Deadline Dilemmas case was at the district sales office, scheduled to coincide with a briefing everyone was required to attend for a major new product. This gave me an opportunity to see the entire district team. After the briefing, I asked Gwen and Dean to leave so I could work more privately with the rest of the team. I asked the team members for written comments (because there was not enough time to meet with each person individually) on what it was like to work at the South Central Office and, more specifically, what it was like for each of them to work with both Gwen and Dean. Here are some of the responses I received:

➤ This office is so chaotic! It seems that all Dean's sales reports and activities need to be compiled at the same time—and usually at the last minute.

➤ We constantly run up against deadlines because several people do not follow standard operating procedures.

➤ Our workload fluctuates between boredom and sheer terror, which obviously causes stress for those of us caught in the mess. If we could have better shipping guidelines with our customers, we might be able to even out the work flow.

Type Clue

From these notes, I guessed that most of the South Central team members preferred a Judging style. The majority of the fingers here were pointing at the Perceptives, especially Dean.

Negative as the team's feedback was concerning the work styles and conflict between Dean, the sales manager, and Gwen, the operations manager, life on other fronts at Donelle South Central seemed to be working out pretty well. On the positive side, the team reported that it was a very pleasant place to work. They enjoyed Dean's insistence on his employees' independence and autonomy, which was helped by the geographical distance to the head office. Most people felt they were treated in a professional manner and appreciated being allowed to set their own daily appointments and schedules; the freedom and variety were mentioned again and again. They also enjoyed the mutual respect that existed among their co-workers.

There seemed to be hope for this office—obviously, Gwen and Dean hadn't yet messed up everything. The conflict appeared to be centered on one area: the question of how best to manage time or whether time should be managed at all! Gwen and Dean's different perspectives on how time could be structured to get work done, what constituted a tight deadline, and the lack of formal procedures to even out the work flow caused most of the mayhem. Before I left South Central, I scheduled a day of meetings for the next week with the morning reserved for Gwen and the afternoon to be spent with Dean.

Because I had sent my interview questions (the list of five earlier in the chapter) to Dean and Gwen in advance, I expected that their individual sessions would go fairly easily and quickly. When the meeting day came, Gwen arrived exactly on time, walking calmly into the conference room set aside for my use. She was the picture of personal organization—everything about her conveyed a businesslike efficiency. As she sat down, she opened her leather folder in which she had two copies (one for me and one for her) of her typed responses to my questions. She had obviously thought them through and prepared in advance for our session.

Gwen said, "I am really looking forward to our time together. So much of my energy goes toward simply keeping all of the balls in the air for this office that I've almost given up trying to communicate with Dean—it's so time-consuming and it doesn't seem to help."

Type Clue

Gwen's preference for Judging seemed apparent almost imme-diately. As we talked further it was clear she didn't leave anything to chance and had even thought about where I'd have lunch! She was known to be very conscientious and tried to do much of the work herself rather than speak up about her own needs. This was especially the case in her dealings with Dean.

"Well, hopefully this process will help," I replied. "If we get a clear picture of what you and Dean each do best and what you need from each other, perhaps the language you need to communicate will develop. First of all, why don't you tell me what contributions you bring to Donelle?"

"Basically," she said, looking at her notes, "I bring stability, calmness, and security to those people who work with me. People around here know that they can rely on me. I'm the one who organizes things here at the office—and frankly, there would be utter chaos without me, or someone who had work habits like mine. Right now, I'm trying to implement standard procedures for processing sales calls, doing follow-up, and handling delivery.

"I also contribute by mentoring the individuals who work for me. I often serve as a buffer between people when conflicts come up. Additionally, I believe that others see me as a source of support, someone they can count on. When the chips are down and there's a customer rush on a product and we have precious little time to get it there on time, everyone looks to me. I only wish," she added, "that I knew how to use my organizational skills in my relationship with Dean. I wish I could mentor *him!*"

Type Clue

True to type, Gwen led by providing the structure for others to follow, then worked behind the scenes to encourage and keep everything running as smoothly as possible. Because ISFJs prefer to lead from the rear, an ENTP like Dean can be especially frustrating to work with, since ENTPs seem to look ahead, not behind.

"In my career with Donelle, I have moved from managing a small city-wide office to a regional office and now to this district office. The increasing amount of responsibility in each office, I think," Gwen said, rather characteristically humbly, "shows the faith the company has put in me to bring order out of chaos. That's really what I do best—develop ways to eliminate these problems at the source. I have a pretty good track record on this."

I said, "Ray [the CEO] said similar things about you and added that he couldn't do without you. Did you get a chance to think about the flip side of your strengths, how your style might be irritating to Dean?"

"It wasn't too hard, given our daily battles," Gwen said. "While I would describe myself as comfortable with routine, the tried and true, I know that others here feel I'm too strict and tied into my current methods. I admit I am reluctant to change some of our work structures, but on the other hand, you can't argue with standardization. This office had a spotty track record until I worked to systemize things. I *know* my approach gets on Dean's nerves because he is not particularly comfortable being tied to anything routine.

"Dean has even accused me of being a wet blanket who sometimes impedes his progress on sales or slows down his ideas. I suppose I do at times inundate him and the office with procedural details. And when I get mad I tend to withdraw and clam up, which I know is especially irritating to Dean. He always wants me to speak up, and do it sooner than I am ready to!"

"It can be tough for those with ISFJ preferences like yourself, who are so conscientious, to get the rest of us to see how much your quiet actions contribute," I said. "You and Dean both said that I could share your MBTI results with the other. Dean's type came out an ENTP. That makes his type directly opposite from yours. I think of ENTPs as the innovators, the people that give us new ways to do things and spur us on to take risks. The ISFJ type, which represents your preferences, is frequently associated with loyal, service-oriented individuals, willing to follow through on *every* detail to support others in reaching practical results. Given your different perspectives, what does Dean do that's annoying to you?"

"Well, I hate to be too negative, but sharing the management of this office with him has been really stressful for me. For example, I can't seem to nail him down on any meeting agenda that's to be jointly issued, so I do the agendas alone while he prefers to wing it. Of course, that means extra work for me. I wouldn't mind, but after I've planned things out he comes along and omits items, changes them, or goes off on tangents. It's hard to reel him in.

"Also, his sense of time bothers me. If we schedule a meeting for 1:30, he shows up at 1:50. I'm sure the twenty minutes don't seem like very much to him, given his work habits, but to me those twenty minutes mean twenty minutes less to cover my responsibilities."

Type Clue

The differences between Judging and Perceiving display themselves so concretely sometimes. Here, Gwen's frustration is justified from her viewpoint. But Dean, given his world view, probably considered himself on time. What he did in those twenty minutes he perceived as a *necessary* last-minute schedule change, whether it was another customer phone call or contract revision. Both saw their different uses of time as appropriate in bringing success to Donelle.

"Then," she went on, "there are his files and his piles. His office is overwhelmed by paper; the only place I dare set something he *has* to see is on his desk chair where he'll at least notice it when he sits down. The other day I saw a file from a customer that stopped doing business with us two years ago! I hate to think what might be lost in his office that may need my follow-through."

Type Clue

Often Perceptives will tell you there's order in their chaos—it's just a Perceptive type of order. Usually they know just where to look in their piles and files, even if others can't figure out their "system."

"Our hottest disagreements come when Dean makes commitments to customers with time lines that are unreasonable. He excuses himself, saying we need to be customer-focused, but we in the operations area are caught in a real time bind. We get it all done because we, too, believe that the customer comes first, but I don't think it needs to be at our expense quite so often. For him, doing things at the last minute is exciting, but for me it's crazy—I'm afraid we may lose a sale.

"Maybe he doesn't think about our schedules because *he* rarely keeps normal office hours. He seems to be in here a lot after everyone leaves and tends to work nights and on weekends. This makes me feel guilty because I believe that life isn't just work. I like to work a regular schedule from eight to five with as little overtime as possible because I, for one, need to schedule family time and some time to do other chores. His schedule tends to be erratic: He lets things pile up and then does them all at once."

Type Clue

Whereas Judgers like to plan their work and work their plan, Perceptives often work best under pressure, sometimes procrastinating in order to create that pressure! Judgers tend to want to separate work and personal time, seeing each area as distinct. Perceptives generally mix work and personal time, seeing the boundaries between the two as quite permeable. Frequently, when one side is forced to adapt to the style of the other, the quality of their work suffers.

We moved onto the next question, what Gwen valued about Dean. "Well," said Gwen, "I'm relieved to get through all the complaining about Dean because he does have some good qualities. He is one of the most creative people with whom I have ever worked. Somehow or other he's able to close sales even if it means using overnight mail, e-mail, and faxes, which you know are more expensive than regular mail and delivery services, but which *do* meet the deadline.

"Dean also seems like the classic entrepreneur: He goes out and finds new markets that often yield new sales. Many of these sideline calls have resulted in huge contracts for us. He is also able to find ways to adapt the sales, marketing, and customer service we provide to changing market needs. His ability to anticipate those changes is uncanny. I often envy his ability to read the future.

"I respect him for being able to eventually get things done—even if it frazzles me and forces me to live with chaos. He always seems to have an unusual remedy or solution that just exactly fills the bill. Without his energy and enthusiasm and his way of working with the customers, I think we'd be in bad shape, however frustrating it is to work with him back here in the office."

I asked her what she would see as some hoped-for outcomes in her relationship with Dean. Gwen had clearly given thought to this as well and glanced at her typed notes. "First, I wish Dean would stick to a structure that more closely matches my schedules, policies, and procedures—even if it's a very loose structure. I also wish he would stop reorganizing the sales force—they barely get used to a new configuration before he has another new idea. Also, I wish he'd realize that he could benefit by paying attention to the operational aspects of this sales office.

"It seems to me we need to be more clear in our relationship with each other, too. If we *could* get clear about our different roles and my need for more accuracy in project timing, we could probably be a pretty good team. I think we need to make it clear to everyone and to Dean, too, that I have the *final* authority for the operational aspects of this sales office. I believe that Dean often doesn't see my role as an equal to his sales management role, but I maintain that indeed it is!"

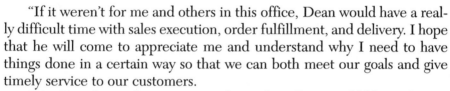

Type Clue

Whoa . . . this is an ISFJ pushed to the limit. They generally consider self-sacrifice acceptable, but Gwen had had enough.

"If it weren't for me and others in this office, Dean would have a really difficult time with sales execution, order fulfillment, and delivery. I hope that he will come to appreciate me and understand why I need to have things done in a certain way so that we can both meet our goals and give timely service to our customers.

"Finally, I know that many people in the office would like to have a firm direction and a general course of action for the sales side of things for at least a six-to-twelve-month period. That way, all of us would know what the priorities are and could adjust our work and schedules to meet those priorities. All the events, from the sales call to the order fulfillment and delivery, should follow the same standard operating procedures. That will reduce mistakes, people will know what to expect, and we won't have to do things at the last minute.

"I've said before I do respect and admire Dean but I sure wish he were more like me."

"How's that?" I asked Gwen.

"Well," Gwen chuckled, "I suppose I don't want him to be exactly like me, but I wish he were more planful. I wish he were more methodical and able to follow through in a timely manner so that any mistakes could be rectified without causing so much stress for everyone."

When we had finished and exchanged some final thoughts on personality type, I thanked Gwen for her candor and honesty and for the information that she had shared with me about herself and Dean.

After lunch it was time for me to interview Dean. Our meeting was scheduled at 1:30 and Dean came in at 1:40, breathless. "I just got off the phone with my newest account and I've been looking for your questions," he said. "I know I have them somewhere, but I just haven't been able to find them. I've read them through and they've been on my mind. I remembered that you wanted me to talk about my contributions and things that annoy me, especially in my relationship with Gwen, and what I want to have happen. I know I'll have some ideas as we go along." He took a deep breath, adjusted his notes in his jam-packed daily sales recorder, and said, "I can start from scratch and wing it, so I think I'm ready to go whenever you are."

Type Clue

What a contrast to Gwen, who appeared on schedule with typed responses! Dean seemed attentive but somewhat unprepared. Having a preference for Perceiving myself, however, I was not surprised at Dean's approach to our time together. I tend to function better "in the moment" and would most likely not type out my answers to these kinds of interview questions as Gwen had. Too much could change in the interim, so why not go into the meeting fresh?

We started out with an interpretation of Dean's personality preferences. He readily agreed that the ENTP type suited him well, especially the parts about energy and enthusiasm. He acknowledged his ability, as he said it, "to pull rabbits out of hats!"

When I asked him to describe the contributions he brought to Donelle, he was hardly at a loss for words. "I've spent fifteen of my twenty years of experience in regional and district sales offices. One of the things I appreciate about myself is my ability to get things done without anyone looking over my shoulder. I believe that I bring a sense of independence as well as responsibility to the work I do. I provide my staff with lots of flexibility and the opportunity to do challenging work.

"Next, I think, comes my ability to adapt to change. We are in a tight market with ever-changing customer needs and I think I have an uncanny ability to read those needs. I pride myself on being able to respond quickly and immediately to what the customers want. I pretty much take things in stride when surprises come. You know, those surprises and unexpected opportunities often yield new business possibilities for Donelle. Because I have my ear to the ground all the time, I repeatedly know where to go to make the next sale. Some people say I have a sixth sense when it comes to finding new markets. I've been told that I'm bright and have lots of great ideas and a good sense of what's going on in this business.

"I also value the fact that if people give me a problem, I can usually figure it out. I enjoy gathering a lot of information about all sorts of things, especially anything that relates to Donelle's business. You know, I belong to several organizations that look at future trends and conduct market surveys for our products."

Type Clue

One of the gifts of Perceiving is the joy that comes with finding out about things, ideas, or people. Gathering new information from many available sources and incorporating it into existing plans is characteristic for Perceptives. Notice how often Dean mentions his adaptability in one way or another.

"I have a lot of integrity because I know that what goes around, comes around. I don't sell products that the manufacturing companies Donelle represents could market better on their own. I'm pretty clear with people here in the office about maintaining the kind of integrity Donelle's name stands for in this industry.

"Finally, I think I have good rapport with just about everyone in the office but Gwen. I've been here since South Central opened and people have learned how to adjust to my style—or at least I *think* they have. I know I can cause some tense moments for them, but at times it's the only way we can really serve our customers."

Type Clue

Because last-minute stress can facilitate task accomplishment for Perceptives, without a knowledge of psychological type they may not appreciate just how detrimental this "rush" at the end of a project can be to others, especially Judgers. Also, Perceptives can be so reluctant to be tied to procedures that they may underestimate just how much those procedures can benefit themselves and their customers.

I said, "Your staff described you as an effective leader in that you allow them lots of independence to do their jobs as they see fit. They also recognize your ability to outguess the competition regarding market changes.

Ray really values your innovativeness and marketing sense, but he also wants to see less conflict between you and Gwen. I think Gwen told you at lunch that her MBTI preferences are exactly opposite to yours. Partly because of her natural ISFJ preferences and mostly because of the person she is, Gwen excels at getting things done and ensuring that all her commitments are met in a timely fashion. I'd like to know your thoughts about the things you do that are irritating to Gwen."

He laughed. "That's pretty easy because I know I do lots of things that irritate her. I wouldn't be in sales if I couldn't get a read on other people. I know she thinks I'm too crisis-oriented and she often says that I am the driving force of the business—ready to drive us off track, that is! My last-minute ways are hard on her and some of the staff, but that's how I prefer to operate.

"I know I seldom give advance warning about changes. And I'm aware that I constantly push against deadlines. I suppose I can go overboard in my zeal to give our customers what they want.

"People tell me they're not sure what's going to happen next. Then Gwen once told me that I talk too much, commit too much, and seem to be a stress-giver to others in the office.

"Finally, I know Gwen thinks I have too many new ideas and that I often rush off and do things in haste. She's said that my way of putting things together at the last minute often looks sloppy to our customers. I know she would like me to be more realistic and stable *and* predictable in the way I go about doing my work. Saying all this, I guess I must irritate her in a number of ways," he concluded.

"Well, it seems like you have a good read on what's irritating about you. That's a pretty thorough list! I've kept notes for our later meeting with Gwen and the others. Now can we move on and have you tell me what Gwen does that annoys you?" I asked.

"I guess," said Dean, "she tries to make me as organized and structured as *she* is. She constantly makes suggestions on how I could rework my calendar or set up response reminders. But frankly, most irritating to me is her expectation that I should follow her office policies, procedures, and time lines. As far as I'm concerned, her system doesn't apply to me and the way I do sales best. Gwen and I have our own separate areas of responsibility and while I can appreciate that she may need to have things more planful, it doesn't always work to Donelle's advantage.

"Also, it appears to me, although I may be wrong, that she obstructs my progress and resists changing things that will keep us current and up-to-date. She seems so set in her ways that when I'm around her I lose my energy and spontaneity.

"Things just go back and forth between us. She doesn't always tell me what's on her mind, or worse, she gives me so many reminders that I forget which items were *really* important or what it was that she wanted me to do.

"She asks me to put things in writing like she does. But I don't especially like to spend time writing. I'd much rather talk to her face-to-face.

"I know that she wants me to stop leaving things to the last minute. But I'm not *always* last minute. Besides, I wish she'd lighten up and relax a little along the way. If I do as she asks, list out deadlines and shipping dates on a piece of paper, she gets rigid about meeting those dates. You know, last week she had some products already in boxes with the mailing labels on them before I'd given her some new information from the customer. And furthermore, she was going to ship the stuff out without the latest changes! I wish she'd wait for the full story instead of doing something just because her calendar says it's time to do it."

Type Clue

Clearly, Dean felt restricted and hemmed in by Gwen's office procedures and her way of doing things. Her quiet persistence and methodical ways were in direct contrast to Dean's loose and laid-back style. And yet, Gwen provided the behind-the-scenes framework that helped Dean to close his sales. He was just moments away from recognizing that.

I next asked Dean if he would tell me what he valued about Gwen. "I can't deny," he said, "that when all is said and done, I really do value the fact that she is an implementor. She seems to be able to take the mixed-up jumble of things I bring to her and put them in some sort of manageable order, develop a work plan, and find the most efficient way to get things done.

"More than once she's saved my neck by reading the fine print and coming up with a specific maneuver that carries the day. She's also able to do things in a sensible, step-by-step way—something I've always admired in her and others like her. Occasionally I've tried to imitate her and plan my work using her methods, but it never quite works for me. Do you know what I mean?" (Since this was Dean's time to talk to me all I did was acknowledge that yes, I frequently felt that way, and that I also had similar experiences.)

I asked Dean what his hoped-for outcomes were in his relationship with Gwen. "I guess that in the time we've worked together, we've managed to get on each other's nerves repeatedly. It would be great if we could both learn how to use the strengths the other brings to get our job done more smoothly. So I hope that we can learn how to work together and that we can establish some clarity about what to do that doesn't fence me in too much and doesn't frustrate Gwen too much. A smoother working relationship with her is well worth my while, you know, because with her organizational skills I'm sure it won't be long before she's moved up in the organization. Since I predict this will be the case, I'd prefer she looked back fondly on this district sales manager rather than remember all the headaches I gave her!"

Type Clue

Notice most of Dean's outcomes were more general than those of Gwen. Gwen's list included specific changes in how they worked together, while Dean simply wanted to establish clarity about how things should be run.

As I had suspected, I could summarize most of Gwen's and Dean's conflicts in just three words: Judging versus Perceiving. Both their strengths and their shortcomings flowed from their skillful use of their preferred styles.

Using Gwen's typed notes plus my notes, I put together an overall report of both conversations for each of them to read. I flew back to Donelle the next week for a daylong meeting with both Gwen and Dean to further review their psychological type differences and to offer my report on their individual conversations with me.

In setting the ground rules and agenda for my meeting with them, we decided to focus on the five interview questions in order to clear the air and establish a common set of perceptions with which to move toward their future working relationship.

As I am frequently delighted to experience, using the language of personality type helped provide for a productive discussion between Gwen and Dean. Our meeting together had its lighter moments as well as a serious probing of the issues they faced. We went over specifically what each found irritating about the other, what they valued about the other, and, finally, their hoped-for outcomes.

"It is generally true," I summarized, "that what we value most about someone also has a negative side to it. Gwen, you value Dean's insight, his sales abilities, and his innovativeness, but these characteristics go hand-in-hand with his not wanting to be saddled with procedures and schedules. His rush to address new customer concerns or new markets also means that he may forget what he needs to do right now. And Dean, you admire Gwen for her ability to follow through, to keep things running on course, and to organize the office efficiently. And you see, these results are due to her careful adherence to those procedures that she knows will produce the tried and true results you want."

Dean said, "You know, this difference in Judging and Perceiving gives me a way to keep our disputes in perspective. If I want the benefit of Gwen's ability to have things in the right place at the right time, I need to accept that she may not want to change the proven way she's always gotten them there."

"That's true," said Gwen. "And if I'm enjoying South Central's profitability and our usually large bonuses, due in a large part to your entrepreneurial drive, I may need to accept that deadlines could have different meanings for you . . . well, at least I can accept that *occasionally*."

Type Clue

Not all conflict resolution tasks proceed as smoothly as this one did. While learning about the Judging versus Perceiving preference gave Gwen and Dean some mutual understanding, it was not the only factor that helped them move closer to conflict resolution. Their shared motivation and their CEO's and their office mates' desire for them to have a better working relationship was also crucial to the success of our working together.

We spent much of the morning reviewing my report, expanding upon their comments about each other, and beginning to develop a to-do list for the short term for each of them. In the afternoon, we changed our focus to their future working relationship. "Let's start by listing some ideas that would adequately meet the needs each of you have. Then you can each suggest what you can individually do to build your future relationship."

Dean and Gwen agreed to address the following needs:

➤ Create further role clarity so that each knew what the other's tasks and responsibilities were for Donelle's South Central Office. This discussion was predicated on their mutual understanding that sales management and operations management needed to dovetail together in order to create an effective, yet not too rigid, office environment. With this agreement, they established distinct roles, responsibilities, and reporting relationships.

They decided that Gwen would be solely in charge of the operations side and could therefore make demands on Dean to: follow mutually agreed-upon standard operating procedures, check in advance with Gwen before committing on delivery dates and other services to customers, and determine realistic time and work schedules on a case-by-case basis when Dean's situation called for special handling.

Gwen agreed that Dean was responsible for the sales management area. Gwen understood that client and customer needs could be in the moment, very conceivably falling outside her standard operating procedures. However, she and Dean agreed that Dean could consider no more than 20 percent of his requests as extremely urgent in any given month's time. Gwen would monitor Dean's special requests and tell him when he was nearing his limit. Dean committed to this standard as reasonable and stated that he would work very diligently to train himself to follow these guidelines.

➤ Gwen and Dean decided that sales growth needed to be better managed and that Dean would be responsible for communicating new customer or product changes to Gwen within three to five days so that she could manage the increased back-office workload, hiring temporary or permanent workers if needed. A contingency budget was established from Dean's sales budget to cover these hiring needs as a way of keeping Dean in check and allowing Gwen more certainty about her own budget for operational costs.

➤ Dean and Gwen decided to use customer surveys to find and detail all the steps in the Donelle sales cycle where customer interface was crucial to both operations and sales. Up until this point, much of that information on follow-ups was too general, was not communicated widely, or resided in Dean's head.

Type Clue

The goal-setting process took quite a bit of discussion because Dean was more motivated by challenging, nearly unreachable goals, while Gwen stated that she was motivated by more realistic and concrete goals. When we concluded, Dean stated that whenever possible, he would give more advanced warning to Gwen so that any new or "stretch" goals could be set. He also agreed that once Gwen approved the deadlines for these goals, they would be strictly enforced.

Dean concurred that it was hard to organize a sales office when products and procedures were continually changing and therefore Gwen's standardization of key accounts and products was absolutely necessary to helping Dean make his sales quotas and commitments. He agreed to work with Gwen to create a manual on key customers and key products that would detail their methods in a step-by-step fashion. With the manual, any new hires for both sales and operations could be more easily oriented as to how the office ran and how sales were processed.

Dean tended to have sporadic work habits, periods of extreme productivity juxtaposed with periods when he seemed to coast, that were hard on operational staff morale. As a partial solution, Dean and Gwen agreed that Dean would work away from the office several days a month and in essence stay out of Gwen's way. His using a more discretionary schedule, both he and Gwen believed, would minimize their constant friction with each other. Gwen stated that in exchange she would work standard business hours, putting in no more than 10 percent overtime in any given week. Gwen said, "I like this particularly because it respects my boundaries about work being work and family and play time being time for family and play . . . and well, you, Dean, can mix your work and play more to your liking now."

Both Gwen and Dean found it useful to know that their MBTI results confirmed their differences (they had not invented their conflicts!). The theory of personality preferences offered them a way to work through those differences and build on their respective strengths. While Gwen could not expect that Dean would ever be as organized, planful, and decisive as she, she could also appreciate that his flexibility and adaptability were key business assets to Donelle's sales organization. Dean also stated that while Gwen could sometimes seem to be too by-the-book and structured in her way of doing things, it was important to quality and consistency that Gwen maintain standards that would keep the behind-the-scenes operations running as smoothly as possible. Using both styles and acknowledging the contributions of the other seemed to be vital for the future of Gwen and Dean's working relationship. Both felt the freedom to contribute to Donelle in a way that matched their style—and that dispensed with many, if not all, of those pesky deadline dilemmas.

TYPE TAKEAWAY

Is there a Judger in your office trying to herd the Perceptives into a more orderly, structured procession? Or is there a Perceptive trying to open the eyes of the Judgers to the value of searching for new, last-minute information? Yes, we can learn to benefit from the best each style has to offer.

Type Solvers to Try

When you suspect an Judging-Perceiving problem, try these ideas.

☑ Use the following questions to guide discussion among those in conflict:

> ➤ What contributions do you bring to the relationship?

> ➤ What actions or habits do you have that may be unsettling or irritating to the other?

> ➤ What does the other do that annoys you?

> ➤ What do you find valuable about each other?

> ➤ What outcomes do you hope for as a result of this conflict resolution process?

By giving positive as well as negative feedback to each other, you may find some areas for negotiation and peace!

☑ If your team is divided between Judgers and Perceptives, the following group exercise may help:

> ➤ Divide the team into two groups based on each person's preference for Judging and Perceiving.

> ➤ Ask each group to think of two projects or decisions that suffered from a one-sided approach. For example, a market opportunity may have been missed because Perceiving team members were reluctant to come to conclusions about the trends they were investigating. Conversely, a product may have been too quickly introduced because Judging team members reached their conclusions as to the features it should have too quickly.

➤ Each group should then list specifically how they would have handled the incident differently. The goal is to give concrete examples of how each side might benefit from the processes of the other side:

It is more natural for Judgers to:	It is more natural for Perceivers to:
➤ Place value on timetables and schedules	➤ Leave room for late-breaking changes
➤ Decide on project steps before beginning	➤ Allow for what is necessary as they go
➤ Make decisions without revisiting each nuance	➤ Search for options, not wanting to overlook anything
➤ Find surprises tend to upset their plans	➤ Find last-minute changes or interruptions helpful in maintaining flexibility

For personal development, consider the following.

If your preference is for Judging, you can practice Perceiving:

☑ Schedule one day per month at work to go with the flow. (I know that's asking a lot, but see what happens. Trust me!) Note what turns up that may add value to your tasks.

☑ Give yourself some extra time to gather more information, both factual and insightful data.

☑ In solving a problem, think of several options in addition to the one you think is correct. Make a list of positive, interesting, and negative characteristics of each option. Challenge your original choice.

☑ In a low-stress area or low-risk situation, ask someone to interrupt a plan of yours so you can evaluate your tolerance for delays and ambiguities and your ability to handle unforeseen events.

☑ Expect some contingencies to your planned processes. If you have some extra time, use it to gather more data.

☑ If someone wants your opinion, try giving several alternatives and then let them decide for themselves.

If your preference is for Perceiving, you can practice Judging:

☑ Schedule in at least half an hour between meetings; plan backwards; use good time management techniques.

☑ Look at a calendar year and ask yourself what five things you need to accomplish. Then schedule them in, planning backwards to ensure that you have allowed ample time, then add a bit more time. (Yes, I know I'm pressing you, but trust me, you'll experience less stress and perhaps increase your effectiveness.)

☑ Remind yourself that contingencies almost always arise—allow for them in your work. Resist the temptation to attend to "just one more thing."

☑ Place limits on your information-gathering, by setting either an imaginary deadline or goal for the number of ideas or amount of information to be found. Then *stop* when you reach the limit.

☑ Determine what tasks in your life could be done in a consistent manner, then develop a routine and follow it. Realize that this can give you more time to explore, enjoy, and "coast."

☑ Choose some small or less important tasks and try to complete them a day or two *before* the deadline.

When You're One or Few Amongst the Many

When you have a preference for Perceiving and your teammates have a preference for Judging, consider:

☑ Explaining the need to collect information prior to making a sound decision

☑ Recognizing that deadlines set by the organization may not be negotiable

☑ Becoming active in projects where the process is just as important as the outcome

☑ Keeping your surprises to the team to a minimum and reducing the number of options you consider

When you have a preference for Judging and your teammates have a preference for Perceiving, consider:

☑ Seeking out projects that have a definite milestone and a final deadline

☑ Trying to wait on a decision for a few days and pay attention to other ideas that may crop up

☑ Understanding work is progressing despite the style differences

☑ Making your own milestones or deadlines along the way

The Case of the Clashing Cultures

"We Just Don't Function the Same"

"That meeting was a waste of my time—we never discussed three of the agenda items." (ST)

"That meeting was confusing—I don't understand how these changes will affect Chris and me, not to mention the team." (SF)

"That meeting was great—we got a firm grip on the training and development plan that will set us on the right path for the next two business cycles." (NF)

"That meeting was okay, but we needed to spend more time deliberating our underlying rationale and coming up with an effective strategy." (NT)

Of course all four of the people quoted above were at the same meeting. However, they each came away with very different impressions of its value and what they had heard and accomplished. Each person's understanding of what went on was affected by their natural way of functioning psychologically.

How you perceive (Sensing or Intuition) and how you judge (Thinking or Feeling) determine how you function. The four combinations of perceiving and judging (ST, SF, NF, and NT) represent the columns as well as four types each of the type table:

ST	SF	NF	NT
ISTJ	ISFJ	INFJ	INTJ
ISTP	ISFP	INFP	INTP
ESTP	ESFP	ENFP	ENTP
ESTJ	ESFJ	ENFJ	ENTJ

Isabel Briggs Myers considered this four function framework one of the essentials of type, influencing our styles for communication, decision making, and leadership. Each part of the four-function framework has its own unique style. The STs are generally practical and logical. They prefer direct communication, factual decision making, and leaders who are experienced. The SFs are often compassionate and friendly. They prefer personal and warm communication, people-centered decision making, and a leader who cares. The NFs are typically enthusiastic and insightful. They prefer empathetic communication, values-focused decision making, and inspirational leaders. Finally, the NTs are generally logical and innovative. They prefer objective communication, analytical decision making, and an ingenious leader. My own work, as well as research conducted by many others,[9] confirms that these groups can have difficulty understanding each other, especially across the pairings: STs and NFs have the most difficulty understanding each other, as do the SFs and NTs.

Put an ST who values efficiency and practicality with an NF who values inspiration and idealism, or an SF who values being of service with an NT who values achievement-oriented tasks, and you have a clash of cultures! Frequently each one hasn't a clue as to the motives behind the actions of the other. These differences in preference can hinder communication, cause friction in the office, and distract quite thoroughly from the jobs at hand. Such was the case at Investment Partnership Services (IPS).

Type Story: Investment Partnership Services [IPS]

Cast of Characters

Julie, IPS Founding Partner	**ENFJ**
Nira, IPS Founding Partner	**ENTP**
Frances, Office Manager	**ISTJ**
Barb	**ESFJ**
Lee	**ISFJ**
George	**INTJ**
David	**INTJ**

IPS was successful. Very successful. But the growth that came with success led to other problems. IPS started as a full-service financial planning firm in the boom times of the 1980s, founded and managed by two extremely competent women, Julie and Nira. They targeted women, particularly those who were a part of a dual-career couple, tailoring their marketing to the concerns of the women. Additionally, they worked with those who were widowed or divorced and in need of financial planning. Because the field of financial planning was relatively new, because they used niche marketing to focus their energy on the growing financial clout of women, and because the two founders were extremely aggressive in the marketplace, their success came quickly and relatively easily.

A hallmark of their organization was that they treated these women with respect, considering themselves stewards for, yet partners with, their female clients, working together to establish and reach financial goals. Julie, one of the founding partners, viewed her financial planning work as a means to help women overall gain a more equal financial footing. She wanted to see women more involved as investors in the marketplace, earning more of their income from sources unrelated to their day-to-day efforts, and increasing their retirement nest eggs.

Nira enjoyed exploring the marketplace potential for the services of their organization, IPS. She loved the challenge of playing the market and of pitting her financial savvy against that of more traditional brokers who focused on their male clientele. She was astute at seeing trends and predicting future earnings for stocks and other sources of investments. She was also adept in promoting her ideas to her clients and in applying her financial ingenuity to the stock market.

The two women began their business on solid principles of steward-ship, service, and profits for themselves while they made money for oth-ers. As part of their initial marketing strategy, they became involved in women-focused organizations such as the League of Women Voters, Financial Women International, the National Association of Women Business Owners, and their own universities' women's associations. Additionally, they were both involved in professional societies—restaurant and hotel management for Nira and accounting for Julie.

Generally, once a woman expressed interest in financial planning, she was invited to the office for a visit with either Julie or Nira. This first session was largely educational, but Julie and Nira also used these opportunities to assess the person's financial situation, to evaluate whether their services fit, and to determine if a financial plan could be drawn.

Whenever the opportunity arose, Julie, and occasionally Nira, con-ducted community workshops on the need for financial planning. I encountered Nira at one of these workshops and was immediately struck by the financial planning possibilities for myself. Additionally, I applauded their female-oriented service.

As with many fast-growing businesses that suffer from their own suc-cess, IPS was experiencing growth pains. The client base increased so rapidly that "by the seat of the pants" became the basis for many of IPS's business methods and the underlying policies and procedures. Nira and Julie quickly realized they needed to hire an administrator. After a long search, Julie and Nira found another woman, Frances, for that position. Frances soon added a full-time assistant, Lee, and a half-time assistant, Barb. Additionally, Julie and Nira hired two experienced investment ana-lysts, George and David, who were familiar with the latest computerized investment models. The firm contracted with a larger brokerage company to carry out their stock purchases and receipts.

Julie was the one who called me. "There's simply too much tension between me and Nira and I'm not sure why, given that we share common goals for our company. The tension appears to be contagious—Frances and Lee seem on edge with us and with others as well. Do you think the *Myers-Briggs Type Indicator* might help shed some light on our struggles? Our personal difficulties are starting to cause problems in how we service our customers, and I don't want our feuds to destroy our organization's growth or our bottom line."

Although I won't go into the entire intervention, I will tell you about each of the key players at IPS and how we jointly used the concepts of psy-chological type—especially the four-function framework, ST, SF, NF, and NT—to increase teamwork and to make sure everyone was working toward the same goals.

Julie (NF)

I met with Julie in her office and my first impression of her quarters was of papers and books—in neat piles but covering just about every flat surface. The office was decorated in a warm and comfortable style with numerous pictures of Julie's family and an occasional motivational plaque or affirmation for financial success. Julie, however, looked exhausted! There were dark circles under her eyes and a general spirit of weariness in her voice and appearance. She seemed older and more tired than when I had seen her in months past.

After a few pleasantries, I asked her to fill in some background for me about her relationship to IPS. "Why were you interested in beginning this business?" I inquired.

"I saw IPS as an opportunity to realize some of my life goals—especially that of increasing women's share of the financial pie. You know," she went on, "women earn only fifty-nine cents for every dollar [at that time] that men earn. In that kind of situation, it's imperative for women to use their smaller proportion even more prudently than men. I am deeply committed to helping women establish themselves financially and to making sure that the divorcees and widows who entrust their funds to me gain a fair financial return for the faith that they've placed in me.

"I feel I know the market and the needs of women. I pride myself on the S for service in our company name. I hope to develop and have long relationships with my clients—play a large role in their financial planning and their financial future and well-being. I think I'm able to read people well and discern their particular needs—especially their emotional needs. You know, investing says as much about one's emotional and psychological life as it does about one's financial life."

Type Clue

I was immediately struck by Julie's altruistic responses regarding the founding and operation of IPS. Her chief motivation seemed to be what she could do for others. This increased the pressure she put on herself to ensure that her financial goals and those she jointly set with her clients were met. NFs frequently set idealistic goals for themselves and wish to serve others in the process. Then they work to create a future where potential growth and development is possible for themselves and others.

"Usually I end up acting as a facilitator between our woman client and her partner, either male or female, if she has one. Many interesting emotional and relational dynamics play out in the area of financial investing. Because of this I make certain that my client gets my full attention. I don't talk or direct my comments only to the man as many investment counselors do. I want to show my expertise with the couple and in particular the woman, who may for the first time be starting a more fiscally independent course.

"Being a teacher at heart, the public workshops and the presentations are fun for me. I got my MBA with an emphasis in accounting and finance only after teaching home economics for years at a high school, but I've always been good with numbers. Doing these seminar sessions and seeing the sparks in women's eyes as they realize opportunities for financial success and security provide me with a lot of intrinsic returns and rewards. I really love this part of our business!"

Type Clue

NFs are the natural communicators of the psychological types, so it was no surprise that Julie enjoyed teaching and talking to others about financial planning. I could feel the sense of commitment and purpose in Julie's voice. She lost her tiredness and became impassioned when she was speaking about the financial possibilities for women.

Because I knew that there were other things on her mind, I decided to turn the conversation to the internal workings of IPS. "So what's it like to work here?" I asked Julie. Almost immediately, there was a change in Julie's demeanor; her weariness became as apparent as when I first walked in the door.

"Well," Julie said reluctantly, "I may as well start with my difficulties with Nira. Nira and I founded this company and have worked together successfully for the last five years, but I am beginning to feel like most of the responsibility is falling very heavily on my shoulders. I have the most client contact, schedule client follow-up, and oversee account administration. While I'm here interacting with clients, Nira is out getting information from vendors—being wined and dined by the various companies who want our investment dollars. A part of me shouts, 'I'm being taken advantage of' and I don't like that feeling. When I try to discuss this with Nira, she reminds me that I am the better educator and the better person to manage client contact while she is the better person for investment opportunities. Still in all, it doesn't seem like an equitable distribution of the partnership responsibilities."

Type Clue

Julie and Nira had naturally selected tasks that reflected their psychological type and the four-function framework without even knowing it. Julie, an NF, probably *is* better matched to the tasks of client education and interaction while Nira, an NT, probably *is* better at focusing on the external investment environment, using her Intuition to find possible financial products and her logical Thinking to judge how lucrative those investment products might be.

"Often when companies grow as fast as yours, fairness gets set aside in the rush to keep up with the demands of the business. How else has this job affected you?" I asked Julie.

"Well, I've been having problems sleeping at night. The market has recently seen a slight shift and a downturn; I feel responsible for so many clients and their funds. I have guaranteed a modest 5 to 8 percent return on their investments, but when the market comes down I can't even deliver on that. So at any given point I live with apprehension that a client may call and ask how well her portfolio is doing vis-à-vis the plan we'd made for her. Because many of these women are novice investors, I worry that they will panic and want to remove their money even though most of their stocks need to be held long-term, through downturns and upturns, to see a long-range appreciation in their portfolio's value. You know, I hate having to give disappointing news to any of our clients! When I do so, I feel as if I've personally let them down."

Type Clue

My ears perked up at this. ENFJs often feel personally responsible for the well-being (both emotionally and financially in Julie's case) of others.

I asked her if she had discussed this with Nira. "Nira believes that as long as we are doing the best we can, we shouldn't sweat it. There will always be some market adjustments and because of this I shouldn't take the gains or losses in anyone's portfolio's personally."

She sighed, "I know that I'm going to sound like I can't get along with anyone, but I've been having some problems with Frances, too. Frances seems to regard the job here as just a job. I see all of us in this organization as mission-driven. The purpose of IPS is to increase the financial well-being of our clients. It really bothers me to see Frances show up at work with an approach that is all business—not much of a mission for her and little for me and the client.

"When Frances asks me questions about office costs, how long a call will take, or if we really have any room in the schedule for another new client, it feels like she's throwing cold water on all my plans. She wants operating procedures and systems for everything and she runs the office in such a tight way. I'm not sure that her streamlined procedures meet the needs of all the IPS team members or the clients. But Frances constantly argues her points. She insists on making sure deadlines are met, costs are kept down, and work flow is well managed, regardless of what stands in the way."

Type Clue

Sounds like a typical ST–NF clash. NFs often feel as if STs are judging them by asking questions about their ideas—questions that NFs might avoid, such as those relating to costs and schedules. STs usually believe that the NFs have forgotten the basic how-to's needed to get a project going. And both are at least partly right in their thoughts.

Before ending my session with Julie, I chatted with her a bit more about the other team members and her own role and relationships with each of the team. Then it was time for me to talk to Nira.

Nira (NT)

Nira's office was such a contrast to Julie's—sleek and sophisticated. It reflected her former career in upscale restaurant and hotel management with its muted colors and stylized, modern furnishings. The walls displayed expensive art and the floor was covered with oriental rugs. The entire office spoke of status and a feeling of "I've made it!" Nira's dress was similar. She seemed self-confident and self-assured. I asked her to tell me a little bit about why she wanted to have a business such as IPS.

"The focus on women as a primary customer base was initially my idea," Nira began. "With the trend of more and more women in the workplace, I predicted a need—and a big one at that—that many of these women would want vehicles for financial investment. You know I'm one of the first women to get a CFP [Certified Financial Planner]. I saw lots of financial opportunities for myself and have done extremely well in the market. Therefore, I wanted to build a business where I could pass on my knowledge and make a nice return for myself as well. While we of course want to serve our customers, our business at IPS is selling investments. To do this well I need to keep abreast of market trends and to find areas with the highest return for the lowest amount of risk.

"I love this job. I love visiting oil fields and other potential investment sites, going to brokerage house meetings. There are so many possibilities for making money and for expanding and developing our business. I only wish I had more time—I'd enjoy forty-eight hours in every day to keep up with all the investment potential I see out there."

Type Clue

NTs often come up with new ideas, more often ideas relating to systems and things than solely to people. New challenges, possibilities, and things outside the ordinary are the playgrounds of NTs. They usually "know" what's on the horizon that will benefit them and others, too. Finding a niche, creating a market, and developing a model to put it all together are key strengths for NTs.

"It's hard for me to understand why more people haven't jumped into the financial services or planning arenas. If they knew what I know, many, many people would want to be involved. Financial planning is such an exciting world. When one is willing to tolerate risk as I am and when one has some money to invest, this is the time and I hope IPS is the place."

Type Clue

Clearly a visionary, in the early 1980s Nira predicted the growth industry of financial planning and services. Typical of many NTs, Nira also had the gumption to take risks to pursue her vision for herself and IPS.

After discussing with Nira her attraction to the financial service field and her reasons for leaving hotel and restaurant management, I asked her (from her perspective) to tell me about some of the relationships in the office. Specifically I inquired about her relationship with Julie.

"Julie . . . " she said, "I think Julie's getting too soft and is too concerned about the impact of small financial gains or losses on our clients' portfolios. She seems to take any downturns in the market very personally. We all know that the market has its peaks and valleys. We *tell* our clients there will be ups and downs in the value of their portfolios and they need to stay in the game for the long haul if they want to make a profit.

"I think Julie wants to see the firm grow, but she seems to be spending more time with the clients holding their hands than I think is appropriate. After all, we do have a business to run and an important part of our business is managing it and bringing in *new* clients. This is also a fun part and I think Julie needs to tend to these areas rather than baby-sitting our *current* clients."

Type Clue

As an NT, Nira had obviously tried to discern and logically deduce the causes of Julie's frustration. Sometimes NTs can be bothered by the NFs' concern for the welfare of the world—or at least that's how it appears to *them*. NFs, on the other hand, often feel that the NTs operate as if everything can be reduced to an analytical calculation that a computer could perform—or at least that's how it appears to *them*.

I asked her about her relationship with Frances and she responded, "I initially thought that Frances was a great hire, but she can be a real pain in the neck. She always wants me to document my expenses and to turn in specific requests for travel advances. Here I am, one of the founding partners, having to fill out a form to get money for travel advances! It just doesn't seem to make a lot of sense to me. I know we asked her to streamline things and improve our effectiveness, but I'm finding some of her careful scrutiny a real bother—she's just too picky!"

Type Clue

It was no surprise that Frances's ST need for accountability (especially about time and money) was getting on the nerves of Nira. NTs often find such things to be just too meticulous.

"Barb, our office assistant, seems to want to attend client meetings, too. I think it might make sense for her to be trained by Julie to do initial sessions with them. I know Julie enjoys those first sessions because she can get a read on what the client needs, but because she already has a written outline of her sales presentation, Barb could be taught to do that, saving Julie for closing the deal.

"Then again, Barb annoys me with her frequent questions regarding specifically how Mrs. Jones or Ms. Brown or even her cousin Jenny, who's also an IPS client, has fared. I can't keep track of all those nitty-gritty things. I don't keep specific clients' plans in my head! I'm more concerned with the aggregate performance of all our clients' portfolios, not each individual one. These details are not what I pay attention to. Julie and the others can do that."

Type Clue

NTs often have great difficulty with SFs' need for specific and often personal data because they focus on the big picture and trends in a less personal way. The SFs' concern and regard for *each* individual person within their purview can irritate the NTs. And just as often, NTs can make SFs feel like pawns in some giant NT chess game. Plenty of fuel to fan those four-function framework fires!

"Otherwise I feel pretty good about the office," Nira said. "I seem to be able to get along really well with George and David, the investment analysts. Those two guys were a needed addition to our talent pool. They do their work well and we hardly ever hear from them unless something big is up or about to happen. I really click with them. We see where the market is heading and move our clients' funds from the slow-moving vehicles to the faster-moving vehicles, all the while generating more commissions for IPS. It's a win-win for all!"

Type Clue

NTs often enjoy other NTs, especially competent ones who bring their own expertise to the other's. Most NTs enjoy jousting intellectually with each other and playing with words, especially "Can you top this?" games of metaphors.

"Lee, our other office assistant, is pleasant and a good worker, but she seems to be quite cautious. She sure is methodical and I can count on her doing just what she says by the time she says. She needs a lot of work direction now, but I think with time she will get better and better," Nira added.

Frances (ST)

My next task was to visit with Frances, the office manager. Frances was cordial but reserved and seemed concerned about the purpose of the session. I told her about the team-building process and said that the information she told me would be treated confidentially.

After very little chitchat, Frances suggested that since we only had approximately an hour for our meeting, we'd better get started. "I have some other very pressing business concerns that need my attention. I have to get all the documentation ready by noon for a client's financial plan. You know," she said, "we have a good track record of selling financial vehicles but I have a terrible time getting Julie and Nira to do simple things such as making sure that their clients fill in and sign all the forms at the close of any transaction. I think they would be surprised if they knew how much money gets lost and how antagonistic people can be because we have to call them back to get a signature, or we haven't gotten the forms to the banks or brokerage houses in time. Often IPS loses sales or misses the marketplace's momentum. You know, people hate to drive over here a few days after the sale has been consummated, just to sign a document that *should* have been signed at the time of the sale. Even worse is when the market changes and because paperwork isn't complete the client misses the valuation of their investment on that particular day."

Type Clue

STs find it very frustrating when NFs and NTs either don't follow the formatted plan or handle standard operating procedures haphazardly. Most STs decry inefficiency and many have had experience cleaning up behind the NFs and NTs, so their frustration is understandable.

I said to Frances, "Sounds like a hassle for all sides. What would you suggest? I'm sure your input would be useful to IPS."

"I think I'll start to keep a record of those times when procedures aren't followed. It could be very convincing data for Nira and Julie and may help them understand my perspective." So we agreed at this point that Frances would keep a record of forms that were not filled out, processes that were delayed, deadlines for investments that were not met, and clients who felt dissatisfaction at missing the timing of the market— things that should have been taken care of during the clients' planning meetings with one of the partners.

Frances went on, "I find working with Julie to be easier. She seems to know some of the struggles I go through and relates well to the clients, too! Yet, I can find her frustrating from time to time."

"How so?"

"Well, she acts like a missionary out to convert the world, especially the women of the world, to financial planning. Worse, she seems to regard anyone who doesn't talk the same line with the same degree of enthusiasm she has as not being as committed to IPS. I want you to know that I truly *am* committed. After all, it's my duty to do all the follow-up and to make sure this office runs smoothly. I work very hard to do that—how could she say that I'm not committed? Just look at the hours I put in on this job. Surely that's a sign of my commitment!"

Type Clue

STs like "just the facts," and concentrate on the job at hand. When a task makes sense and has a logical rationale to it, they'll do everything that is needed to see that it gets done. That is *their* style of commitment.

NFs like the big picture, and see it as their role (and that of non-NFs as well!) to be a persuasive communicator about people's futures and their personal growth. To them, "just the facts" is too narrow a focus.

"Commitment" looks very different depending on which part of the four-function framework a person represents. NTs show their commitment by strategizing and demonstrating for others the interconnectedness of different paths or things. For SFs, commitment is shown by providing loyal help and service to others.

"And then there's Nira. She sure is out of the office a lot. I'm never quite sure when she's going, where she's going, or even *why* she needs to go. So many of her trips are last minute, too. She wants me to come up with expense money at a moment's notice because she suddenly needs to leave town to attend some new meeting. She doesn't give me advance notice so that I can have her travel funds ready. I don't think she's aware of how very little cash we keep on hand here in the office, nor how disruptive and costly it is for me to leave work to make a special trip to the bank for her money. This and other spur-of-the-moment errands often interfere with my work, especially when I'm trying to concentrate on a specific product or client file."

Type Clue

NTs and STs often have different ideas of what constitutes doing a good job. This is especially noticeable when there is also a contrast of *Introverted* ST with *Extraverted* NT. Introverted STs tend to stay in their offices, leaving the workplace only when there's a bona fide reason for doing so. Many ISTs work straight through their lunches, eating at their desks. Extraverted NTs, on the other hand, feel compelled to be out and about getting new information or exploring new opportunities or customers.

NFs see communication as an integral part of their job and find that they need to interact with others. SFs work to make sure people have what they need when they need it.

"One last thing about Nira that bothers me," Frances added hesitantly. "She sometimes seems to have a superior attitude that goes with her elegant clothes and fancy car—a bit too much. I know she need to impress clients but. . . ."

After noting Frances's concerns with the IPS partners, I asked, "Now how about the others who work here?"

"I never see George and David. They're often working behind closed doors. They seem to enjoy being locked away in the research room with their computers and market analysis newsletters. I guess that they're at work but I'm pretty clueless about their direct contribution to IPS. When I do check in with them, they're manipulating numbers on the computer screen."

Type Clue

NTs, especially Introverted NTs, can get lost in thought as they ponder models, schemes, future ideas, and such. The outside world may see little of them. Often their ideas are not readily communicated to others until they've worked them through. When the internal conceptual work is done and when they have something important to share they will, but not before, and only if they're asked.

Introverted STs will do their inner work as well, but they are more dutiful to their schedules and others. If a meeting is on their calendar, they may resent the interruption, depending on their workload, but will also most likely suspend their own thought process and/or schedules in order to not be late to anything involving other people.

"Lee is new and I'm working on getting her up to speed. I think she is going to be very effective. Every now and then she or Barb will remind me of some individual client need like a specific report on a certain investment, so I'm glad she is here. However, sometimes her focus is on only one client or two instead of how we are managing all the clients and deadlines we have for that day. It can drive me crazy! I wish she spent as much time making sure that the previous day's portfolios are complete as she spends on giving clients her personal attention. Maybe she *should* do some customer contact and sales work, but at present I need her fully engaged with the back-office paperwork to help me keep up with IPS' growth."

Type Clue

SFs see helping *specific* people as their work. They want to give each person his or her due and do it in a pleasant way. SFs' "service with a smile" approach can be extremely valuable in a project involving others.

NFs can appreciate the SF focus on specific people's needs, but STs and NTs often misunderstand the SF contribution because their own focus is on the tasks to be done.

As I finished interviewing Frances, I felt as if the final piece of a puzzle had snapped into place. It seemed that IPS was a successful organization in need of fine-tuning rather than a major overhaul. If I wasn't mistaken, each of the four functional pairs was represented: NF (Julie), NT (Nira, George, and David), ST (Frances), and SF (Barb and Lee). Each of these functions has its own way of communicating, leading, and working. What one functional pair sees as necessary, the other functional pairs may see as picky or unimportant. What one sees as helpful, others may see as nosy. What one sees as good business sense, the others may see as rude or impersonal.

The concepts of psychological type, especially the four-function framework (ST, SF, NF, and NT), could help this team understand the different yet valuable approaches each of the players brought to IPS. If the IPS staff became "type-aware," they would start to see their colleagues' actions as flowing from their personality, which has its own reason for being, rather than from spite or lack of understanding of the work at hand.

After administering the MBTI inventory, I met with each team member to go over their results and to clarify with them which type was their best fit. After that I worked with the four-function framework to see if the theory would be useful in explaining some of the conflicts they had with each other. The opposite pairings (ST and NF, and SF and NT) generally have the most trouble understanding each other's driving force and point of view. This is how the IPS team appeared:

ST	SF	NF	NT
Frances	Barb	Julie	Nira
	Lee		George
			David

STs perceive themselves as practical and accurate. If they try to pin down those idealistic, growth-oriented NFs in order to establish accountability and control, the NFs may complain that the STs are "raining on our parade." And when the NFs display a natural interest in the personal growth and development of an ST, the ST may feel that the NF is prying and trying to expose his or her inner, private self. Instant replay of Julie and Frances?[10]

As for the other set of opposites, what is the SFs' version of the NTs? SFs like to think of how their actions affect individuals—just like Barb and her client files—and think that the NTs are too concerned with achievement-oriented tasks and projects. The SFs often feel as if they are giant pieces of the NTs' chess game—to be moved or changed at will to suit some grand strategy. The NTs , however, find the SFs' personal interactions with others and their focus on each individual to be too narrow. When SFs are dealing with people and particularly with other SFs, the NTs view these discussions as perhaps falling into the realm of gossip. Remember how Nira reacted to Barb? While Barb, the SF, felt success was to be found through more customer contact, Nira, the NT, wanted less of it.

So there you have it, a small company lucky enough to have representatives of all four functions of the framework, yet pulled into conflict because of the separate and distinct focus of each function.

The Team-Building Session

At the first team-building session, after an introduction to the four-function framework, I asked the team to group themselves into the function category that best fit them (ST, SF, NF, or NT) and to write on a piece of flip chart paper what they thought was characteristic of their style. After working at the task, Julie, the NF, volunteered to share her list first. "This is a lot of fun for me," she said, and listed as her enjoyments:

➤ Envisioning where we are going
➤ Acting on issues I feel strongly about
➤ Knowing I can make a difference for people

"You see," she said, "I really care about the people we serve and think of myself as a steward, providing the important service of financial planning to the people who need it the most—women in this culture."

I added, "Intuition combined with Feeling provides special contributions in an organizational setting. The NFs of the world like environments where important goals for people's well-being can be worked at and hopefully attained. Julie, as others of you have described her, is a crusader about women's financial needs; that is a strength the company ought to expand upon. Your customers often cite her convincing, authentic, and sincere sales presentations and her teaching of financial principles as the major reason they chose IPS over other financial planning firms. Her facilitator style and the mediator role she plays between the spouses and partners she works with are beneficial to the effective execution of her responsibilities. She works to help strengthen the women's financial assets without undermining their personal relationships and with the goal, as well, of bringing to IPS any cash for investments that the woman's partner might have."

The NTs went next, with Nira, George, and David listing:

➤ Individual initiative, being able to take risks
➤ Discovering or "sniffing out" opportunities well in advance of trends

➤ Drive and energy to achieve breakthroughs in financial dealings and profitable results

Nira said, "Taking risks is who I am. You all know I left Lebanon for the United States to strike out on my own. In the process, I not only found opportunities for myself but brought all my siblings here and put them each through college. It was hard work, but I liked the challenge of setting a goal and reaching it. Now I have the same drive for IPS' success. To do this, one needs individual initiative and a willingness to take risks."

George nodded, "All three of us can sniff out opportunities way in advance of others seeing them. Dave and I do it with our computer models and Nira does it as she interacts with businesses, investors, and vendors firsthand. Our computer-based timing model serves us well—and Julie, while I now better understand your missionary stuff, if you were to spend more time understanding our system, you'd realize our uniqueness and be better able to sell the process to our customers—for a nice service fee."

"You'll have to come out of your office cave and explain it, though," Julie replied with a grin.

David laughed and Nira added, "I know some of you want to see more of me, too. I *am* gone a lot but I think it's important to the business that I establish our presence in the financial community. I'm pretty energetic, too, and when all the red tape around here slows me down, I feel stifled. It amazes me that we have a new form for when we see the client and another for the one-week-later follow-up! If I knew more about why these forms are necessary, I'd be willing to give them a good try."

Frances spoke up. "I think this is where I come in—the one who wants all of those forms!" After the chuckles died down, Frances (ST) listed her strengths as:

➤ Dependability and reliability
➤ Being efficient
➤ Ensuring that each necessary step toward IPS' goals is followed explicitly, specifically, and accurately

"People can count on me and they know it," added Frances. "You can set your watches by my arrival because I'm always here on time, 8:30 A.M. I *like* the implementation part and if you want something from me, you're sure to get it from me in a timely way. And Nira, if you knew how many deals we've almost lost because a client had to come back for some small yet crucial detail, you'd be surprised."

Before having Nira and Frances discuss the topic of procedures, forms, and near misses for the business, I asked for time to add some thoughts about STs.

"STs are the ones most likely to focus on costs and schedules, using time efficiently, and making sure that t's are crossed and i's are dotted. They can easily spot inefficiency and waste and believe that it is their job to uphold and be responsible for any organizational aspect where they have accountability. The day-to-day, step-by-step attention STs give to the technical aspects of their work provides real value to any work setting. Personally, if a project I am working on is being overseen by an ST, I find it much easier to sleep at night!"

Frances added, "Maybe I don't see the big picture, but if you tell me where you're going, I'll make sure you take the right steps to get there."

Barb and Lee went last with their list of what is valuable to an SF:

➤ Servicing IPS customers in a personal and practical way
➤ Being accurate and helpful
➤ Working to keep the office harmonious

Barb added, "If only we could be nicer to each other. You know, I really miss people saying please and thank you, and hello and good-bye at the beginning and end of the day. If we were to do this, it would make this office much more pleasant."

Julie chimed in, "Well, that's certainly easy enough to do. Let's make it a goal for this week."

"Hey, I do that with my customers," Nira responded. "You mean I have to do it in the office, too?" Everyone laughed at this comment, even Nira, who then affirmed she would give "office niceties" her best shot.

I added to the description of SF cultures. "SFs make people feel like part of a large, extended family; they are the social glue that binds individuals together. They want to support others and in turn to be supported. Cooperation is their hallmark, and teams where the SF strengths are ignored often say that it can feel as if everyone is only out for him or herself. Because people's needs matter to them, SFs often will go out of their way to create a work environment for others that's cooperative and orderly."

I then asked the group, "Which of the functional pairings do you think IPS can do without?" There was quick agreement that all were useful to IPS. Then I asked them to consider how those irritating actions of others, particularly of those most opposite to them (ST and NF, and SF and NT) may also serve to balance their own weak points.

Julie spoke up, "Maybe we could post signs outside our offices. Mine could say, 'NF spoken here. Beware of zeal and a missionary idealism.'"

Nira laughed, "And mine could read, 'Beware of big-picture agendas while details are swept under the rug.'"

"Not to put a damper on the fun," I interrupted, "but I'm sure Frances's sign would say, 'Beware of exacting time frames.' And in keeping with *that* spirit, it's time for us to wrap up. For homework I want you to consider what you value most and need most from your opposite style. Then come up with a very specific list of what the others need to know in order to work most effectively with you." I asked them to read through their type descriptions again. The meeting adjourned amidst lots of discussion.

When we met three weeks later, there was a noticeable improvement in the office working relationships and a reduction in tension between many of the individuals. During this team-building meeting, the following agreements were reached:

➤ Julie affirmed to the group that she would be slightly less crusading in her approach to selling financial planning to women; that she would work on putting more distance between herself and the effect of stock market changes on her clients' portfolios; that she would accompany Nira on several trips to brokers and vendors; and that she would begin to turn over to Barb some of the smaller clients (in terms of portfolio monetary value) and other clients whom she had nurtured over several years. Barb's help would relieve Julie's workload somewhat and give Barb vital work experience, interacting with clients and managing accounts.

➤ Nira acknowledged that some of the "junkets" she took were not profitable to IPS in the long run, and because of this she would be more focused and strategic in selecting from the many opportunities. She would offer daily pleasantries not only to clients and customers but to the folks at IPS. She would spend more time on client relations and on taking some of the day-to-day operations burden from Julie. Also, she agreed to initiate her requests for travel advances earlier and stick with the systems that Frances established. She asked Frances and Julie to remind and help her when she started to backslide.

➤ Frances did her homework as agreed on logging inefficiencies and came to the meeting with a list of clients who were dissatisfied and financial deals that were not consummated because of overlooked details. She developed an excellent client-tracking form modeled after one she used at her previous employer to monitor current and future IPS customers. She urged both partners and anyone else who had client contact to follow the outline and procedure with each client interaction. To help with this process she planned to staple a flowchart on the inside of each client folder. Any documents that needed work in a timely way would be clearly marked with due dates and procedures needing completion. She told the group that she would train Lee and Barb in the most efficient office management procedures. Because Lee was new, it was agreed that Lee, Julie, and Nira would meet so Lee could see how her responsibilities related to the overall goals of IPS.

➤ Barb said that she would be delighted to work with long-term clients as well as those with relatively small portfolios and that she would also enjoy watching and learning how Julie and Nira evaluated clients in their initial meetings. Prior to this meeting, she listed the existing clients with whom she had good working relationships and asked to manage their files.

➤ George and David agreed it was important to let the rest of the office know in a straightforward way what the two of them were working on in the research room. They offered to do a brown bag lunch seminar to explain the intricacies of their task to their colleagues. David promised to prepare a one-page weekly update that detailed more specifically the market trends and strategies he and George were using in their timing work.

Julie and Nira pointed out how follow-through by each person on the commitments they were making in the session could have a positive impact on IPS, each person's work life, and each person's part of the corporate prof-it-sharing plan. With everyone working toward these objectives, IPS soon developed a cohesive rather than clashing four-part culture.

Reviewing the Four-Function Framework

Can you place yourself or your team within this four-function framework? See if you can find your own and your teammates' strengths and possible blind spots as you review each of the four functional pairings below.

ST: Let's Be Objective and Matter-of-Fact

ST organizations tend to want answers to questions about costs, schedules, efficiency, precision, and accuracy. They like to build hierarchical organizations with a place for everyone and everything in its place. They believe they are earning their keep when they are critiquing broad, general ideas in order to focus everyone realistically and practically.

Because the focus of STs is day-to-day, they may sometimes overlook the long-term implications of their work. However, their orientation to the present keeps the team from misusing its current resources—both human and financial. STs also prefer to work in organizations with products and services that are reliable and of high quality. You can often identify STs because they want details on specifics and logical answers to their questions (usually tactical and procedural).

SF: Let's Be Practical and Service-Oriented

The SF organizational environment may resemble a varied and extended family. Most SF organizations also have a hierarchy, but a friendly one. SF organizations (such as schools or hospitals) are structured in such a way that a person's level in the hierarchy reflects his or her qualifications or skills for the services he or she is to provide. This division of labor in a broad hierarchy allows for a particularly SF flavor—to have the right person in the right place to do the right thing for others.

"Service with a smile" is quite characteristic of SF organizations. SFs feel like they are worth their salt when they use clarity and direction to meet the needs of each specific individual and group. SFs' attention to people makes them very cognizant of how things will affect others. They are unlikely to be very wrong about a customer's needs.

Because they are busy serving others, they may overlook the strategic plan, the big picture, and sometimes their own needs. They may, therefore, need help in these areas.

SF organizations are typically pleasant, sociable, and enjoyable places to be. Efficiency is important to SFs but only if that efficiency still allows for carefully handling people's concerns.

NF: Let's Be Insightful and Inspiring

NF organizations are characterized by their mission and values focus. Generally, NF organizations set goals for an improvement in the circumstances of people and communities. While the SFs might focus on specific people, the NF approach is to help people in general. NF organizations are often about fostering growth and development, inspiring people to greater heights, developing human aspirations, and, in general, making the world a better place for people to live.

NFs tend to set up collegial organizations with an interchangeable leadership format, because often NFs are reluctant to elevate any one person over another. Instead, they allow people to take turns as leader and follower. This is probably one of the reasons that NF business organizations are rare, but that seems to be just fine for NFs, who tend to avoid being a part of business bureaucracies. Business organizations generally have only a few places where NFs can express themselves as they'd like.

Working for the values that one believes in and having, as Isabel Myers said, "a purpose beyond the paycheck" is an important attribute of the work environment for NFs. Work must have meaning; when it doesn't, NFs become less productive. Like SF organizations, the work environment is best when it is filled with harmonious people who enjoy each other's company while striving together toward a common purpose.

NT: Let's Be Theoretical and Entrepreneurial

The NT organization is characterized by meeting challenges: mental, financial, conceptual, and sometimes physical. NTs set broad goals for themselves. They are not very patient with detail; however, like STs, they tend to like things to be logical. While the ST may focus on the day-to-day specifics, the NT focus is the big picture and long-range possibilities.

NTs are most happy when they can be in an environment that is filled with others who like debate, rigor, and intellectual work. They are most effective in situations that involve the complexity of orchestrating various systems together to achieve a common objective.

NTs use a hierarchy when it is the most effective organizational format but tend to prefer a structure of matrix organizations and project teams where roles are more fluid. They often overlook interpersonal niceties, thinking of people as only *one* of the facets in their systems and structures. Of course, NTs believe people are an important component of any system, strategy, or structure but it's up to people to fit into the NTs' structure.

TYPE TAKEAWAY

The following chart may be helpful in summarizing the four-function framework and in introducing these type concepts.

Characteristic	STs	SFs	NFs	NTs
Like work that is	Practical Crisp	Social Personal	Idealistic Insightful	Theoretical Complex
Establish teams that are	Efficient and data-oriented	Friendly and service-oriented	Creative and growth-oriented	Effective and competition-oriented
Establish team structure that is	Hierarchical	Fraternal	Collegial	Entrepreneurial
Team focus is	Predictable and stable	Traditional and affiliative	Dynamic and ideological	Achieving and competent
Seek	Permanence Accountability Control	Membership Personal interaction Support	Personal meaning Development Growth	Rationality Opportunity Long-range plans
Often found in	Military Industry	Service Health care	Arts Communication	Sciences Start-up

Source: Reprinted by permission from Hirsh, Sandra Krebs, *MBTI Team Building Program*. Palo Alto, Calif.: Consulting Psychologists Press, 1992.

Type Solvers to Try

When you suspect a clash in cultures, try these ideas.

☑ Review the four-function framework. After discussing the basic concepts, have each person identify which one of the four functions best describes them (ST, SF, NF, or NT). Then, either individually or in groups, answer the following questions:

➤ What should the other groups know about what we value and contribute to the workplace?

➤ What do we need from the three other parts of the four-function framework to have a more effective working relationship?

☑ If appropriate, meet again as a large group. Depending on your needs, the following topics could be discussed:

➤ List the tasks where each person or group works most naturally and with the most energy and enthusiasm. Ask, does our work division follow these lines?

➤ Conversely, which tasks is it best for each person or group to avoid? What are the ways we could team across the four-function framework to better cover these areas?

➤ When communication has been problematic, take two or three recent written communications and let each person or group report on the aspects of the communication that made it easy or difficult to understand. Look for concrete examples of the different communication styles and needs within the four-function framework. List any necessary changes to be made so communication will bridge the four cultures.

Tips for Persuading Each of the
Four Function Pairs—ST, SF, NF, and NT

ST

➤ Show me that it works.

➤ Indicate how it saves time and money.

➤ Demonstrate a good cost-to-benefit ratio.

➤ Show how the results can be measured.

➤ Allow me to try it before I buy it.

➤ Offer specific applications and benefit.

➤ Answer all my questions.

SF

➤ Indicate its practical results for people.

➤ Show how it will clearly benefit me and those I care about.

➤ Use personal testimonies from those who have benefited from it.

➤ Show that it provides immediate results.

➤ Set it in a personal context.

➤ Show respect to me and others in your presentation.

➤ Explicitly state the benefits; don't just imply them.

NF

➤ Show how it will enhance relationships.

➤ State how it helps people grow and develop.

➤ Focus on my own and others' giftedness.

➤ Show how it gives new insights and perspectives.

➤ Indicate that people will like it, and, by implication, will like *me*.

➤ Point out how it will help me find meaning.

➤ Say it's enjoyable and fun.

NT

➤ Discuss its research base.

➤ Highlight its theoretical background.

➤ Demonstrate how it fits a strategy.

➤ Show how it will increase competency.

➤ Indicate its broad and far-reaching possibilities.

➤ Show that it has intriguing and fascinating possibilities.

➤ Be a credible source of information.

Source: Reprinted by permission from Hirsh, Sandra Krebs, *MBTI Team Building Program*, Palo Alto, Calif.: Consulting Psychologists Press, 1992.

Of <u>course</u> I see the big picture.

The Case of the
Lurking Inferior Function

The Shadow Knows

Type Key

Type is a poor excuse for inexcusable behavior!

What a natural place for stress the world of work is. You know the week just is not going your way when:

➤ You learn your most important client's daughter is marrying your competitor's son.

➤ Your computer guru informs you that his dog ate the only copy of the password changes he made over the weekend.

➤ Your associate tells you not to worry, but everyone at your level is invited to a free seminar on job search skills.

➤ Your new boss announces all vacations are canceled because of a rush project—two days before you are to leave on your nonrefundable prepaid trip to the Greek islands.

All kidding aside, new bosses, new policies, and restructuring can trigger the inferior function if the right (or wrong) ingredients for stress, conflict, or illness are present. Carl Jung saw that even our inconsistencies can be predicted by type, which is why understanding the symptoms of being in the grip of the inferior function can be extremely useful to team members. As we mentioned in chapter 1, for each type there are a dominant function and an inferior function—aptly described as inferior because of our inability to do two things well at the same time.

Type Chart 3 shows the dominant (in bold) and inferior function for each personality type.

Type Chart 3

ISTJ **Sensing** Intuition	ISFJ **Sensing** Intuition	INFJ **Intuition** Sensing	INTJ **Intuition** Sensing
ISTP **Thinking** Feeling	ISFP **Feeling** Thinking	INFP **Feeling** Thinking	INTP **Thinking** Feeling
ESTP **Sensing** Intuition	ESFP **Sensing** Intuition	ENFP **Intuition** Sensing	ENTP **Intuition** Sensing
ESTJ **Thinking** Feeling	ESFJ **Feeling** Thinking	ENFJ **Feeling** Thinking	ENTJ **Thinking** Feeling

If a dominant Intuitive is guided by insights and possibilities, he or she naturally relies less on information from the senses (facts and current realities). If a dominant Thinker depends on logic, hunches or "feelings" are not seen as trustworthy. Hence, the way one comprehends and experiences the function opposite to the dominant truly feels inferior.

There are ways to learn about and benefit from the inferior function, and this becomes especially interesting at midlife. For example, Feeling types often explore intellectual coursework and logical analysis of their decisions while Thinkers often reflect on what is meaningful and of value to them. However, no matter how aware you are of your inferior function's gifts and common pitfalls, add an overdose of stress to life and guess what happens? The inferior function sneaks into your behavior! For example, someone with dominant Intuition may, under stress, begin overeating or indulging in mindless television-viewing, both of which involve an exaggerated use of the senses. In contrast, a dominant Sensing person may begin to conjecture about the future and fear that a prime customer will leave or that a new product launch will fail when neither is likely. (Clues about the common manifestations of the inferior function for each type are found at the end of this chapter.)

Learning about the inferior function can give you ways to:

➤ Recognize its manifestations
➤ Understand your own blind spots
➤ Make sense of your behavior and the actions of others during stressful or changing times

The following case at Impressions, Inc. shows a concrete example of what can happen when the inferior function lurks.

Type Story: Impressions, Inc.

Cast of Characters

Penny, Director of Quality	INFJ
Jason, Vice President of Marketing	ESTJ
Leya, Quality Control Analyst	INFP
Wesley, Quality Control Analyst	ENFP
Josh, Purchasing Liaison	ESTJ
Kendra, Materials Quality Specialist	INFP
Ellen, former Vice President of Quality	ESFJ

The call for help came from Tanya, the director of human resources of Impressions, Inc., a furniture company. "Would you be willing to come in and read the riot act to our Quality team? It's having lots of trouble. You've worked with us before, you've traveled to many organizations, and you know both the theory and reality of organizational life, so you'll be able to tell this team how good they have it here at our company. The team is mostly women and they're behaving like children."

"Whoa," I responded, "I'd be glad to meet with you and the team leader to see what's going on, but I'm not sure I'll take you up on the reading the riot act part."

"Okay," she laughed, "come in on Thursday and I'll arrange for you to meet the team leader, Penny Klein. She just joined our company and she's great—best credentials we could find. We snatched her away from our competitor. She knows every aspect of the furniture business and has even written articles about quality standards regarding household furnishings;

but she's never managed before, so she may need some coaching in that area. I just wish her team would give her the backing she deserves. From an HR perspective, she's dynamite—just the kind of hire we want for our senior positions. But I'm hearing rumors of discontent . . . I'm sure your help and intervention will get Penny and her team to become better acquainted with each other."

Impressions had been a client of mine before; this was part of the reason I was asked to see what I could do. I knew the business from the top down (I had worked with several senior management teams) and I was a fan of their particular kind of quality discount furniture. The mood of the company was very upbeat with a positive, can-do attitude; hence I was surprised that this one team would be in such turmoil and experiencing, according to Tanya, such a negative climate.

Tanya's office was the site of my first meeting with Penny, a troubled-looking thirty-four-year-old. "I want this team to cooperate with me and accept the fact that I'm the leader, but they are either apathetic or act like college kids hazing a newcomer. I know I'm not an experienced manager, but I do know my technical stuff and I've read all the latest management gurus. I've already demonstrated my abilities to Jason, my boss here at Impressions, and I know I have his solid backing."

"And she has our backing too," added Tanya.

I asked, "Tell me about your first weeks at Impressions."

Penny continued, "Well, here's what I've done so far: I've created a vision statement for the department; reworked the department's mission with Jason; conducted interviews with each of my direct reports; delineated the new quality standard; audited departmental practices top-to-bottom; and tried to be motivational. After all this, the team treats me like the new kid on the block, balking at everything I ask them to do! There's Leya, she's especially difficult for me to fathom—and there's Wesley, too. Why Wesley doesn't jump at the chances I've given him is a mystery to me!"

When I asked Penny further questions about her new position, she responded hesitantly, "I've moved clear across the country for this job—left my family, friends and a very comfortable house—not to mention a sure promotion at my old company. But I'm heading towards thirty-five; I wanted the senior management post Impressions offered—and the salary treatment and director job title are great, too. But I sure don't feel great. Most days I leave this place with a headache. I keep losing my glasses and wristwatch— me who likes being organized, acting as if my brain has left me.

"I feel like I'm working better in some areas, though, but the detail work really drains me. I've read *all* the reports, really gotten into the department's finances, and checked over the warehouse inventory reports.

I'm filled to the brim with all the details of the Quality function and of Impressions, Inc.! I feel I'm getting to the bottom of everything—but there's one thing that I can't figure out and I've been thinking about it every minute when I'm not occupied with something else."

"What's that?" I asked.

"Page six, paragraph three, of the quarterly Quality report deals with a group of occasional chairs from our best suppliers in North Carolina. They met our standard and I don't understand why Leya rejected them. They are great quality, for the price. But I'll get to the bottom of this yet . . . even if I have to work around Leya."

Type Clue

Hmmm . . . possible clues that the inferior is lurking in Penny's world. Lots of changes in her life—geographical, organizational, personal, and managerial. "Things," she said, "feel out of control." Penny's symptoms were similar to those I see in other dominant Intuitives under stress, experiencing their inferior function through obsession with detail and often having physical symptoms: in this case, Penny's headaches.

As time was moving rapidly, I felt the need to talk about what kind of intervention we thought necessary—other than "reading the riot act" or asking the team to "shape up or ship out." "Things haven't only changed for Penny," I remarked. "The role and mission of Quality has changed, too." Because of my work with other senior leaders at Impressions, I knew that the person to fill the lead position in Quality had to create a new vision and carry out Quality's new mission—to partner with and support Marketing. Additionally, that person would have to implement the strategic direction handed down by the Marketing vice president (Jason, Penny's boss).

I restated this information and added, "You know, Penny, they could resent you as a newcomer, resent the new policies, and resent all the changes in general. They probably feel they've lost the old, comfortable team atmosphere and the relationship they had with Ellen [their previous boss] and the more independent status the department had as opposed to its new ties to Marketing. Let's start with a fresh look at the impact of the changes. I'll want to see everything you can give me: job descriptions, the new mission statement, your vision, and anything else about Quality that would give me a clearer picture of the department—especially the new corporate direction for Quality that I understand your boss Jason wants to see implemented."

After more discussion, we three decided on a full-scale team-building approach. I made arrangements to interview Penny, each team member who reported directly to her, and Penny's boss, Jason.

"And, of course we'll do the MBTI," added Tanya.

"Well, let's hold on that just now," I said. "I don't want to use the MBTI inventory in group sessions at this time, because I'm concerned that in their present mood they might use the MBTI information to nail each other rather than to rebuild their work relationships." We therefore decided to do an individual MBTI interpretation for each person as a part of my investigation but use the results in team-building sessions later on, *when and if* it seemed appropriate. They quickly understood how the MBTI could do more harm than good if it were introduced to the team at the wrong time.

The MBTI data could help explain to Penny and possibly to the others some of the mental and physical reactions they might be having to all the changes. I also wanted to see if Penny's stress and her headaches were a result of her lurking inferior function. Additionally, I requested a chance to attend the next staff meeting to see Penny at work with her department firsthand.

At the next Quality staff meeting, I explained the team-building process to the team members and fielded questions about it. The group was professional but seemed to lack enthusiasm for the team building we were about to do. I noticed how compliant they were to Penny's agenda—not much commitment or feedback to her—until she mentioned the quarterly Quality report.

Wesley blurted out, "I was shocked to see that you sent it on to Jason under your signature! I was in charge of the whole project; you only rewrote a few pieces. We put a lot of work into that report, all of us. How can we be a team if you go over every detail of our work and then ignore us and put *your* name on it! Don't you trust us? You know, we did just fine for fifteen months without a leader! Ellen would never have taken our names off a report and put her own name on it!" Heads around the table nodded in agreement.

"Well," stammered Penny, "it is my responsibility to check things. Besides, you know I'm new here and getting to the detail is one way I can familiarize myself with the way things are done. I am the head of this department; it is the department's quarterly report; and my name *should* be on it. If there are errors in it, my neck will be the one on the line, not yours! That's part of a leader's job too, you know, to protect the team. Heck, I'm really being a team player. Now that we're clear about this, let's move on. . . . "

"Team player," I heard someone murmur under their breath, "Yeah, right."

"Hey, let's move on," said Josh. "Cut Penny some slack, you guys! She's new—we can live with the report that way. We've got other things to do, like go over the flammability standards."

With Josh's help, the meeting moved on, but only halfheartedly. I expected another incident because it seemed as if antagonism ran just below the surface—especially between Penny and Wesley and to a similar extent all the other team members except Josh. Okay, I thought to myself as the meeting adjourned, no doubt as to why they called me in.

I started my MBTI interpretation and interview process with Penny. Her MBTI reported type came out ENTJ but with just slight preferences for Extraversion and Thinking. As we discussed the Extraversion–Introversion scale Penny said, "I need to be an Extravert in this job! I'm pleased to see my Extraversion score because that's what I'm working on—being more action-oriented and outgoing. One of the reasons I was hired is to be an advocate for the new quality standard."

Type Clue

When people take an instrument such as the MBTI, they can affect their scores by responding as they need to be at work or in a socially desirable manner. Therefore, when doing an interpretation I listen for clues to mindset such as "I have to" or "I should" either when they are filling out the Indicator or when they are listening to my interpretation. Penny wanted to make an impression as an Extravert, but doing this does not necessarily make her one. As both preferences are good and equally valid, when I hear that someone is working on or trying to shift their preference toward one or the other, I begin to wonder if their reported type reflects their true preference.

The S–N decision went quickly. "I know this is me," Penny said without delay, but on the T–F scale I noticed her hesitation. "Oh yes, I *have* to be logical and analytical in this job—my decisions *have* to be fair and firm. I've worked on this, too. I *have* to hold people accountable to the new quality standard—'quality for the price'—that Impressions has. My team sure doesn't understand or appreciate my efforts, though. I used to be more on the 'heart' side, but I don't think that works in management."

Type Clue

Again, Penny seemed to be trying to change her natural preferences. Note her frequent use of the words *have to*. There is a world of difference between *have to* and *prefer to*.

The J was also a quick decision for Penny. "I like to decide," she said, "and I don't feel comfortable about any endeavor unless I establish a timetable." When she read the ENTJ type description, she especially liked "being goal-oriented and organized, and delivering results as projected." When I told her many senior managers had ENTJ preferences, she stated that she knew she'd made the right choice in answering the MBTI in what she called her "tough guy" mind-set.

Although I had an educated guess that Penny was an INFJ, it is not ethical (or a very effective practice) to select a person's type for him or her. Also, I try not to let people place all the weight on the MBTI scores themselves, especially given the tip-offs of "working on" a preference or the "have to" comments that Penny made. Because of my doubts about the accuracy of her type, I gave Penny some homework. "This week, why don't you read through Extraversion–Introversion and Thinking–Feeling more carefully and then monitor yourself during this time with these preferences in mind. If you can, sense the 'should do's' you place on yourself. Try to see how often you feel like your 'I should do this or that' manager self versus your 'shoulds-off' self.

"Because of your comments and the specific language you used and your slight preference scores, it might help if you were to clarify your dominant function, the major gift of your personality, by monitoring it as well. Of the four functions, Sensing, Intuition, Thinking, or Feeling, which one do you think comes easiest; which one do you rely on most; and which one do you remember yourself doing most easily as a young person? Do people say you:

➤ Have common sense, which is one way to think about Sensing
➤ Are insightful, which is one way to think about Intuition
➤ Are quick to discover a flaw, which is one way to describe Thinking
➤ Are the type of person who likes to please others, which is one way to describe Feeling

Which one feels most like you? Think about this because it may help you determine your dominant function and therefore your best-fit type."

Even though I said this was part of her homework, Penny said, "That's easy, I've often been called insightful. Also, I'm pretty good with people, but you'd never know it now given this team." I asked her to think about these things because given the way she had just responded, her answers to the question sounded like she could more likely have preferences for Introversion and Feeling.

During the interview process, Penny stated that she was trying hard to do things by the book to no real avail. "Life would be so much easier if I didn't have to play the tough guy," Penny lamented.

"What does playing the tough guy mean?" I asked her.

"It means monitoring people in a detailed fashion as they work day-to-day. I keep track of all the specific requests I give them and how they follow through." She further elaborated that getting tough meant ignoring their protestations when she second-guessed them and when they complained about her style.

Type Clue

Being a dominant Intuitive myself, I know that monitoring specific details on a daily basis is not typical for a dominant Intuitive and can lead to stress. Further, we tend to have trouble keeping track of details over an extended period, leading to frustration at our ineptness. Penny was setting herself up for a good case of distress.

After interviewing Penny, I had a chance to talk with Jason, her boss. I knew from my previous work with Impressions that Jason's type preferences were for ESTJ. Jason reiterated some interesting facts about the Quality department and about Penny's arrival on the scene that helped explain some of what I had observed. "I can't say enough about what Penny has done so far; she certainly has my endorsement. I suppose she is a little green in her management capabilities, but her understanding of the technical aspects of furniture design and quality is stellar.

"You know, the Quality department was initially chartered by the founder of Impressions and was managed for sixteen years by his administrative assistant, Ellen. Originally, Ellen simply answered customer letters and complaints about their furniture purchases. As the store grew, her function grew as well. Over the years, Ellen hired every person who is currently in the department. She selected people who were experienced in quality analysis and who had the technical expertise she lacked."

"Oh, yes, I remember Ellen," I said, recalling past meetings with Impressions. To myself I thought, I remember her type preferences were for ESFJ.

Type Clue

The ESFJ management style is usually outgoing, warm, and personal. ESFJs tend to reward loyalty and consistency. Therefore, for some team members Penny's "tough guy" act must have been a difficult contrast to Ellen's nurturing atmosphere. And if Penny were imitating a Thinking style, there's a good chance she might not be doing a very good imitation. It's hard to act consistently like another psychological type for any length of time and do it well.

"Ellen had a great knack for responding favorably to customer complaints while maintaining Impression's integrity. She left Impressions on family leave. I think she fully intended to return, but after spending three months at home with her new husband and stepchild, she decided that she needed to be a full-time wife and mother. In the interim, however, her position was held open for three months of leave and for the twelve months it took Impressions to do a national search to replace her. You know, the department almost managed itself for those fifteen months, with Wesley acting as informal department leader reporting to me."

"Was Wesley ever considered as a replacement for Ellen?" I asked.

"Well, we sounded him out on that. He said he didn't want all the responsibility because he is so involved with his extended family and in community theater, which besides his family is his first love."

"That's good for me to know. What about the job title change from vice president to director and the new reporting relationship?" I asked.

"That was a rather big change—Quality reporting to me as VP of Sales and Marketing. In the past, Ellen, who held the title of vice president, reported directly to our CEO, whereas Penny as a director reports to me, a VP. I guess the Quality department saw this reorganization as a real loss of status. I know there has been a lot of turmoil in the department, especially since Penny arrived. I think it will sort itself out eventually, but I am glad you are here."

Type Clue

I felt certain, after hearing Jason's description, that I had correctly recalled Ellen's type as ESFJ. Certainly ESFJ characteristics were evident: the personal touch for each employee and the concern about their problems.

The situational leadership model of Hershey and Blanchard[11] quickly flashed into my mind. The Quality department had very experienced followers now being led by a relatively inexperienced leader. Given that the department had almost run itself and fairly successfully at that for fifteen months, *any* newcomer would have faced resentment. To most of her direct reports, Penny's "tough but firm" management style probably felt like salt rubbed into wounds.

"I know of one major mistake Penny made since coming on board," said Jason. "She changed the quarterly Quality report so that only her name was on it. Because I had a good working relationship with Wesley and the others in the department for that long interim period, at least three members in the department voiced their resentment to me loud and clear. I've already talked to Penny about this and have coached her on the way we here at Impressions acknowledge team efforts.

"The other issue in the department was the change in the quality standard. After a strategic planning session with all of the company officers, we determined that quality would no longer be defined as Ellen had defined it."

I asked what the former definition was, and Jason replied, "Quality was interpreted in a very personal way. Ellen trained all her team to look at quality with these questions in mind: 'Would I buy this? Would I want my friends to buy this? Are the materials durable and sturdy and structurally sound? How would I feel about Impressions if I bought a chair, for example, and something were wrong with it? What would that do to Impressions' reputation as a provider of high-quality, low-cost furniture?' As I said, Ellen's was a very personal standard.

"For our continuing nationwide expansion, we wanted new standards of quality that can be measured empirically. Penny was asked to endorse our new standard, which is now very directly and succinctly stated as 'quality for the price.' This means, for example, that if customers buy a lower-priced swivel rocker, they should expect that it might wear out sooner than a swivel rocker purchased at a higher price. Our new standard is uniform and consistent and based on a strategy of comparable pricing of all of the items in our furniture stores."

Type Clue

This sounded like a Thinking–Feeling difference in determining furniture quality. By this time, I knew that most of Penny's team had a reported preference for Feeling. So did Ellen, and Jason's description of Ellen's policy had a decidedly Feeling flavor to it. The new standard of "quality for the price" probably did not conform to the values held by most of the Feeling types in the department.

Jason, an ESTJ, was new to Impressions in the last four years. For his type preferences, the new "quality for the price" made sense. His new quality and pricing structures, which were measurable and more easily replicated, fit his Thinking preference for making quality and pricing decisions—so more type pieces were falling in place for me.

I was now beginning to have some thoughts about how the full team-building intervention might go. It seemed to me that a discussion of departmental history and situational leadership might explain some of the issues that Penny was having with her staff. Particularly for Feeling types, past history as well as past and current relationships are important. In addition, it is extremely crucial to those who have a psychological preference for Feeling to know that the standards they use for making work decisions are a suitable match with their values. Perhaps "quality for the price" wasn't measuring up to Ellen's more Feeling quality standard. I made some mental notes and moved on to my interview with Wesley.

We reviewed Wesley's type together and he confirmed that his inventory results, ENFP, were a match with his own self-perceptions. Like Penny, I asked Wesley to do some homework and think about his type over the next week to see if he could gather more evidence to support that ENFP was indeed his best-fit type. When I asked him a question about how others viewed him, he said he was definitely known as an innovator, one who provided creative ideas.

As we moved from type to the interview questions, Wesley's stress began to surface. I asked him to tell me about his role and function in the Quality department and he complained, "I don't know why I was given the job to assist Marketing in setting up a display room of furniture samples and fabrics for a trade show!" He whipped out a copy of his job description and jabbed at it. "I want you to read this and show me where in my job description it says that I am to set up a furniture exhibition room. I can't find anything about that in here and I don't want to do anything not in my job description!"

"You know, in order to set up this room, I will have to travel to various furniture manufacturers, attend the trade show near Hilton Head, maybe even go to Mexico and who knows where else to find examples of the styles and fabrics that Impressions uses in our furniture. I'll have to be sure that quality is high, too. I know I have a decent budget to carry this out but there are no specific directions anywhere on how to do this! A display room like this has never been set up before and I am breaking new ground. Frankly, I'm very unhappy that there's no detailed information or a model for me to follow. If this is what they want me to do, then I specifically want to see it in writing."

Type Clue

Hm, this could be an ENFP under stress. Because I have ENFP preferences, I know the stress signs well, especially in others! Wesley wanted specific, detailed information in his job description for his new, uncharted assignment. Generally, one is hard-pressed to get ENFPs to read their job description, let alone to follow its directives! Wesley was also overlooking the fact that this new assignment contained a lot of creative challenge. It would expose him to many parts of the furniture-making world and give him the broad overview that many ENFPs love. He could also count on an exciting travel schedule at Impressions' expense—something many ENFPs fantasize will happen to them in their work settings.

I asked Wesley how things were going in his life in general. "Not well," he responded. "I have these terrible stomach cramps and I ache all over. I'm afraid I may have cancer, so I've put myself on a very strict macrobiotic diet. I've been on it about a week, but it sure is hard to follow. I find all the cooking a real chore, but I follow the recipes to the letter and I think I am feeling somewhat improved. If not, the cancer may have just died down."

"Cancer!" I said. "Have you been to the doctor?"

"No, I just diagnosed myself. After all, it must be something serious if I feel this badly."

"Perhaps it could be stress."

"Well, that's too easy—something else must be going on."

Type Clue

When aches and pains mean dreaded diseases and when dominant Intuitives obsess over some bodily symptom until self-diagnosing a major life-threatening illness, it sounds like their lurking inferior (and negatively cast) *Introverted Sensing* function is hard at work.

After talking about Wesley's stress and several more questions, we ended the session with my gaining a commitment from Wesley to see his doctor to check out his stomach symptoms, to give himself some downtime to reflect on his new assignment, and to leave the office each day at normal times for the next two weeks. In this way I hoped that he could get more fresh air (literally!) and perhaps change his perspective. "Is this job important to you overall?" I asked.

"Oh, yes," said Wesley. "Overall it *has* been great! It's just that now there's too much stress and too many changes. I really miss the good old days with Ellen and our old approach to sizing up quality. And I'm having a hard time with Penny. You know, of course, that she took my name off the quarterly Quality report and signed it herself." I asked him to tell me more about his relationship to Penny and his thoughts now about not taking the Quality leadership role. I found our time together was up just as we finished the last question.

The interview with Wesley confirmed to me that the environment in the Quality department was stressful. Penny and Wesley both seemed to be under a great deal of stress and pressure. Now it was time to interview Leya, another team member.

As Leya entered the room, I thought if looks could kill, I'd be dead. A strange greeting, given that I remembered Leya's reported type came out clearly as an INFP on the MBTI.

Type Clue

Leya's glaring, hostile eyes caught me off guard. INFPs are usually pleasant to interact with and seem to meet others with the assumption "hail fellow, well met." However, the woman about to begin an interview with me was anything but pleasant—she was downright angry and nasty. Another team member under stress; perchance the lurking inferior *Extraverted Thinking* function.

I decided to let Leya vent her frustration by doing the interview questions first and then later discussing her MBTI type with her.

I started with the same question I asked the others, "Tell me about your job and what it's like to work in the Quality department at Impressions."

Leya sat silent for just a short time and then blurted out, "This department is the pits! I think the company is going to hell in a handbasket and I don't want to be a part of it. The new policy of 'quality for the price' is one of the worst moves Impressions has ever made. I can't imagine changing the way we do business to incorporate this new quality standard. The old standard we crafted with Ellen worked so well. Under the old policy, I used great criteria as I did my analysis, considering how I'd feel if the piece of furniture fell apart, or if some such problem occurred. It worked well, too, because we got letters day in and day out from satisfied customers who loved the way we did business. I think we are going to lose most of our loyal customers—not to mention loyal workers [my ears perked up with this aside]—with this new policy."

Type Clue

Aha, an INFP experiencing her inferior function. The stress of having a new boss and a new policy that crossed her values seemed to be pushing the expression of Leya's inferior *Extraverted Thinking* function. When INFPs become stressed, fatigued, or ill, as with all the other types, the inferior function emerges—in the INFP's case inferior Extraverted Thinking. However, inferior Extraverted Thinking involves negative thinking. In this situation, Leya was finding fault with everything in a company where she had worked devotedly for sixteen years. Nothing and no one at Impressions nor the company itself seemed to please her. She talked at length about the organization's "stupidity" with the new quality policy and about Penny's "Attila the Hun" leadership style.

I gave Leya quite a bit of time to talk out her frustrations, simply nodding at her perception of things. She became less agitated as the interview progressed. However, it was clear to me that Leya was feeling very hurt and defensive about the changes at Impressions.

With a sigh, she said, "In the last month, I started looking for opportunities in other departments at Impressions. I can't see myself agreeing wholeheartedly with the new quality standards. 'You get what you pay for' may be good advice for purchasing from another company, but I can't be a part of peddling 'quality for the price' to Impressions customers. Given a choice of going along or getting along, I'd prefer to move along."

We then debriefed Leya's MBTI inventory and she readily endorsed the INFP preferences as her best-fit type. When she read the type description, she remarked how uncanny it was that the description fit her so well. She said, "It's interesting to see that INFPs tend to be loyal to people and causes. I sometimes feel very misunderstood by Jason because he is so adamant about doing things differently than in the past. I can't help but appreciate the successful way Ellen handled things, so I feel disloyal to Ellen, too, when I try to go along with all the changes.

"I guess Penny might work well as a manager once she gets her wings. Maybe I could even work for her under other circumstances, but not in Quality the way it is currently evolving. 'Quality for the price' is really distasteful to me!"

"You sound so sure."

"I'm positive," she said, "and you know after all these years, it may be time for a change."

I asked Leya to read more MBTI information, particularly that relating to the expression of the inferior function when individuals are under stress. I suggested to her that it seemed as if she were in the grip of her inferior function and therefore might want to take more time before implementing a transfer. I fear for people who make a big change while in the grip of the inferior function because they are not at their psychological best and therefore might make a flawed decision. Leya thanked me for listening and for the suggestions to take care of herself.

Next on the interview list was Josh, the newest member of the department and one of Penny's two male direct reports. I noted that Josh's type clearly came out ESTJ and when we reviewed the MBTI he said, "Yup, that fits me to a T—no pun intended. I do like to see things happen and I work hard to make sure that I and others follow through on commitments."

"What is it like to work in the department?"

"To me, it's only common sense that the organization is shifting. We're growing, we have a new vice president, a new quality standard, and a new director, Penny. I don't see why the others in this department find it so hard to understand and accommodate to these things. They should know that new leadership *always* wants to put their own stamp on things.

"I love my work—it's a good match for my talent and skills. I used to be a buyer, but I wanted to be a liaison person between Purchasing and Quality because I saw firsthand how mistakes were made in the past between the two functions. I wanted to get involved proactively in the Quality side of things so that we could 'buy right,' you know, correct the mistakes before the customers are involved. Now I have what I wanted, a liaison role among the vendors and sales personnel and Quality. Because I was once a buyer and I started out as a salesperson, I know from experience what we need to do to keep things working well."

"What are your views on the climate of the department?" I asked.

"You can't miss the problems between most of the team and Penny, but why we just can't get on with things puzzles me. Families don't always get along, so it only makes sense that people at work won't always get along, either. Logically, you have to expect the good and the bad, the highs and the lows. We are simply in a low time because of all the change. When things get back to normal and when Penny gets used to her role and our new standard for quality is even more widely implemented, things should be okay."

Type Clue

An ESTJ actually sounding like an ESTJ. Josh objectively analyzed the situation and made sense of the many changes and new relationships for himself. Because of their logical approach to assessing new problems, their ability to adapt prior experiences to new situations, and their not allowing their emotions to get in the way of their logical assessments, ESTJs often add stability to their work environments. Josh seemed to meet all these criteria.

I asked him if he personally felt much stress in the department.

"Well, yes, there is stress in the department, but I don't personally feel much of it. You know, the disruption with Penny hasn't affected me all that much because I have a good grasp of Jason's overall strategies. Jason and I are on the same wavelength. I thought we needed a tighter Quality standard and a clear linkage to Impressions' new marketing thrust. And it's only logical for me to support Penny as the director he chose—that's how you get ahead."

Type Clue

No surprises here that Josh and Jason were on the same wavelength, as Jason was also an ESTJ. Josh seemed able to provide a possible scenario of what life could be like on the Quality team *if and when* things stabilized there. It also appeared during the interview that Josh was not experiencing an activation of his inferior function.

The rest of the session with Josh went according to plan. He was anxious for the team to move on and wanted to incorporate all the "sensible" changes as quickly as possible.

I had only one more of Penny's direct reports to go. Kendra, the materials quality specialist, was next on the interview schedule. In going over her MBTI results, Kendra affirmed that the INFP reported type seemed to fit her. "I love these kinds of things—taking self-assessments to find out more about myself," she said. "I wish I had more opportunity to work with others because I love the people part of Quality—pleasing them by providing good merchandise. I'm really good at what I do—I have studied textiles and have a good eye for texture and fabric. I screen all of our products using the highest standards, so I know that only the best furnishings are sold in our store. I enjoy knowing my care makes a difference for people who are of modest means and I always appreciated the fact that Impressions, Inc. cared, too. You've heard about the new quality standards, I suppose? Well, they are disheartening to me. 'Quality for the price' just won't serve Impressions in the long run. Once the policy is fully launched, our loyal public will catch on and find that they may not be able to rely on getting durable, high-quality furniture at Impressions anymore. I bet our customers will move to other furniture stores that will give them the value that they need.

"I just plain miss Ellen, too. She started the department and brought it to its high level of professionalism. We had a wonderful sense of camaraderie that's gone now. I think we lost status, too, because Ellen reported directly to our CEO and Penny is only a director reporting to a VP. I think we've also lost on the 'quality for the price' issue. I'm not sure how much can be done about all of this. I feel a sense of loss. I have openly warned the company about its new policies. I'm at best lukewarm toward Penny because she symbolizes all the new changes that don't sit right with me. I guess I need to make peace with everything or take this job and . . . well, you know."

Type Clue

INFPs are characteristically loyal to people or a cause. They tend to go with the flow until something or someone violates one of those closely held values. When that happens, the intensity of their efforts to fight back can surprise those around them.

Therefore, it was no surprise that Kendra missed Ellen and the old quality standards.

I asked Kendra if she were doing anything to relieve the stress she was feeling and she vigorously nodded yes. "I'm getting out of here on my lunch hours. A brisk walk seems to improve my attitude. This weekend I picked out fabric for a new quilt, too—a quality project I can control! I also made a list of what I still enjoy about my work. I pull it out whenever I feel upset or whenever the fireworks start because I know I'd prefer to remain here. It is tough to separate my feelings about the changes from my feelings for my job, but deep down I know it is worth it in the long run for me to try to support Penny and to give the new policy a chance."

Type Clue

Aha, Kendra is different—an INFP experiencing stress but dealing with it in several different ways, getting away from the source of stress, engaging in a hobby where she can control quality, and listing her reasons for staying. She is still using her Feeling function to decide what's important to her, to others, and to Impressions. Although the changes may be hard on her, she isn't spinning out of control like Leya.

I said, "You've come up with some great ways to cope with your frustrations." After we talked some more, I asked her to review as homework her type description to affirm the ways in which she was using her type's gifts in this stressful time.

This meeting with Kendra concluded my interviews. After I processed all the information (type, interview, and additional materials), I met with Tanya and Penny to discuss my findings and to plan the team-building session. I detailed several key findings from the interview data:

➤ Penny's newness to management and the department's mature stage of followership (the department ran itself for fifteen months). The team needed to see if the situational leadership model applied to their situation.

➤ Penny's self-imposed "tough guy" style contrasted with Ellen's more "tender" style.

➤ Penny's probable INFJ preferences contrasted with her ENTJ "wannabe" style.

➤ The new policy of "quality for the price."

➤ The conflict between Penny and several team members, especially Wesley and Leya.

➤ The distrust and lack of faith that Wesley and Leya had in Penny and in the new Quality procedures.

Next I discussed the MBTI data and focused especially on the inferior function. "One of the reasons I like to work with personality types is that I can use their clues to understand how much stress people are experiencing and why. Frequently, the inferior function—the preference opposite your dominant function—comes to the fore. For example, my inferior function is Introverted Sensing. When I observe people with dominant Sensing, I see that they have a gift of being able to take in all the data the senses provide. Aesthetic and sensual experiences are appreciated in all their richness. There is a wonderful delight in the physical world.

"However, when I am in the grip of my inferior function, the gifts of Sensing get twisted. Instead of processing data, I become obsessed with detail and perhaps paranoid about errors. Instead of seeking pleasure, I tend to overindulge. Instead of enjoying the physical world, I avoid it or complain about it. And instead of evaluating accurately what's going on with me physically, I tend to overreact and think I'm really sick!

"Frequently, too, stress, tension, illness, etcetera, will trigger everyone's inferior function. Change, as well, does that. And you and your department have had rather an overdose of change."

Without disclosing any team member's type, I ran through some general examples I saw of lurking inferior functions on the team. "When there is as much change as this department experienced after a stable sixteen-year history, when a new leader comes on board, when there is a new quality standard that does not match the values of some of the team members, when there is disharmony on the team and when a lack of clarity exists, the situation is ripe for the inferior function to emerge.

"Several of the team members have a dominant function of Feeling. They believe that their values have been compromised by the new standards for quality. For some, the values conflicts are enough that they almost feel a need to leave Quality rather than work with the new policy."

Penny and Tanya heard the news about discontent with a mixed response. "I'd hate to lose good team members, but I can understand that some might find it easier to leave than to stay around and work through the changes," commented Penny. "It would be rather nice to have the opportunity to hire and train a few people myself—maybe I could even gain a loyal follower or two!"

Tanya nodded in agreement. "Let's not precipitate any moves, but if anyone expresses a desire to leave the department, we will work to help them find new assignments within Impressions." The three of us did a preliminary design for the team-building session before Penny and I met privately.

"Penny, since you specifically asked for feedback, the team wants you to view them as competent and they want more appreciation for their efforts. Your need for detail and your 'tough guy' management style is perceived entirely differently from what you intended. I think your ENTJ style may be the problem because it may not truly be you."

Penny said, "I'm beginning to be a bit skeptical about my ENTJ results, too, especially given the level of stress I feel in trying to be more Extraverted and outgoing as well as being more tough than I really am."

Type Clue

Penny was onto something. It is important to remember that psychological type deals with one's preferences, not with one's competencies. In my experience, having a psychological type that serves as a home base allows one to adapt more easily and to adopt job behaviors or characteristics that may be outside a person's preferences.

"Perhaps your true preference is for Introversion. If you honor that preference by giving it time and its due, I think it will allow you to behave in a more Extraverted, more energetic, and more outgoing way with others when you need to do so because you will have more energy for it when you use your true energy source of Introversion.

"Also, being consistent with your own typology gives your followers a consistent way of understanding you and therefore of working more effectively with you. Since all eight preferences, Extraversion–Introversion, Sensing–Intuition, and so on are positive, and all sixteen types are positive, it is important to find those that best describe who you *truly are* rather than those that describe what you think you *should be*. Even though it may appear counterintuitive, being true to one's self generally leads to being a more effective leader. As we discussed before, many managers have preferences for ENTJ, but remember, great leaders are found in every type."

Penny thought a moment before speaking. "On the E–I preference, Extraversion is what I think I *should* be, so I guess it's not my true preference.

Even as a child, I was admonished by people to be more talkative and more outgoing. I took this to heart and even now I continue to strive to make these changes in my behavior."

I asked Penny, "What do you think some of the gifts of your Introversion might be?"

Penny was somewhat at a loss. "Well . . . before I start on a project I usually have the process and rationale nailed down since I've thought it through so well in advance. I also tend to have the last word because I've listened to others and taken the time to think through situations."

"You see, Penny, Introversion can be advantageous to a leader. Being an Introvert doesn't mean you can't Extravert. Lincoln gave great speeches because they were so well thought out." After more discussion, we moved on to the Thinking–Feeling preference.

Because her score showed only a slight preference for Thinking, we spent time talking about her understanding of Thinking and Feeling. She said, "My management courses impressed upon me the need to be fair to all employees and therefore I hold fairness as a high value."

"'Value' is an interesting word choice here. Perhaps you are a person who has a preference for Feeling and uses logic to support your values."

Upon hearing this, Penny said, "Oh, that could be it! Logic does help me support what I truly and deeply believe in."

"The Feeling preference can be of high value in a leadership position—knowing what matters to people, having a service orientation, and being mindful of the needs and wants of others while working to get the job done has merits, too. Acting tough because you think you have to probably works against your own natural style. And your 'tough guy' hasn't brought the desired results, has it? In fact, it seems to polarize you and your staff, especially Wesley and Leya, even further."

Penny took a moment to reread the INFJ type description. "INFJ really fits with me over the long haul and as I see myself in the future as well as how I remember myself as a child—an imaginative kid. I can see how an INFJ, looking for possibilities for people and making decisions based on values, could make an effective manager—if I work to inspire rather than irritate!"

Continuing with our meeting, Penny and I went over the effects of the inferior function for the INFJ. "The inferior function for Introverted Intuition is Extraverted Sensing. One way it often makes itself known to INFJs is when they obsess on details. I remember in our first meeting, you seemed obsessed with that one section of the quality report."

"Oh, yes," Penny laughed, "page six, paragraph three!"

"You also were reading *all* the fine print, all the job descriptions, and all the policies and procedures for Impressions as well as the quality function. Did any of this reading prove of benefit to you?"

Penny sighed, "Only slightly."

"Making oneself attend to lots of detail, working to be more like an Extravert (having to share your thought process before you are ready), and using a tough, logical style instead of your more natural people-oriented style can cause stress, particularly for INFJs. All this works to bring your inferior function to the surface."

Penny said, "I don't usually see myself as a detail person, but I *need* detail at this point in time."

"You have a valid point, but the detail is driving you nuts, isn't it? You also have a competent staff with gifts that complement yours. They are losing out on your type's characteristics, such as an ability to envision possibilities. You are missing their depth of experience and understanding of Quality. With your gift of Introverted Intuition, why not guide your department from where it *was* to where you *envision* and want it to be? As you do this, however, be sure to include the other team members in your thinking even before you know your thoughts are finalized. Ask them for their input—it will help to increase their ownership and implementation of your plans."

The team-building process had several steps. For the first phase, Penny and I agreed upon the following outline for the full team-building session.

➤ Jason as vice president of Marketing would start the team-building session by giving a history of Quality's role at Impressions, Inc. and the strategic goals of the senior management team. He would then briefly review the rationale for Penny's selection, add his endorsement of both Penny and the new quality policy, and stay for an open-ended, no-holds-barred question-and-answer period about his remarks.

➤ Penny would follow, stating her goals for this team building, her vision for the department, her understanding of the mission for the department, and lastly her thoughts about the new quality standards and then lead a discussion on these topics. We agreed that this plan would fill most of the morning and that toward lunchtime I would report my interview findings.

➤ In the afternoon, we decided to divide the Quality department into subteams to work on the issues. I would also introduce the situational leadership model to help the entire team understand why Penny, or any other leader for that matter, might have experienced difficulties managing this team.

For the second phase of the team-building process, we planned a subsequent daylong session three weeks later to hear progress reports and, if the time were right, to debrief the MBTI inventory results with the entire team, focusing on the lurking inferior function.

The phase one meeting took much longer than we anticipated, especially Jason's and Penny's segments. There were many questions and much gnashing of teeth as the new directions and polices were challenged, yet firmly upheld. During this meeting, however, committees were put in place to address the specific concerns identified in our joint analysis of the issues holding Quality back. These committees were charged with further analysis and action planning. The team members were beginning to feel hopeful and even enthusiastic about the prospect of a department that functioned smoothly.

In the following three weeks, I mediated a session between Penny and Leya where we hashed out many of their difficulties. Leya's natural compassion surfaced as she remembered Penny's situation as a newcomer and identified with that. Leya felt better knowing that Penny understood how her feigned "tough guy" style had been untrue to her real nature.

I also coached Leya individually. Leya realized how much she valued her role in the Quality department and how deep her relationships were with the other team members. She recommitted herself to staying in the department, working to improve things there. Also, as Penny and Leya had talked, Penny grasped Leya's difficulties with "quality for the price." Together they explored a new role for Leya—working directly with Jason to monitor the impact of the new policy on customer satisfaction.

I also met with Wesley, who found out from his doctor that he did not have cancer—just a case of severe stress induced, he surmised, by "inferior functionitis." He was in the process of setting up the showroom and enjoyed partnering in the project with Marketing and Sales so much that he approached their director about moving to their area. Wesley revealed his future position, a new marketing liaison role, at the following team-building session. Privately both Tanya and Penny told me that they were relieved to know that Wesley had found a new place for himself.

The second team-building session went as planned and the concepts of psychological type helped the team understand Wesley's and Leya's frustrations as well as Josh's easier acceptance of the new order. Kendra was excited about being managed by another NF and thought she could better support Penny as she worked to manage in her more natural style. The team also learned more about Jason's ESTJ needs for a specific, consistent quality standard. And a farewell party was planned for Wesley.

In affirming her INFJ preferences, Penny did two very important things. First, she acknowledged that her overdone "tough guy" stance was a poor imitation of an ENTJ. Second, she admitted that she should not have taken Wesley's name off the quarterly Quality report. She apologized to Wesley and said that he had taught her a valuable lesson in leadership. Penny closed the meeting by reviewing her future vision, incorporating the changes the subteams and total department had agreed to and asking for their support. She told the group, "You can help me, an INFJ, by having me to tell you my thoughts before I move to carry them out." This reminder would keep them included in her thinking process—something that she and the team all thought would be desirable.

TYPE TAKEAWAY

Now you may ask, "How do I recognize the signs of a lurking inferior function and how can I keep it at bay?" Here are some suggestions for you as an individual and for your team. The chart on pages 178–179 should help you in implementing them.

Type Solvers for You as an Individual

To reduce the effects of an activated inferior function, use your auxiliary function. If you are dominant Sensing or Intuitive, concentrate on your Thinking or Feeling, whichever is your other middle letter of your four-letter type description (check chapter 1 if you are unsure of your auxiliary function). For example, when I as an ENFP realize (generally after too long) that my inferior Sensing function is lurking, I make a conscious effort to use my Feeling preference to get myself out of trouble. I need to ask myself, How do the nit-picking behaviors of my inferior Sensing make others *feel*? What are my most important values here? What good does all this insistence on perfection or detail provide to me and to those about whom I care? Answering these questions usually brings my lurking inferior function into broad daylight where it can act within a reduced arena.

An ESTJ friend of mine says that when she's feeling overly emotional and undervalued ("poor me," she calls it) she uses her auxiliary Sensing to help her get clear about which of her feelings about her present situation reflect reality and what the situation clearly calls for.

The following questions may help you focus on how to use your auxiliary function in order to escape the grip of your inferior function.

If your auxiliary function is Sensing (ESTJ, ESFJ, ISTP, ISFP):

☑ What can my senses verify about this situation? What is real versus what I have imagined?

☑ What can I learn that is concrete? What can I do that is more sensible?

If your auxiliary function is Intuition (ENFJ, ENTJ, INFP, INTP):

☑ What new ideas might be helpful? Could I take a different approach to a current activity?

☑ What possibilities for growth or renewal could come out of this situation?

If your auxiliary function is Thinking (ESTP, ENTP, ISTJ, INTJ):

☑ What logical steps can I take to change what is causing me stress? Which area can I fix first?

☑ What are my guiding principles? How can I align with them?

If your auxiliary function is Feeling (ESFP, ENFP, ISFJ, INFJ):

☑ How are my actions making others feel?

☑ Am I being too hard on myself? Would I judge others as harshly given the circumstances?

Type Solvers for Your Team

When your team seems unduly stressed, and perhaps the inferior function is lurking in the dark, consider the following team-building ideas.

☑ Interview each person using a common set of questions. If you are concerned about whether responses will be honest, consider bringing in a representative of your human resources department or an outside consultant to gather the information. Sample questions:

➤ What's it like to be a part of this team?

➤ What would you change if you could?

➤ Do you receive clear direction? If not, give some examples of times where you have not had clear direction for your area of responsibility.

➤ Are employees treated fairly? If not, give examples of unfair treatment.

➤ What does this team do best?

➤ Where could the team improve?

☑ Consider conducting a commercially available team attitude survey. These surveys can provide specific and quantifiable data about the various issues facing teams (leadership, support, clarity, roles, and so on).

☑ Talk with external customers, vendors, and others who interact with the team for their comments as to what is going well for the team and where improvements could be made.

☑ Brainstorm with a mentor or senior manager to explore the history of the team. Look for reasons for the team's current reality. Could resentment of newcomers or promotions be found? How does this team differ organizationally from the past (reporting relationships, status, etc.)? [At Impressions, an examination of the team's history showed a long period of self-management, a new quality standard, a new manager, a change in reporting relationships, and status.] What contrast exists between the management styles of the new and previous team leaders? Type can help tremendously here.

☑ Assess what the team can and cannot change and/or what the team "needs" versus what the team "wants." [In the case of Impressions the fact that the new quality policy was permanent needed to be firmly communicated to dissenters along with an emphatic statement about the new organizational reality despite the longing to have the "good old days" back.]

☑ Consider your own communications in times of stress. Are you sending clear messages? Remember that you may need to communicate time and time again in order to be understood when people are in the grip of their inferior function.

☑ Think of general ways to relieve stress around your workplace. What efforts can be made to relieve stress for your team? Some stress reducers are: noise reduction, private spaces for people to go when they need to concentrate, keeping surprises to a minimum, or making sure people keep regular hours and take their vacations.

☑ Be careful if you say, "I'll bet your behavior is a result of your inferior function." No one likes to hear that they are acting like they got up on the wrong side of the bed!

What stresses you? Get to know these trouble spots in advance. The following chart on pages 178 and 179 lists some typical triggers as well as manifestations and routes to recovery from the inferior function for the sixteen types.[12]

Clues to the Inferior Function

Type and Dominant and Inferior Functions	In Their Dominant Function	In the Grip of Their Inferior Function	Common Triggers of Their Inferior	What Can Help
ESTJ, ENTJ *Extraverted Thinking; Feeling*	• Make decisions • Look for truth, effectiveness, and commitment • Enjoy leadership	• Hypersensitive to others' criticism • Prone to emotional outbursts • Uncomfortable with their own feelings	• Violation of their core values • Accusations of coldness • Remorse for one's unfeeling actions	• Solitude • Rest • Assessment of limitations
ISFP, INFP *Introverted Feeling; Thinking*	• Known as trustworthy and affirming • Focus on the best in others • Maintain inner harmony	• Judgmental • Critical attitude toward others • Acting before thinking things through	• Negative atmosphere • Fear of loss or failure in a relationship • Violation of values	• Time • Acknowledgement of the effect of criticism on others • Emphasis on established skills
ISTP, INTP *Introverted Thinking; Feeling*	• Observe objectively in order to find truth • Adeptly use logical analysis, applying that analysis to people and events • Known for depth of knowledge	• Overly defensive when trying to prove the "logic" of their feelings • Excessively sensitive about relationships • Too emotional	• When others are overly emotional • Situations that appear arbitrary or uncontrollable • Having no time for reflection	• Solitude spent on activities they enjoy • Physical activity • Having others give them space
ESFJ, ENFJ *Extraverted Feeling; Thinking*	• Depend on feelings as more rational than logic • Known for sensitivity to the needs of others • Able to easily and appropriately express emotion	• Overly critical and domineering • Sidetracked by poor logic • Compulsively search for answers through books or unusual philosophies	• Being asked to compromise a value • Misunderstood or belittled by others • Too much conflict as opposed to harmony	• Change in routine • A new project • Confiding in an understanding friend or self through journaling

Clues to the Inferior Function

Type and Dominant and Inferior Functions	In Their Dominant Function	In the Grip of Their Inferior Function	Common Triggers of Their Inferior	What Can Help
ESTP, ESFP *Extraverted Sensing; Intuition*	• Take in and sort all the data the senses provide • Accept the world at face value • Enjoy everyday life	• Imagining doom and gloom • Misinterpreting the motives of others • Obsessed with mystical life views	• Overcommitment • Being forced to make decisions about the future • Having too much structure at work	• Contingency planning • Solitary activities such as gardening, exercise • The help of others to adjust priorities
INTJ, INFJ *Introverted Intuition; Sensing*	• Demonstrate intellectual clarity • Sort intuitive hunches accurately • Have long-term, novel perspectives	• Overindulgent in sensing (TV, food) without enjoyment • Approaching the world as an enemy • Overwhelmed by sensory data	• Dealing with details • Experiencing unexpected events • Too much Extraverting	• "Space" • Quiet, natural surroundings • Using Thinking to find solutions or Feeling to allow oneself to be less serious
ISTJ, ISFJ *Introverted Sensing; Intuition*	• Exhibit efficiency, calmness, and attention to specifics • Focused on the present and perfecting the tried and true • Aware of their sensory experiences	• Anxious over facts and details • Reckless and impulsive • Worried about possible future disasters	• Experiencing change, prospect of the unknown • When others deny reality (especially dominant Intuitives) • Overdoing reliability and efficiency	• Finding others who will take them seriously • Delegating details • Working through auxiliary Thinking or Feeling to find solutions
ENFP, ENTP *Extraverted Intuition; Sensing*	• Focus on their vision or the big picture • Pursue new ideas optimistically • Identify future trends with uncanny ability	• Depressed and withdrawn • Obsessed with details and information • Focused on physical symptoms	• Overcommitted and tired • Attending to details • Violation of important values or principles	• Meditation • Positive use of Sensing—physical exercise, sleep, healthy diet • Using Thinking or Feeling to lend perspective

Then the boss told me to go fly a kite . . . so I did.

The Problem Is the Boss— Or Is It?

Influencing Upward

Type Key

To influence others, try speaking their language.

It's a fact: Your boss is the boss. She or he is in control and your relationship may not always be smooth. Given that all of us go through life and work interacting with many different people, there is ample opportunity for problems. You can approach these problems with seminars and books about how to deal with micromanagers, procrastinators, show-offs, and other difficult people *or* you could learn to look for Type Clues about what information others pay attention to, what factors they consider in making decisions, and their preferred approach to solving problems—especially Type Clues about your boss.

One way to do this is to identify your boss's dominant function—Sensing, Intuition, Thinking, or Feeling. (See chapter 1 for more information on the dominant function.) Each dominant preference has different styles of problem solving and decision making. Understanding these styles can help you provide the right tools and information to your superiors and others as well as help you discover more effective ways to communicate. Compare your boss's preferences with your own for gathering information, making decisions, and solving problems. If it's a match, you're in luck because you have methods in common. If it's not a match, there are ways to adapt your style to influence upward. (However, even when it *is* a match, remember, there are a lot of individual differences within psychological preferences and types. Thus the clues here may still apply.) So this chapter may provide you with some ideas to boss your boss—well, at least to play to his or her strengths!

Solving the Mystery of Getting Your Ideas Heard

Dominant Sensing (ISTJ, ISFJ, ESTP, ESFP)

Kyri, a dominant Intuitive, thought she had developed a brilliant way to handle her division's monthly client review process. When the computer generated its list of trouble accounts, she carefully marked those that appeared on the problem list for the first time. For those accounts, Kyri had her assistant pull the client's complete file. She or one of her colleagues then filled out a summary analysis form, recording the pertinent financial information and review comments. For repeats on the problem list, her assistant pulled only the information placed in the file since the prior review, thus eliminating several hours of review work that duplicated the efforts of the previous month. The existing analysis form was then updated and passed on to Kyri's manager for review and approval.

Sara, Kyri's manager, disliked the new system. She still wanted to see all of the data, especially the background information on which the summary form was based. Before Kyri came up with her idea and review form, the entire folder on a client, three to five inches thick, went to Sara each month with a written analysis form placed on top. Sara told Kyri, "I can't tell if you've captured all the important information. Besides, what if you missed something last month? What if that information is important now?"

Kyri replied, "You don't have time to review all this stuff . . . and we don't have time to redo the same items month after month. My way allows us to save time checking on clients that seem to provide repeat business for our surveillance screens."

Type Clue

Dominant Sensors such as Sara usually have a unique ability to find pertinent facts in the midst of voluminous files and notice what needs attention. So, Sara preferred her style of review—all the facts. However, Kyri, a dominant Intuitive, had a legitimate point, too. As a manager, Sara really no longer had the time to do this type of in-depth, detailed review.

Even though Kyri had an idea that could save considerable time and effort, Sara will not be comfortable with it unless Kyri pays attention to Sara's preferences and needs as a Sensor. Here are some Sensor characteristics and suggestions for dealing with them:

DOMINANT SENSORS TEND TO:	AS A DOMINANT INTUITIVE, KYRI COULD:
➤ See the facts at hand and want to know *exactly* what the factors are	➤ Increase the amount of data shown on the summary sheet *or* spell out in detail the policies and procedures for reviewing client files so that Sara can be assured that nothing has been missed.
➤ Rely on their past experience	➤ Prepare several files using both the old and new method. Review them with Sara and point out how the new method covers the same data needs as the old.
➤ Want realistic time frames and schedules	➤ Quantify the time savings under the new system (once it has proved to be reliable).
➤ Have all necessary information at their fingertips	➤ Set up a flag system so that more information could be pulled quickly if Sara needed it. Also, Kyri could use her Intuition to look for patterns in Sara's informational needs.
➤ Look for the details first to ascertain what is essential to the problem	➤ Back up the conclusions with the details in plain sight so that Sara can quickly review what needs attention.

The Party or Picnic Puzzle

Dominant Intuition (INTJ, ENTP, INFJ, ENFP)

Mutual Benefits Corporation, a large insurance company, had just completed merging with Trimark Corporation, one of its competitors. Hannah, the head of employee relations, asked Andrew to meet with her.

Hannah began, "Now that our merger with Trimark is complete, I want to make sure that the annual employee gathering serves to welcome everyone, including our newcomers. Let's make it a stretch this year, something really special to help them transfer their loyalty from Trimark to Mutual Benefits."

Andrew asked, "What kind of budget do I have for the event?"

"I'll negotiate some extra funding from senior management after I review your ideas. Why don't you get back to me next week with your plans? You can put your other projects on the back burner until we have the site reserved and our plans roughed out."

Andrew spent the next few days thoroughly checking out the traditional company picnic site—a beautiful, multi-use park complete with beach, playground, picnic area, and nature trails. He verified that by renting two adjacent picnic shelters, the park could accommodate the increased size of the group. Their favorite caterer, a popular Mexican deli, also assured Andrew that they could easily serve the larger group.

Andrew reported back to Hannah, "We can get the park on the first Sunday in August, as usual. I found two new entertainment acts so that we could divide the children into groups rather than have one magician or clown try to keep the interest of so many. Also, with two picnic shelters, we can add more games and activities. This should make for a great employee appreciation event."

Hannah looked at the information Andrew had given her. "Did you check out any other possibilities? What if we did something other than a picnic?"

"Something else? We've been at Mears Lake Park for twelve years and most employees circle the first Sunday in August when they get their yearly calendars. It's a tradition that lots of people look forward to. Over 200 employees and their families attend annually. That shows how popular the event is."

"I hear, though," replied Hannah, "that it's the same employees every year. Those without children aren't interested and others don't like Mexican food. Did you find out if Trimark had any traditions?"

"Well, no. I thought it would be better to welcome them in our fashion."

Hannah paused a moment before speaking again. "I want some new ideas for this event. Some companies rent recreational facilities, theaters, hire professional entertainment, take evening cruises—what would generate some excitement here? What would make this an event no one would want to miss?"

"I'm really not sure we *should* change it. It's always been a *family* event. You could lose as many employees as you gain, all for a lot of bother and cost," Andrew replied.

Type Clue

Andrew, a dominant Sensor, didn't understand that Hannah, a dominant Intuitive, wanted information that considered other possibilities for the annual employee event. Andrew, knowing that the picnic had been popular, built on his past experiences to come up with what, to him, was a bigger, better, more exciting event.

To meet the needs of Hannah, Andrew might consider these tendencies and ways of addressing them:

DOMINANT INTUITIVES TEND TO:	AS A DOMINANT SENSOR, ANDREW COULD:
➤ Explore new possibilities	➤ Research several alternatives, either by calling his counterparts at other companies or by checking library resources on corporate events.
➤ Look for patterns other than the obvious when reviewing data	➤ Seek other reasons why picnic attendance has been consistent. Talk to other employees about their likes and dislikes.
➤ Use analogies to solve problems	➤ Review how other meetings and events have been handled since the merger. Are all consistent with Mutual Benefits style or have Trimark elements been added? Use the findings to augment the planning process.
➤ Tackle new problems with zest	➤ Remember that Hannah may be a better advocate for a novel event than for the "same old thing."

➤ Focus on the big-picture aspects of a problem

➤ Keep the broad scope of the event before Hannah: Select a theme and show how the site and the people come together via this event. Save the details until they are needed.

Solving the Mystery of Who Should Go

Dominant Thinking (ISTP, INTP, ESTJ, ENTJ)

For Edge Electronics, a manufacturer of consumer electronics products, early advertising and exposure for its new developments were vital to success. Edge's strategies included showcasing new lines and ideas at the major trade conventions for the electronics industry each year.

Chris handed a folder to his associate, Gerri, and said, "Here's the scoop on the upcoming digital electronics convention in Orlando. I have clearance from above to send one sales representative from your team of eight and one rep from my National Accounts team. Everyone realizes that two people are slim coverage for our booth, but Edge's travel budget won't handle sending more reps than that. Given that our three major customers plan to attend, I think that I as the head of National Accounts should be there to provide them with red carpet treatment. I'd like for you to decide who the other rep should be—no reason it couldn't be you, if you think that's best. Otherwise, take a look at everyone's sales records this year, which sales representatives' customers plan to attend, and whatever else you think will make your decision as fair as possible."

"You and I certainly don't both need to be there," replied Gerri, "and you know, my husband and I just took our kids to Orlando last year, so I have no interest in attending. My first thought is to send Roxanne. She needs this type of experience in making contacts and spotting potential clients."

"Roxanne? She's too new; I don't think she knows enough about our upcoming consumer products to work a convention. I won't say no to her yet, but let's consider our other options. Which rep is furthest ahead of budget so far this year?"

Gerri thought for a moment. "Kyle, but he just got back from the Las Vegas show. Sending him would only hurt the morale of others who've worked just as hard. You know, given that the convention runs over the weekend, it would be a shame not to send someone who has children."

Gerri went on, "Perhaps we could set this up as an annual opportunity, with the idea that the chance will rotate among our top achievers. That way, no matter whom we pick, everyone will feel motivated by future opportunities to go."

"The problem with setting a precedent like that is finding crystal-clear criteria so that we don't get accused of playing favorites. If it's set as a percentage of budget, someone will say his or her budget was unfairly high. If it's seniority, the same people will go. If it's perfect attendance, then we might not like the choice. The people who go should be the best ones to represent our firm," Chris concluded. "Set up your criteria and let me know your choice."

Type Clue

Chris, as a Thinker, needs a logical rationale to reach his decision; whereas Gerri, as a Feeler, wants to maintain harmony in the organization. Gerri has quite a job, trying to set objective criteria for Chris that will also meet *her* needs.

If Gerri, as a dominant Feeler, wants to reach a decision that also contributes to harmony in the office, here are some suggestions:

DOMINANT THINKERS TEND TO:	AS A DOMINANT FEELER, GERRI COULD:
➤ Seek objective, measurable criteria for decision making that can be fairly and consistently applied	➤ Create a matrix that lists the decision-making criteria, covering both Thinking and Feeling aspects. Then rank each team member against the criteria. If the "wrong" person is selected, revisit the criteria.
➤ Identify the flaws in ideas or processes	➤ Show that the logical criteria, such as sales records, might be less than effective, and point out that fact early on in her report to Chris. She may then be able to introduce less "logical" criteria.
➤ Desire consistency, considering it more important than the feelings of others	➤ Decide this is the time for her to articulate a framework for choosing future convention attendees. (Although Orlando is a "great site," the same criteria need to work for a January meeting in the snow zone—not at a ski resort, either!)

➤ Look at the principles involved in the situation

➤ Meet Chris's need to know that the best people *are* being considered by making a list of the objective qualifications of each member such as product knowledge and convention experience before moving to the values-based criteria.

➤ Weigh the pros and cons of each choice

➤ Make sure to consider the negatives, hard as it may be, about each person.

The Search for a Significant Site

Dominant Feeling (ISFP, INFP, ESFJ, ENFJ)

Tender Toys manufactured and distributed nonviolent toys that emphasized creativity and met the needs of people of different ethnic origins in the United States. Dale had worked for Tender Toys and its founder, Ramón, from the firm's beginnings. Ramón's timing for Tender Toys had been perfect; they were ahead of the market in realizing the importance of multiculturalism and the concerns of parents in selecting long-lasting, worthwhile products for their children. Because the company had outgrown its suburban facility, Ramón asked Dale to meet with him to begin relocation planning.

Ramón began, "This has been such a great spot for our company, with its easy access for our employees and Oak Field Park just down the way. I know the staff often walks there at lunch, and I personally like the view. I've also enjoyed being housed with that nonprofit organization—this is all in keeping with our image as a values-driven company. Dale, your job is to find us a new spot that will keep our employees happy and be good for our business. I'd like to have a small museum-style showroom in the new building so that customers and their children could stop by and see the development of our toys. We've had a lot of mail recently from teachers who think this could be a good field trip spot and I'd like to provide that opportunity. It's good business and good customer relations, too.

"So what I'm looking for is a place like this, but one with more space. Cost effective and convenient, of course, but also personifying the mission of Tender Toys."

Ramón concluded, "I feel that you're the right person for this assignment. You handled our space planning so well last year, keeping shipping, manufacturing, and our customer service staff happy! Let me know when you find some possible sites."

Dale left the meeting with her head full of considerations. She immediately thought, "If Tender Toys could be near the airport, rather than on the opposite end of town as we are now, that would reduce our trucking costs by about 50 percent and save headaches on rush shipments. And sharing a warehouse facility again could decrease overhead. Perhaps the new office park next to that spacious compound the defense contractors developed. . . ."

Two weeks later, Dale returned to Ramón's office with a neatly bound report on relocation sites. "My report delineates the top five choices, weighted on the criteria of leasing costs, distance from the airport, and available space for future expansion. Various other factors such as neighboring tenants are listed in narrative form. Actually, there is considerably more information on the top three sites since the last two are significantly more expensive and, therefore, pretty much out of the running. I'm especially excited about the first one in Quadrangle Office Park. It's close to the airport, yet a new building that could be turned into a showpiece."

Ramón scanned the report summary. "We can't move to the west side of town. Most of our employees live here in the eastern suburbs and wouldn't want that kind of commute. The second one—isn't it next to the National Guard armory? I served in the Guard myself, but I'd imagine that Tender Toys customers don't want to drive their children by the military display as they head to the premier maker of nonviolent toys!"

Dale looked a bit perplexed as she replied, "But anything on this side of town will double our transportation costs as well as lessen our chances of finding a newer site. Everything around here is occupied by established businesses that are not likely to move out; the other side of town is full of empty space—that means more choices and lower costs. We're at the top end of the toy market already and we can't afford to increase our costs. The fifth site on my list is close to here. You've already eliminated sites one and two, but I can't see choosing number five over sites three and four."

"Well, the third one isn't in the greatest part of town for our workers. Am I correct about that?" asked Ramón.

"We'd have our own secured facility and the building already has most of the modifications we need," replied Dale.

Ramón shook his head, "I want my employees to feel that we look out for their best interests. Remember, key factors for me are, in no special order, proximity to a park or nature area, having business neighbors with values similar to ours, and a space that reflects our image back to our customers. So, that leaves just two of your five choices and I'm not sure about the fourth one. I think you'd better come up with at least two more that meet our needs. Will that take much longer?"

Type Clue

Ramón as a dominant Feeler did not have the same priorities as Dale, a dominant Thinker. Dale had placed a higher weight on the logical, measurable criteria for the decision than on the values-based criteria that Ramón had outlined.

Here are some suggestions for Dale to locate sites that Ramón would find acceptable:

DOMINANT FEELERS TEND TO:

➤ Consider foremost the impact of a decision on the people involved.

➤ Be values-driven. Often these values seem vague to Thinkers. For example, the image of cotenants and the ambiance of nearby parks matter greatly to Feelers like Ramón whereas cost and efficiency criteria tend to be more important to Thinkers like Dale.

➤ Make exceptions to rules if people or circumstances warrant it.

AS A DOMINANT THINKER, DALE COULD:

➤ Restart the process with Ramón, listening carefully for his concerns for his employees such as commuting distance and pleasant surroundings. For Ramón, cost considerations will probably not outweigh the impact of the move on Tender Toys' people.

➤ List Ramón's nonnegotiables such as commute distance and the "feel" of the approach to their facility for visitors. Understand that it is extremely difficult to change a Feeler's position on a value.

➤ Carefully list the pros and cons of each site using both the "logical" and values-based points. The best choice may be made on a combination of values *and* logical criteria.

➤ Try to keep harmony among all players and may therefore understate their position.

➤ Remember, when a Feeler like Ramón says a spot wouldn't be his preferred one, or that he isn't sure, chances are the Feeler may really dislike the choice but is unwilling to hurt anyone's feelings by being so direct. So Dale as a Thinker needs to listen closely to any hesitancies or cushioning terms that may indicate she's on thin ice with the Feeler!

➤ Want group consensus.

➤ Perhaps let the employees vote on the two or three most reasonable choices that meet all of Ramón's criteria. Thinkers, bite your tongue about how "illogical" this approach would be!

TYPE TAKEAWAY

Has this chapter piqued your curiosity? Would you like to see if providing information in a different way or paying attention to different factors can indeed influence those around you?

Type Solvers to Try

When you suspect differing dominant functions, try these ideas.

☑ If your problem is with the boss:

➤ Determine your boss's dominant preference (S, N, T, F), either actual or your estimate.

➤ Recast your messages using the suggestions for your boss's dominant preference given in this chapter.

➤ If you know someone else with the same dominant function as your boss, have him or her coach you as you practice the communication. Incorporate the suggestions and *then* approach your boss.

☑ If your problem is with your team:

➤ Consider one of the scenarios from this chapter: introducing a new process, planning a company event, choosing the right person for an assignment, or moving to a different location, *or* work on your team's current "hot button."

➤ Divide into four groups, based on dominant function (Sensing, Intuition, Thinking, and Feeling).

➤ Ask each group to outline the process they would use to go about solving a problem and record the factors they consider most important in doing so.

➤ As each group reports back, use the statements on page 17 of chapter 1 to analyze how closely each group's answers reflect their dominant functions.

➤ Discuss as a full team the implications of each group's style for adequately dealing with problems that face the team.

➤ If any of the dominant functions are absent from your team, discuss ways your team can compensate.

☑ Another graphic way to demonstrate the use of the dominant functions in problem solving is to work as a full group on a topic such as purchasing new computers for everyone.

➤ Starting with the whole group in one corner of the room, list three factual information needs for the decision (Sensing).

➤ Move to the next corner, having the Sensors remain in the first corner to listen. Come up with three possible "outside-the-box" possibilities for addressing the issue (Intuition).

➤ Moving on, leaving the Intuitives behind to listen, consider the pros and cons of the informational needs and the possible methods (Thinking).

➤ Finally, move the Feelers to the last corner. With the other three groups listening, have the Feelers address the way the process may affect individual team members.

This exercise illustrates in a concrete way how important it is to consider the domains of each of the dominant functions (Sensing, Intuition, Thinking, and Feeling) in making decisions and solving problems.

Note: If your team has had considerable training in formal approaches to problem solving, the differences among the dominant functions in these exercises may not be as striking because all good problem solving involves using all four dominant preferences.

TYPE-CASTING

Accountant
ISTJ

Nurse
ISFJ

Writer
INFJ

Scientist
INTJ

Coach
ESTP

Receptionist
ESFJ

Clues to Strengths, Clues to Growth

Putting the Type Clues to Work for You

Type Key

Growing in type awareness adds an extra edge.

Helping Tony, the software entrepreneur, soften his critical edges; tutoring Penny, the new director of Quality, to use the strengths of her personality type; watching Malcolm pull his team back together—one of the great pleasures in the work I do is the privilege of coaching individuals.

The MBTI and the concepts of psychological type open many previously mysterious aspects of an individual's self-awareness. The theory of psychological type allows the people I coach to apply type concepts at a deeper level. In doing this, they understand more of their own personality, their individual work situation, and the way they want to live their lives. For the *Sensor*, psychological type gives a practical and meaningful way of understanding human interaction. For the *Intuitor*, it offers a conceptual framework to think about human potential and possibilities. For the *Thinker*, it provides a logical model to explain some of the nuances of human interaction. And for the *Feeler*, it presents a system that honors the values of individual differences and the complementarity of opposites.

There are several common scenarios that lead to my being asked to coach an individual. Coaching often occurs:

➤ As a result of a team-building process where either the leader or a team member needs specific skill development, support, or more intensive one-on-one time. Remember the public speaking needs of the Systems Design team?

➤ When the person appears mismatched with the work he or she is required to do, with others on the team, or with the organizational environment in general. Remember Wesley?

➤ When personality clashes exist and people need some mediation or conflict resolution. Remember Dean and Gwen?

➤ When an individual seeks coaching because of feeling like a "square peg in a round hole," being caught in a no-win situation, or finding that work itself is no longer meaningful or rewarding. Remember Leya?

Appendix B outlines my coaching process in detail. However, if you are looking to coach yourself or perhaps want a few tips for working with someone on your team, this chapter contains general suggestions for each of the sixteen types: typical areas for growth along with suggested steps one might take to improve in that area. Also included is a story of a true coaching situation (names and identities disguised, of course) for each personality type, representative of that type's typical needs.

If you wish these tips for *self-coaching*, try the following:

➤ Before reading the pages for your personality type, think of two recent situations that didn't go as smoothly as you might have wished. Ask yourself if type may have been involved.

➤ Look through the *Typical Areas for Growth* for your type. Were any of these a factor in the recent situations you identified?

➤ Using the *Coaching Suggestions*, record specific areas where you could have acted/reacted differently. For example, listed for growth areas for ISTJ is "Accepting more responsibilities rather than delegating them or saying 'No.' " One might record the specific tasks that could have been delegated.

➤ Review your self-critique with someone you respect or a trusted colleague. Does he or she agree with your conclusions? If so, what might that person recommend you do differently?

➤ List the areas for growth most appropriate for you on a 3x5 card, placing it somewhere that will allow a daily review of your "hot buttons."

➤ Broaden the coaching suggestions by reading other management texts or finding specific training opportunities. Again as an example, for the ISTJs, a *Typical Area for Growth* is "Not being able to see the 'forest for the trees.'" A person who struggles in this area might consider reading books on creative thinking or brainstorming techniques and/or attending a creative problem-solving course.

If you wish to use these suggestions to coach a *teammate* or *someone who works for you:*

➤ First, review your own type description to see if problems between you might result from your *own* shortcomings or from honest differences in your personality style and that of the other(s).

➤ Allow the person you are coaching to self-select his or her own type, either by taking the MBTI, reading the first chapter of this book, or reviewing another resource.

➤ Make sure that you are giving constructive feedback, using the following suggestions for people with each preference:

Sensing: Describe the actual and specific unwanted behavior or unfulfilled responsibilities you have observed. Be concrete. Use factual data.

Intuition: Relate the actual behavior to the big picture (team productivity, for example) and give your impressions about how this behavior or unfulfilled expectation has affected outcomes. Present your interpretation of the facts.

Thinking: Determine and express the logical outcomes of this behavior. Discuss the consequences of this behavior on you and others in the work unit. Consider the pros and cons of any actions you might take.

Feeling: Disclose your values and feelings. Explain why this responsibility is important to you and why it matters.[13]

➤ If the difficulty was between yourself and the person you wish to coach, let him or her work through the areas for growth and coaching suggestions as discussed above.

➤ If the difficulty was between different members of the team, consider having each work through the above suggestions. Then mediate a session to discuss from a type perspective what went wrong and how things can be done differently in the future (see pages 114–117 in chapter 5, "The Case of the Deadline Dilemmas," for an example).

➤ Together, adopt an action plan that gives specifics yet allows for adjustments as the process continues.

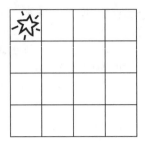

ISTJ
Salt of the Earth

Ruth came to see me for coaching as a result of her seeming inability to say no to requests from her boss. She tended to assume that she must, by herself, do every assignment that she was given. As with many ISTJs that I've coached, Ruth worked too hard, put in long hours, and consequently lost sight of the big picture. Not surprisingly, as her work mounted, her enthusiasm wore down; Ruth felt burned out.

In discussing Ruth's situation with her boss, he commented, "She does everything I ask on time, so I naturally thought she could handle more." What the boss didn't realize was that Ruth completed the new assignments by working evenings, Saturdays, and on what should have been her vacation days.

As I coached Ruth, we reviewed her duties to assess what could be reasonably accomplished in a normal work week. I then helped her determine options for delegating tasks to others and we strategized how to say no to unreasonable requests. By periodically pausing to stand back from her work, Ruth was able to gain perspective and to appreciably lower her stress level.

General Strengths

➤ Once something is learned and practiced, few will do it better
➤ Trusted with every detail: contracts, documents, etcetera
➤ Stick-to-it-iveness—schedules, commitments, completion

Typical Areas for Growth

➤ Not being able to see the forest for the trees

➤ Holding on to your own truth too long—becoming inflexible in the views you hold

➤ Accepting more responsibilities rather than delegating them or saying no

➤ Making few exceptions for yourself or others with regard to standard operating procedures

➤ Failing to express your deeply felt approval or appreciation

➤ Being serious—even at inappropriate times

Coaching Suggestions

➤ Ask yourself, What do the facts add up to? What do the details mean? What inferences can I make from this data?

➤ Ask yourself, What is the other stakeholder's perspective? How might other people interpret the same data?

➤ Practice questioning if a new task is reasonable. Could someone else do it just as easily and perhaps benefit from the experience?

➤ Recognize extenuating circumstances. Before you resist making an exception, think again about whether the exception will really harm anything.

➤ Test, with people you trust, *saying* how much you appreciate or value their contributions. Remember, it probably won't spoil them.

➤ Open up to others—share your own internal wry sense of humor and your joy.

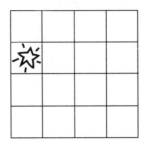

ISTP

Walking Encyclopedia

If most ISTPs that I've encountered could have their way, their positions would allow them to do their work in the way they want without much interference from anyone. Many ISTPs prefer working alone and enjoy taking a task from start to finish. Fred was just one of those ISTPs. His supervisor, who thought highly of his technical work, asked me to coach him because he found Fred difficult to read.

Fred was indeed a man of few words who believed his work should stand for itself. However, he needed to understand the rationale for being more politically savvy and then develop those skills.

Because Fred was a practical man who liked his current work, he was willing to take my advice. He believed it would, in the long run, yield him more job satisfaction and perhaps some of the "finer" things in life. Fred took several short courses in interpersonal relationships. We also video-taped role-playing activities, using recent experiences from his work. He role-played the situation, we noted what he did well and brainstormed how he could have handled things differently, and then redid the exercise to try out the new skills. On seeing the videotapes, Fred found that he liked his new ability to act more warmly and persuasively. He was motivated to practice his skills even more outside of our sessions.

We also determined that it would be important for Fred to give *brief* daily updates to his supervisor, along with weekly and monthly reviews of his work in progress. This way he could communicate outwardly to others the richness that was going on within him.

General Strengths

➤ Repository for facts and specifics, which can be readily retrieved
➤ Work around or through red tape toward a "mission impossible"
➤ Realistically adapt to extenuating circumstances

Typical Areas for Growth

➤ Being indifferent to people's needs and wants (especially your boss, co-workers, or family)

➤ Trying too hard not to care what others think

➤ Having unrealistic expectations or being overly concerned that all things be logical

➤ Taking the expedient but not necessarily the most effective route to getting things done

➤ Not completing what was started

➤ Dismissing a troublesome relationship rather than trying to fix it

Coaching Suggestions

➤ Let others into your world; share your hopes and dreams with a trusted other; offer time to your boss, others, or family and respect their needs.

➤ Realize that your laid-back style might be misconstrued as not caring or not being committed.

➤ Remind yourself that many things in life are not subject to rules of logic. After considering logic, factor into your formula the impact on self, others, or organizations.

➤ Ask yourself, Am I responding to the urgent or the important? or If I do it quickly, what might I overlook? Consider taking a project planning course.

➤ Do an analysis of things left incomplete; how many, why, what was the outcome, what's now important to finish.

➤ Use your logic. List concrete reasons why the relationship should be fixed. If it then seems worth saving, go for it!

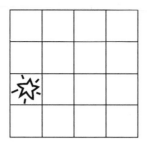

ESTP

"Just Do It," The Action Person

Marcie was recently appointed director of security for St. Luke's, a large suburban hospital. Her career had progressed with the growth of the hospital. She enjoyed her work immensely and was one of the most senior women there. Clearly her boss saw her as a key performer, yet he felt she needed some coaching help. A series of incidents where Marcie acted too quickly had resulted in some costly problems for the hospital.

Marcie loved to live life on the edge and because of this seemed to take precipitous action when she thought hospital security was violated. Her brinkmanship behavior was something that she enjoyed and that others tolerated when she was at a lower status in the organization. However, her boss made it clear that her behavior had to change now that she had assumed the senior security leadership role.

In coaching Marcie, we thoroughly explored the ramifications of her ESTP psychological type. She understood how her preferences inclined her in a direction that was different from the meticulous security procedures established by the hospital board. Marcie was able to see that her natural style was at variance with the powers that be. A simple strategy helped Marcie keep from acting too quickly: We worked on counting to ten before doing anything, making her own checklist for the most frequently occurring security breaches, and then following that checklist to the letter. Also, the vice president of administration agreed to mentor her. By acting as a sounding board, he served as a check on Marcie's rush to action when a potential security emergency loomed. Marcie was a quick study and put the coaching suggestions to good use. Thus her hasty reactions to security emergencies were reduced.

General Strengths

➤ Straightforward, direct, logical problem solvers
➤ Resourceful, flexible, quick to act to save the day
➤ Remind others, by their example, of pleasures of the moment

Typical Areas for Growth

➤ Bluntness—calling it like it is without thought of impact on others

➤ Being overly absorbed in the physical world or with material possessions

➤ Rushing ahead without planning, eleventh-hour heroics

➤ Appearing to others to be too concerned about your recreational pursuits

➤ Pushing others to do things before they are ready

➤ Blaming others before considering the role you played

Coaching Suggestions

➤ Consider, If I say or do this, what will be the impact on others and the consequences to me?

➤ Periodically take stock of life's nonmaterial joys and nuances.

➤ Stop, take aim, think ahead, and see if you can improve your results.

➤ Watch your conversations; let others know how much your leisure heightens your work productivity.

➤ Remember, others may not have the same abilities, skills, or talents to do things quickly. Regard the caution of others as being prudent for them— and maybe even for you!

➤ Think about whether you share the blame, own up, and then suggest ways to solve the problem.

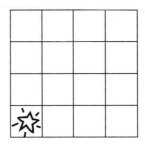

ESTJ

People Who Take Charge

Bill had switched industries, moving from heavy equipment manufacturing to designer clothing manufacturing. An accountant and financial analyst by training, Bill thought his financial experience in the industrial world would transfer easily into the fashion world.

However, Bill's new situation was completely different from his previous position and environment. In his previous job, he was used to giving orders and having them followed. When he sought to use this management style in the new job, it just didn't work. Bill was on the verge of being fired because of his lack of teaming skills. He was at a loss in the new organization's team environment and seemed unable to adapt on his own.

With a strong motivator hanging over his head—his job—Bill was very ready to become more adaptable and more of a team player. My coaching strategy with him was to review his past experience to see what could be applied to his new environment; to evaluate his knowledge and skill level with teamwork; and to help him develop brainstorming and problem-solving techniques with which to anticipate and adjust to his new environment.

At my suggestion, Bill attended several internal corporatewide programs on team development and team leadership. He also participated in an external adventure-style leadership school where he was able to see himself in action and learn teamwork principles that could be applied to his new situation. Eventually Bill met the challenge of adapting to the new job and became more of a team player to his and everyone else's satisfaction.

General Strengths

➤ Step up to task and get people, things, and organizations mobilized for action
➤ Provide structure, direction, and clarity of focus
➤ Results-driven

Typical Areas for Growth

➤ Being too rigid in your expectations of others

➤ Getting so task-focused as to neglect the roles others play in the process

➤ Railroading things through; believing your course of action is the only one

➤ Forgetting to stop and smell the roses

➤ "You can't argue with my success" syndrome

➤ Deciding before collecting all the necessary information

Coaching Suggestions

➤ Practice allowing some give and take. Start in small areas and work to increase your range of openness and kindness.

➤ Acknowledge and reward the contributions of others. Remember, people get things done and may work even harder if their needs and wants are considered in your plans.

➤ Listen to others' perspective to see what you can learn.

➤ Remind yourself, When I'm eighty-five, what might I have missed by not spending more time in the moment?

➤ Clarify with yourself or ask a trusted other, "Could I have been even more successful if I had been less forceful with myself or others?" Check areas of life other than work to see if you are successful there, too.

➤ Learn and use techniques of problem definition, brainstorming, and idea generating before rushing into action.

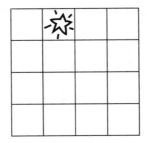

ISFJ

Behind-the-Scenes Helper

Rosa worked in the production section of a large airline parts manufacturer. The organization initiated a total team concept and Rosa's section attended one of the first training programs. Rosa was instrumental in the team's subsequent success in implementing the training concepts while continuing to meet the organization's production goals. She worked in a quiet, yet directive way, and made sure expectations and assignments were clear.

The organization asked me to work with Rosa because, while all the evidence pointed to her key leadership role in the team's accomplishments, Rosa was reluctant both to acknowledge her abilities and to take on an expanded leadership role. For Rosa's boss, the last straw came when Rosa arranged a photo shoot for the three top teams in the organization. Her team was one of them; and the photo was taken *without* Rosa in the picture. She was so busy organizing the photographer and her teammates that she neglected to step into her spot!

After an initial coaching session, I convinced Rosa to take a three-part series on leadership effectiveness offered by a large off-site leadership training organization. The program included videotaping and a thorough assessment of her leadership skills and competencies. Additionally, Rosa and I worked together to find specific ways to enhance her leadership ability. We put a plan in place to meet periodically over several months so that I could provide Rosa with a sounding board on using her newly developed leadership and assertiveness skills.

General Strengths

➤ As good as gold—others can rely on them
➤ Painstaking and thorough in organizing and helping others so that needs are met
➤ "Power behind the throne," especially in administrative areas

Typical Areas for Growth

➤ Not taking the credit that is your due

➤ Feeling you may be taken advantage of—being a doormat

➤ Ignoring your own needs to help others

➤ Neglecting to set priorities, doing things as they turn up or working straight through a to-do list

➤ Avoiding leadership roles

➤ Picking up the balls that others have dropped

Coaching Suggestions

➤ Say "I did that" and toot your own horn; practice seeking the spotlight you deserve.

➤ Show your contributions— present to the stakeholders the things you've done. Find your place in the sun.

➤ Befriend yourself; put yourself on your list of those deserving help and attention.

➤ Ask what's most important to do first; then prioritize those tasks that matter to you and to others.

➤ Consider what projects might benefit from your leadership. Assume a small leadership role at first and then move to larger roles.

➤ Resist doing it for them. *Tell* them it is their job to complete their assignments.

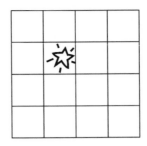

ISFP

St. Francis of Assisi Type

Michael, a lead auditor for an accounting firm, was in career transition when he sought my coaching help. He seemed down on himself and wondered, "Sandra, I'm not sure I did the right thing in following my parents' footsteps in accounting. I spend my days getting information from people who are reluctant to give it or telling people about their record-keeping errors. I don't know if my work is really useful to the clients—it only seems to upset them." After some soul-searching, Michael determined that what he missed most was the chance to give concrete, positive service to people in need.

In coaching Michael, I used a fairly straightforward career development intervention. He completed several vocational assessments, a values clarification exercise, and the MBTI inventory. With this new information and self-awareness in mind, Michael researched the job market thoroughly. After about eight months, he found a job more closely aligned with his service-centered values. He became a business manager in a small nursing home where he used accounting skills in a caring environment that also allowed him to interact personally with the residents and their families.

General Strengths

➤ Know the right word or action that others need and state or do it at *just* the right time
➤ Exemplify kindness and gentleness with others more unfortunate while being aware of the preciousness of every living thing
➤ Use of sensual treats—color, form, texture, music—in service to others

Typical Areas for Growth

➤ Being gullible and too much of a pushover

➤ Being overly self-critical

➤ Sweeping conflict under the rug

➤ Not representing your accomplishments in businesslike terms

➤ Empathizing to the point of not being able to separate yourself from needy others

➤ Withdrawing from others or the scene when feeling threatened; being reluctant to leave your comfort zone

Coaching Suggestions

➤ Consider taking assertiveness training to learn to represent your needs as legitimate.

➤ Make a concentrated effort by consulting with trusted others to find your own value and worth.

➤ Begin to see conflict as a way to clarify your own and others' needs and wants.

➤ Practice, with someone who knows you well, how to talk about your achievements appropriately.

➤ Work on establishing boundaries with people. Give others ample time and opportunity to help themselves.

➤ Seek out supportive others who will help you bridge your comfort gaps until you feel more at ease.

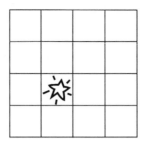

ESFP

Everyone's Friend

He was known as Mr. Sunshine, and he lived up to his name. When I met Nils for the first time, in a restaurant near his office, I could readily tell that he was the one I was to meet for coaching. He greeted me with a broad smile, a friendly wave, and immediately stood up and started coming in my direction. Over lunch, we discussed his coaching needs. He said, "You know, the people in my office don't take my work abilities seriously. Just because I tend to be a little more outgoing and I try to make the office more enjoyable, they don't seem to notice the quality output I produce."

His boss had told me that he wished that Nils could be a little less lively and more serious at work. However, the boss also knew that Nils was a real asset to the organization—on the occasions when he toned down his exuberant nature he was listened to by all.

Because Nils was a realist, he quickly caught on to the downside of being Mr. Sunshine. My coaching strategy was to help him tailor his personal style to his role of marketing office products. He agreed that before a sales call he would ask himself what impression he had to make, keep that impression foremost in his mind, and then act it out during the sales call. His boss also agreed to mentor him in learning the appropriate use of his serious side. Now Mr. Sunshine is earning the respect he deserves.

General Strengths

➤ Generous with others, enhancing any workplace where they're found
➤ Offer grace under pressure, fun-loving
➤ Add enthusiasm, energy, spirit, spunk

Typical Areas for Growth

➤ Being a social butterfly, party person, or "cheerleader"

➤ All froth, no substance—the "class clown"

➤ Busyness—trying to lighten the loads of too many other people

➤ Not looking for patterns or systems to explain your world and the things in it

➤ Being too image-conscious, especially of your own and others' personal images

➤ In trying to be nice, not giving your true opinion or preference

Coaching Suggestions

➤ Ask yourself, Of the roles I have at work, which ones allow others to see my serious side?

➤ Before interactions, consider what kind of impression you want to make. Afterwards, ask a trusted other how you did.

➤ Not everything needs to be done *now* nor by you. Use your person-centered values to determine what's important for others, your work, and yourself.

➤ Stop and ask, What do all my sense impressions add up to? What interpretations could be made? Is there order somewhere?

➤ Take a hard look at what you value. Realize that to many people, "all that glitters is not gold."

➤ Find out more about what you need for yourself. Use your values to clarify your position and then state it!

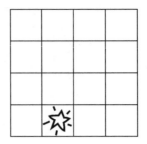

ESFJ

Server of Humankind

A call came from Charlotte, the new executive vice president of a small hotel chain. Because of her service orientation and her loyalty to the company's founder, Charlotte had risen quickly to a senior position. As the hotel grew to be a chain of hotels, Charlotte's role grew as well. She was treated like family by the company founder and had a warm and cordial relationship with him. When he died suddenly and without a succession plan, Charlotte was cast into the role of keeping the business going until a replacement could be found.

Charlotte was not used to making tough decisions because the founder had handled them himself. Because of the uncertainty created by his death, however, several weighty matters arose. Charlotte tried to handle these, but her style in keeping things running smoothly was regarded by family members as meddlesome. She knew the business so well the family wanted to retain her. However, they also wanted her to be coached about her intrusiveness and the appropriate boundaries in the interim position.

I helped Charlotte separate her likes and dislikes from the family's business needs and wants. Charlotte knew that a family member would likely be named as president and that her responsibilities would change. She therefore planned to set appropriate boundaries with the new leader.

I also recommended that for career insurance she pursue a degree in hotel management. She worked hard at her studies and graduated a few years later. In the meantime, she did an admirable job of staying out of the way of the new president unless he asked for her help.

General Strengths

➤ Consistent, compassionate, and careful response to each person's needs or wants
➤ Commitment and loyalty to people and organizations; team players
➤ Offer warmth, practical recognition, and harmonious ways for self and others

Typical Areas for Growth

➤ Attempting to help but instead meddling in others' business

➤ Telling other people what they need

➤ Feeling so much sympathy that you overidentify with others

➤ Focusing more on people's needs and the values to be served, possibly ignoring business needs

➤ Talking or chitchatting too much

➤ Putting yourself at the bottom of the totem pole and forgetting your own needs

Coaching Suggestions

➤ Monitor others' perceptions of your interventions; ask for ways you might help or give options.

➤ Make frequent checks by asking, "Is this information helpful to you?" or "What do *you* think, what do *you* need to do?" Allow others to experience logical consequences— remember, consequences are teachers, too.

➤ Take three steps backward or take time out to do boundary and/or role clarification for yourself and others.

➤ See if your values are getting in the way of business. If so, find out how to change the situation or leave.

➤ At times, consider giving the most terse answer you can find. Remind yourself that you don't need to say everything you know.

➤ Put yourself first occasionally; try once a week for a start!

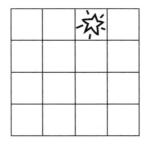

INFJ

Oracle for People

Cecil worked for a large international religious organization. While he was an ordained clergy person, Cecil's main responsibilities were for administration and strategic planning. Cecil, like other INFJs whom I've coached, was very bright, earnest, and dedicated to giving his best effort.

However, Cecil sometimes ran into trouble because his co-workers didn't quite know what was on his mind. He had a reputation for doing things unbeknownst to others, sometimes showing up with a task fully accomplished when his teammates still wondered if anything needed to be done! In one recent incident, Cecil actually developed and began funding a plan that no one else had heard about or passed judgment on. Cecil definitely needed to work on his "surprise" factor to achieve more success in his calling.

Part of my coaching plan for Cecil included his having lunch on a weekly basis with at least one other person from his immediate circle—his boss, a co-worker, someone who reported to him, or someone who represented the people he served. Additionally, we planned for him to take a public seminar on influencing skills. We also determined that he would meet one-on-one with his boss when he had an idea (even if he still considered it to be in the incubation stage). This allowed his boss to interact with him before Cecil worked his idea through to completion. Cecil called me several months later, pleased at the progress he had made in inviting others into his work world.

General Strengths

➤ Insight, imagination sometimes approaching clairvoyance, especially about what matters to people
➤ Understanding how individuals and systems interrelate
➤ Storehouse of integrity; uplifting to those with whom they live and work

Typical Areas for Growth

➤ Not bringing others into your world of ideas soon enough

➤ Being too sure you know what is best for others

➤ Neglecting to let others know how they might help you

➤ Being too optimistic and living too much in the future, forgetting that you have to deal with the present

➤ Not advocating for yourself, thinking others should be able to guess what you could contribute

➤ Not claiming your ideas—even if you don't have the written proof, they *are* your ideas!

Coaching Suggestions

➤ Share some of the richness of your insights and thinking process with people as you go along to gain support for your ideas.

➤ Hear others out and ask yourself, What does it mean if they are right?

➤ Remind yourself that accepting help early on in the idea-generating phase may buy you even more time to go back to that first love—creating.

➤ Find someone you trust who spontaneously lives for the moment and share some of your relaxed time with him or her.

➤ Ask, Where would my abilities make a difference? Then make it known!

➤ Be direct in letting others know that "their" idea was yours originally.

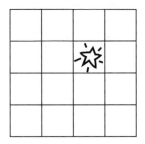

INFP

Joan of Arc Type

Grace was a trust officer at a large banking firm. She enjoyed customer contact and the chance to think creatively for the people she served. However, Grace's supervisor, Anne, was displeased with her lack of attention to very necessary trust formalities and regulations. Anne appreciated the good relationships that Grace had with her customers, yet also knew that rules had to be followed.

As I began coaching Grace, we determined the importance of following bank protocol. Because she valued her relationship with Anne, Grace quickly realized that attention to procedures would not only benefit the bank but maintain harmony between her and Anne.

I tutored Grace on presenting new ideas to Anne, an ESFJ, with concrete, incremental steps, in order to gain Anne's acceptance and therefore make Grace's ideas become reality. In time, though, with the new information about her INFP preferences, Grace decided that her heart was really elsewhere. She loved the people side of the business but resented the time she had to spend keeping up-to-date on the myriad of trust regulations. Eventually she moved to an international economic organization where the focus was on using financial means to help fight world hunger— one of her passions.

General Strengths

➤ Galvanize others and organizations to action
➤ Stand firmly on their values against formidable opposition
➤ Remind others in creative ways about human aspirations and goals

Typical Areas for Growth	Coaching Suggestions
➤ Tending to consider your own values of higher merit than those of others	➤ Ask yourself if another person's values are as appropriate to them or their situation as yours are to you.
➤ Not being straightforward with others	➤ Assertiveness training, especially about delivering the tough messages you *need* to deliver or others *need* to hear.
➤ Perfectionism or procrastination	➤ Decide whether a job is *really* worth doing well before you begin. Let others do some of the work.
➤ Harboring resentments	➤ Talk to the "transgressor" so he or she will have a chance to earn your favor again.
➤ Being idealistic to the point of acting out-of-touch	➤ Temper your idealism with a tad of realism, when appropriate. Remind yourself that both realism and idealism exist and that each can benefit from the other.
➤ Accepting salary treatment that may not match your worth to the organization	➤ Tell yourself that having adequate pay for what you do can create options for you to give or do even more.

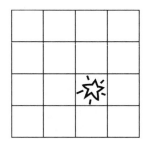

ENFP

Spark That Ignites the Fire

Alex was late to our first meeting, carrying an armful of books and files and wearing an overall frazzled look. Alex had the potential to be a star performer in his organization but was also known for being too scattered, lacking focus and direction. This was most apparent in his behavior at team meetings, where he was often unprepared and seemingly disorganized. Sometimes, through the force of his personality, he took the team way off track. His boss wanted his creativity but also wanted Alex to develop some organizational skills.

In coaching Alex, I asked him to list for me his five key job requirements and to put them into priority order. Then we arranged his daily schedule and appointment book to reflect these five priorities. Alex also attended a personal time management class. Additionally, he started to watch for cues from his teammates that he was promising more than could be delivered, interjecting too many of his own faddish ideas, or otherwise pulling the team off track. While it was difficult at times for Alex to restrain himself, he realized that a less scattered approach, built around his top five priorities, was yielding him more *real* influence at work, something on which he placed a high value.

General Strengths

➤ Initiators and promoters for all kinds of ideas for human growth and potential
➤ Tireless in the pursuit of novel ideas
➤ "Pulls rabbits out of hats" to accomplish the nearly impossible

Typical Areas for Growth	**Coaching Suggestions**
➤ Being considered unrealistic, a "flake"	➤ Watch for raised eyebrows or other verbal and nonverbal clues that you're not being taken seriously. Scale it down a bit.
➤ Following new fads, leaders, ideas, without careful evaluation	➤ Use your values to weigh which new promise really delivers; be wary in your selection of leaders. Conversely, with your charisma, be careful what you encourage others to do.
➤ Not knowing your own physical, time, and mental limits	➤ Remind yourself that you are human, with normal physical and time limits. Adopt good stress and time management.
➤ Underestimating how long or how much effort something will take	➤ Respect reality—on occasion, it can be your best friend, so take a good dose of it as needed.
➤ Overwhelming yourself, others, or organizations with options	➤ Find a trusted person who has a talent for decision making or learn some of the skills yourself—then be sure to apply them!
➤ Ignoring facts	➤ Look for the givens or unalterables in a situation. Don't varnish the *real* truth.

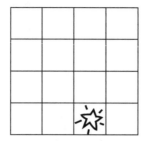

ENFJ

Values Spokesperson

Dale was an entrepreneur in the software design and development industry. His products were extremely user-friendly and, as a result, his business was booming. In the early days, he hired people based on their potential for camaraderie as well as their credentials.

To his dismay, some of the criticisms Dale heard from his employees were their perceptions that he played favorites and that he reacted negatively to anyone's disapproval. His staff felt that these problems made him less effective as a leader. For these reasons and at his loyal staff's urgings, Dale sought my coaching.

Dale quickly grasped the concepts of psychological type and immediately saw that he needed to be more businesslike. He also realized that good business decisions had the potential to affect the bottom line as well as people both positively and negatively. He felt he could make tough decisions when it was important to do so.

I cautioned him that while he might wish to make everyone his friend, not everyone would want his friendship in return. Because he was the head of the firm, Dale realized that he had to be sure he was being fair to all by not showing partiality to some. Additionally, Dale decided that when he needed another senior level person, he would hire someone who would balance him in terms of technical skill.

Notice, I did not say Dale would hire a Thinking type, because hiring on the basis of type preferences would be unethical! And besides, even if Dale did hire a Thinking type, she or he still might not have the requisite skills linked with the Thinking preference. Remember, a person's type cannot guarantee that they will use their type preferences effectively.

General Strengths

➤ Caring, cooperating, and facilitating people's growth within organizations
➤ Articulate messages that people want or need to hear
➤ Remind people and organizations of their mission and core values

Typical Areas for Growth

➤ Ignoring or not valuing your own natural decision-making process, leading to a caricature of logical decision-making processes

➤ Talking too long or not getting to the point when getting down to business

➤ Taking work-related coaching as personal criticism

➤ Thinking that most, if not all, relationships can be win-win and collaborative

➤ Becoming bossy, with many *shoulds* and *oughts,* or being overly zealous on issues

➤ Becoming the emotional sponge for office woes

Coaching Suggestions

➤ Rethink decisions minus the business jargon. Which outcome is *really* better?

➤ Set a mental timer for yourself. Monitor and ask for feedback on how quickly and efficiently you get to the point of the business at hand.

➤ Ask, How would a sensible, impartial person regard this information? Then work to separate your work performance from your personal identity.

➤ Note the factors that allowed "snakes in the grass" to operate in the past. Develop a checklist for yourself to be sure others are playing by mutual rules.

➤ Your gifts of persuasion can be pushed to extremes, so take time to see reactions of others and to ask yourself, What is this stand going to cost me?

➤ Take care of yourself, too: Get away from work, take your vacations, and have some other diversions to rejuvenate yourself.

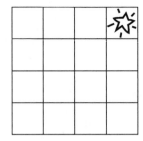

INTJ

Designer of the Future

Shelly was a senior vice president of a large engineering organization. Her area of expertise was technological innovation. Part of her task was to ensure that technical vitality was maintained throughout the corporation. Shelly developed a plan to reduce technical obsolescence for all the engineers and scientists under her direction. Unfortunately, Shelly did not share her plans with other members of the executive team, nor did she gather any input from those who would be affected by the plan, namely the scientists and engineers. In retrospect, she realized that getting buy-in from her staff was crucial to the success of her strategy. Because she was fairly confident of her plan's potential, she called me for some coaching.

I helped Shelly understand that while doing a project herself might be a strength for technical work, it could sometimes be a weakness for projects whose success depended on the involvement of people. Shelly worked to consider the impact of her decisions on others. Specifically, we looked at her technical vitality plan to see what happened to people at each step. With Shelly's concurrence, we also held focus groups to determine what the engineers and scientists wanted to include in the plan.

Shelly set as a goal for herself to involve others earlier in any future plans that affected them. Further, Shelly took an off-site class on interpersonal negotiating skills. At her request, I continued to meet with Shelly on a periodic basis to see how things were going and to serve as a shadow consultant to some of her major projects.

General Strengths

➤ Envision "what will be" so clearly that it's palpable
➤ Paradigm shifters—conceptual breakthrough artists
➤ See relationship of each part to the whole

Typical Areas for Growth

➤ Seeing outcomes so vividly that you can't understand how others miss them

➤ Not letting others in on your thinking until the very end

➤ Locking into ideas and not wanting to budge

➤ Doing team projects by yourself, believing no one can do it better

➤ Failing to take the necessary time to train or develop others

➤ Impatience—lack of awareness of your impact on others; lost in your own world

Coaching Suggestions

➤ Practice patience, reiterating your insights until others catch on. Think about what will capture their hearts and minds, then use this information as you outline your ideas.

➤ Bring others into your process before you work it all out in order to gain their commitment.

➤ Write down others' ideas and ponder their merits before deciding whether to include or toss them out.

➤ Delegate parts of your vision or task as early as possible— someone else may benefit greatly from the delegation.

➤ Practice sharing tasks with others, then spend time training them. Realize that the net outcome is ultimately freedom for you to do more creating while others do the implementation.

➤ Ask trusted others to give you feedback about your impact—no holds barred!

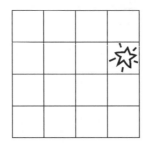

INTP
Blueprinter of Ideas

Nicole was a talented research scientist who could draw circles around anyone in her technical area. However, she was often clueless when it came to reading people's verbal and nonverbal behaviors. She knew that her lack of interpersonal skills put her at risk for not getting the senior project leader assignment in the laboratory where she worked. Because she wanted a crack at setting the course of action for a cutting-edge project with extremely high potential, Nicole sought interpersonal coaching with me.

In coaching Nicole, I wanted her to understand the impact she had on others. We videotaped her interactions with me and with a small group of her team members who were also learning interpersonal skills. As we viewed the tapes together, Nicole listed for herself several hints for better communication. I also gave her reading assignments, as this was her preferred mode of learning.

Once she mastered the concepts of the importance of people to the task, Nicole began to put into practice many of the suggested tips and skills from our coaching session and from those embedded in her reading. Because of her determination to become competent interpersonally and her intentional use of the skills, it wasn't long before she got the project leader assignment she wanted. We agreed that her skillful but *draining* use of these interpersonal skills allowed her more opportunity to lead technical projects—her true goal.

General Strengths

➤ The strategists' strategist—master of complexity
➤ Developer of models and theories
➤ Independent, critical, and logical analysis of new thoughts, systems, and "sacred cows"

Typical Areas for Growth

➤ Intellectual snobbery

➤ Confusing others with complex explanations

➤ Appearing cold and aloof with little awareness of how you affect others

➤ Pointing out flaws in the logic or reasoning of others—even your own boss

➤ Forgetting your own and others' needs when "lost in thought"

➤ Expecting others to behave logically

Coaching Suggestions

➤ Study the other types of intelligence, especially inter-personal, intrapersonal, and emotional intelligences.

➤ Practice "reducing" your thoughts to three to five key, easy-to-understand points.

➤ Remember that most work in life involves others. If you really want resources or recognition for your work, lighten up!

➤ Count to ten before you speak. One or two well-rounded people may appreci-ate your critique, but others may begin to avoid you.

➤ Take people breaks—purposely put yourself on committees or sporting teams to break up your typical "head" work. Get physical!

➤ Recognize the value and strength of emotions by start-ing to know your own feel-ings. Seek self-awareness classes or personal growth opportunities.

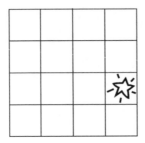

ENTP

Classic Entrepreneur

Britta was on the faculty of an international training organization. She often teamed with two to three other trainers when working with a client company. I was asked by Britta's boss, the head of consulting and training, to coach Britta about her exaggerated Extraverted style and her competitiveness. Britta wanted to be the center of the stage when she co-trained. This was causing problems for her with her teammates, who periodically felt that they were upstaged. Additionally, since many of the firm's client companies were multinationals, Britta needed to learn how to express her ENTP style in a way that was more appropriate for different cultures.

To help Britta understand how to work more effectively internationally, she enrolled in a university course on cross-cultural sensitivity. She also joined an intercultural service organization that afforded her a firsthand understanding of several different cultures' interpersonal norms. Britta was videotaped in some team-training sessions so she could see the impact of her style on her colleagues and learn why they saw her as being competitive.

To control her center-stage tendencies, Britta reviewed feedback from her colleagues periodically during the training day and adjusted her behavior accordingly. Finally, because her energy was so Extraverted, I suggested that Britta do some needed introspection, perhaps making her sporadic meditation practice more regular.

General Strengths

➤ Provide energy and thrust to new projects, products, markets, or tasks; starting things off with enthusiasm
➤ Use synthesis as a strategy to work on or solve problems
➤ See possibilities even in the face of disaster

Typical Areas for Growth	**Coaching Suggestions**
➤ Competitive nature	➤ Evaluate the input of others on a task; practice giving praise where praise is due. Ask others for feedback on your style.
➤ Glib responses to human needs	➤ Remind yourself, How will others feel or react?
➤ Stealing the show or hogging the limelight, needing to be the center of attention	➤ Ask yourself, Who else deserves recognition? Give them some floor space when rewards are handed out. Remember, sharing the limelight with others may increase your "human capital."
➤ Getting tied up in models or structures to explain reality	➤ Remind yourself that not everything is *that* involved and that many people get lost with models and prefer straightforward answers.
➤ Bending the rules, taking advantage of loopholes, and pulling the wool over others' eyes	➤ Ask yourself, Has taking advantage ever gotten me in so much trouble that it was, in reality, more grief than it was worth? List the *actual* costs.
➤ Overextending yourself, your resources, and those of others or the organization	➤ Take time to reflect, recreate, rejuvenate. Ask, What will I need to let go of to make room for this new opportunity?

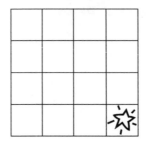

ENTJ
Grand Scale Organizer

Miki was a very focused and direct person. She achieved her doctorate in business management in the shortest amount of time possible by using that focus in her studies. After graduation, she moved into several troubleshooter assignments where she was called in to turn around a situation. However, she often left a wake of people in pain. This caught up with her in her last assignment. She was on the verge of being terminated or plateaued because of her over-controlling style. "But," she told me, "I was told that I had free rein. When I exercised this option, people got on my case. I realize I've been a bit heavy-handed, but I got the job done and in record time!" Rather than lose her, Miki's boss asked me to coach her.

In our first session together, Miki wanted me to establish my competency as a coach. When that was done, I laughingly challenged her to demonstrate her interpersonal competency to me before we moved on to develop a plan. We did a thorough cause and effect analysis of her three most recent assignments and weighed the consequences of her actions not only on the task but on the people involved. Next, we searched for a qualified mentor for her—someone with similar accomplishments but who had reached the same goals in a more humane way. We looked at areas in Miki's work and in her leisure time where she could relax her standards and just enjoy the people or the circumstances. Of her own accord, Miki decided to take a project management course that emphasized the people part of the planning process.

After several months, Miki told me that she'd gotten some positive feedback about "The New Miki" and that she even liked her "new" self better!

General Strengths

- ➤ "No one does it better"—marshaling forces to achieve future goals
- ➤ Think in terms of systems, bring all elements to bear on a situation
- ➤ Find flaws and focus on what could be achieved once they are removed

Typical Areas for Growth

➤ Overstructuring and/or controlling people and processes

➤ Being overly confident of your strategies

➤ Acting impatient with processes when you came up with the solution so quickly

➤ Assuming the world is yours to run

➤ Applying "goal setting" too stringently to your life or to the lives of others

➤ Considering too many complexities and contingencies

Coaching Suggestions

➤ Use the input of others— even that of people not necessarily considered "experts."

➤ Find the person most likely to be your "naysayer" and run your ideas past him or her.

➤ Figure out realistic expectations of others and of resources. Many solutions need to face real hurdles of time and resources.

➤ Develop and coach the leadership potential in others.

➤ Watch your control needs. Practice being in the moment —not every person or adventure needs goals and objectives!

➤ Set some deadlines on your thought process. Remind yourself that at times it's better to "keep it simple, sweetheart!"

I wonder if Charlie is taking his
time management skills to extremes?

10

Case Closed

A Leader Who Put Type to Work

To close, let's look at someone who managed to incorporate all of the nine Type Keys into his management style. Joel was a model student throughout his high school, college, and graduate school days, so it was no surprise to me that when Joel was introduced to the concepts of psychological type, he was a model student there as well. He learned the fundamental principles and used them effectively to increase his already impressive leadership skills.

I first met Joel when he was the director of curriculum for a large suburban school district. At the age of thirty-two, he was one of the youngest people in the state to hold such a responsible position in a large school district. He asked me to work with his elementary principals as they together implemented site-based management. Many of them were concerned about several aspects of the new approach, such as the role of the principal, shared decision making, and how the system would allow them to work with their various constituencies including teachers, unions, parents, and each other.

Joel and I decided to offer the MBTI personality inventory to each individual player, and Joel took it for the first time himself. His type preferences came out INTJ and he confirmed that as his best-fit type. The elementary principals were primarily ESFJ and ESTJ. As we planned the intervention, I coached Joel to understand how his INTJ style would be quite different on two to three of the type preferences from most of the elementary principals.

I was impressed immediately with Joel's desire to use the type information he learned about himself as an INTJ to work with his team. He knew he had a good plan for the way site-based management could work and a well-thought-out model that could be applied in each school. However, he quickly recognized that if he wanted his complementary ES principals to be committed to his ideas, they needed to talk and be active participants in the planning process.

⚷ Type Key

If you understand your own style, you can work more effectively with others.

Joel quickly realized through the concepts of type how he and his team could complement each other.

We structured our team-building meeting to debrief members on their MBTI results, work on issues of collaboration, and determine a plan of action for site-based management implementation.

Joel started off the program with his hopes for the outcomes of the session. He said, "I guess I'll be known as the 'newcomer' here for a long time to come, since the rest of you have at least five years in your positions. As we move forward into site-based management, though, I want to put to rest the issues such as the old guard versus new guard politics that have hindered this team. Those issues will only block each person's individual effectiveness. That's why we're here today: to better understand each other's strengths and how each of us can best be utilized in implementing these ideas."

Many of the team members nodded in agreement. I had interviewed a few of them prior to our session. They were well aware of the issues and appreciated Joel's efforts to address them. The principals, as a group, believed that so far under Joel's leadership, there was more trust and team support than before. However, there was still room for improvement.

After I gave a group interpretation of the MBTI results, we moved on to the issues. Joel had decided in advance that he wanted to participate as a group member so that his thoughts wouldn't unduly influence the others' input, so I facilitated their discussion. We worked on the concepts of psychological type and the following points with each person.

First, the participants listed:

➤ One accomplishment in their current position of which they were proud
➤ What they saw as their strengths and areas for development

➤ What they most admired in each of their colleagues
➤ What their colleagues needed to do in order for them to have better working relationships

Secondly, we worked on setting up priorities to put plans into action. Factors included the interpersonal relationships on the team, based on the information that we gathered in the first exercise and the MBTI. When the action plans were set, we moved on to the following questions.

➤ How do we want support expressed within our group?
➤ How do we want to manage conflict and disagreement?
➤ How can we value team operations as well as highly competent individual performance?
➤ How do we handle competition among ourselves?

We worked through each of the questions in our two-day session and I was impressed at every juncture with Joel's ability to weave the ideas and plans of others into an overall strategy for the district. He did an excellent job of keeping the team on course and listened intently to the input in a nonjudgmental fashion.

Type Key

If you know why you drive others up a wall, perhaps you can help them down.
Joel knew that his tendency to find the flaws in the ideas of others could interfere with the input of his staff—something he really valued.

By the end of the meeting, the elementary principals had developed a code of conduct for their team efforts, a unified plan for each school to introduce the concepts of site-based management, and a partnership system with each other to manage the inevitable difficulties. They saw their ES and IN difference to be a strength for the tasks ahead; "reality combined with vision" is how they talked about it.

Type Key

Perceiving is noticing both the forest and the trees.
While Joel's staff focused naturally on the specifics for the near future, Joel added the big-picture perspective.

The team-building process seemed to work very well in Joel's eyes—at least that's what he reported to me when we met several weeks after the session. Joel and I had monthly one-on-one meetings throughout the remainder of that school year.

It was about two years before I heard from Joel again. By then, he was the new superintendent of a third-ring suburban community with very high educational standards. Joel was clearly perceived as a rising star in the state's educational arena and this appointment was an impressive achievement. Most of the previous superintendents had come to the position as a capstone to their careers.

He had just moved to the district when he called to ask for my help in working with his new school board. He particularly wanted to build on the already existing pride and sense of community in the district's schools. The district took a very progressive approach to education, with twelve educational pilot projects underway when he arrived on the scene. However, he told me, "You know, we're facing a huge bond issue vote and I don't want to alienate *anyone* who might support the bond. We need to be cautious about any more innovations and be unified as a board."

At Joel's request, I met with each individual on the school board and discussed:

➤ Their view of education
➤ What they "got on their soapbox" about
➤ What they wanted to be remembered for
➤ What mattered most to them in establishing their working relationship with Joel

Joel had also already talked in-depth with each board member, sharing with them his vision for the schools. Many of these board members were newly elected and were anxious to support their new leader. I then administered the MBTI inventory to each of the board members and found the board had a mixture of the sixteen types with the majority preference being for Intuition.

The team-building session began with a spirit of camaraderie and mutual respect between Joel and the board. Joel started the meeting by listing some of his hopes for their relationship. We then worked through the MBTI information.

In advance of the meeting, Joel had distributed to the board nine different pieces of information including what the school board could expect from a superintendent, why teams have problems, team commandments, and a self-assessment for each board member on the thoroughness and efficiency with which they as board members went about their task. He joked, "I assigned the advance readings for those of you with a preference for Introversion so that you would be ready to give me your opinions today.

I listed them in priority order and gave a synopsis of each piece for those people (probably those with a preference for Extraversion) who might not learn as well by, or enjoy, reading articles. Hopefully, now, everyone is set to go on to our big task today, crystallizing our vision for the district."

Joel's advance planning paid off. By the end of the day, the group came up with a twenty-point plan. At Joel's urging, they placed each goal and subgoal in priority order for the district. The plan also included time lines and specific implementation ideas.

Type Key

Looking at an issue from all sides leads to good decisions.
Joel created an atmosphere where each of the preferences was honored, allowing for an easy and effective exchange of information.

At the session, I witnessed a clear collaboration between Joel and the school board. Joel was persuasive, yet clearly open to the ideas and influence of the board members. His clear thinking, ability to represent his viewpoints, and strong commitment convinced the others that he was on target. The session was one of the most productive events I've ever seen.

At the end of this meeting, the board discussed what they had accomplished. The team felt that they had moved very effectively and efficiently through the many issues they faced at the start of a new school year with a new superintendent. The board members universally praised Joel for his organizational skills, his ability to listen, and his clarity of vision that was instrumental in helping the board develop its plan. Many commented that they had felt the group's openness as they expressed their own positions. They had enjoyed the humor and trust evident in the session—and there was unanimous agreement that no one had a hidden agenda and that egos had been checked at the door before entering!

Type Key

Behaviors that annoy you in others may be clues to areas for your *own* self-development.
Joel resisted creating the board's plan on his own, as an INTJ might tend to do, because he'd learned from his own past experience how much he disliked leaders who did not empower others.

With such clarity of purpose obtained at the first meeting, Joel was off to a good start. Communitywide, Joel and the board enjoyed being perceived as a solid leadership team.

It was exactly a year later when I heard from Joel again. He had just issued the first annual report of his activities to everyone as well as to the local newspaper. Not surprisingly as an INTJ, he chose to call it "The Road Ahead." He asked me to do a team-building session with his entire administrative council, which included the district's administrative leaders as well as the principals from each school.

Joel's objectives for this team building were similar to the previous one with the school board. The goals for this session were:

➤ To allow members to become better acquainted
➤ To strategize how to navigate "The Road Ahead"
➤ To increase role clarity about each council member's responsibilities (especially those of the district administrative leaders vis-à-vis the school principals)
➤ To establish higher levels of trust
➤ To determine, from the council's perspective, the immediate and more long-term needs for the continuation of educational excellence in the district

Type Key

The world would be a stagnant place if everyone were the same.

Joel had articulated his vision for the district in his report, "The Road Ahead," but realized implementation of the vision called on the strengths of others—his administrative council.

As is often done in team-building sessions, Joel worked with several other council members to define the objectives. We selected interview questions for me to ask each of the council members to gain their views on Joel, their own strengths, challenges they anticipated, and "The Road Ahead."

Several key issues were identified in the interviews, relating to the new people on the council and their comfort and ease in speaking up; selecting the correct group of individuals for different projects on "The Road Ahead"; and lastly, the need for quick communication methods (e-mail, interoffice memos, or voice mail) for effective communication in such a sprawling district.

We also decided to give the MBTI inventory to each team member. After each individual confirmed his or her best-fit type and a team type analysis was completed, the following data emerged: The team type was ES/NTJ and its modal types were ENFP and ESTJ. The dominant functions (selected from the four functions of S, N, T, or F) were Intuition first, Thinking second, and Sensing third. No one on the team was a dominant Feeler. As the meeting progressed, the team decided to work on factoring in the characteristic Feeling emphasis on values and the impact on the people involved before making any major decisions.

Further, in examining the four-function framework, the team had only one SF. The council decided to deliberately invite that person to speak out and to incorporate the SF service focus in its work.

⌒ Type Key

Type is a poor excuse for inexcusable behavior!
Rather than leave out the gifts of Feeling, the absence of which could result in inexcusable behavior, Joel and the council members became intentional about applying their *own* less preferred Feeling gifts.

The NT functional pairing was the most frequent and was Joel's preference, too. The NF and the ST functional pairings were second and third, respectively.

The MBTI data proved to be very compelling to the council members. There was much discussion of Joel's style and that of the group. Many issues focused on the Extraverted style of the team and Joel's preferred Introverted style. After seeking input on how he could better meet the predominant Extraverted communication style of the council, Joel listed some action items for himself for the future.

⌒ Type Key

To influence others, try speaking their language.
Joel appreciated his own natural style but also recognized the value of working outside that style.

Joel's dominant Intuitive style matched the dominant Intuitive style of the team. Someone remarked, "No wonder this district has so many educational pilot projects going on!" To act as a check on Joel's and the council's majority Intuitive process, the Sensors in the group were asked to pay attention to and remind the group about current operations and standards. Without this check, the group might want to spend too much of its time on future planning.

There was a match between the team's preference and Joel's preference for Thinking. Some of the team members with a preference for Feeling wanted a little bit more feedback from Joel when they were starting a new project so that they could know that Joel valued what they were doing.

Joel's preference for Judging matched the team's preference for Judging as well. However, a strong counterbalancing force to the majority of Judgers was the influential senior-high principal, Andy, who had a preference for Perceiving. Andy was a lifetime resident of the school district who enjoyed firm support from students, parents, and community leaders for his enthusiastic and creative ways.

The council members agreed that they would call on Andy and the other Perceivers before anything was absolutely solidified. They also set ground rules to allow time for the Perceivers to bring in new findings before any major decisions were made.

By the end of the day, the council members had used the concepts of psychological type as they established a list of issues, assigned those issues to various team members, and drew up time lines. An overall sense of satisfaction permeated the session.

I occasionally meet with Joel, his board, or his council when issues and problems arise. At one of our one-on-one meetings, I asked Joel how psychological type helped him solve the mysteries of working with people.

Joel said, "You know, I used to wonder why other people didn't think like I did and couldn't catch on to my ideas and brainstorming. I wanted to move ahead, get on to the task, and time and again I'd find that others were digging in their heels on projects I *knew* were on target.

"Now, I understand that I wouldn't *want* them to all think like me. If the world were full of INTJs, there are a lot of things that would get left undone. Further, type helps me communicate with the other fifteen types and explain my ideas in a way that they can understand. Then they ask me the right questions, which helps me.

"I truly can't think of being in leadership without this understanding of those around me—take Andy, for instance. Knowing that one of his gifts is identifying as many options as possible is very different from thinking that he can't keep focused on a single solution. Being a student of type, I think, is one of the things that makes me an effective leader."

Type Key

Growing in type awareness adds an extra edge.

Yes, Joel was a model student when it came to psychological type. Joel found that his INTJ preferences and his understanding of type *clued* him into the fifteen other valid styles and ways of doing things. This self-knowledge and understanding of a model that takes the mystery out of working relationships has allowed him to meet with success. And that is what I wish for you!

The Team-Building Process

A team can be defined as two or more people who coordinate their activities regularly to accomplish a common purpose or task. Team building, as I see it, is a process for working with a group of two or more people to facilitate and make possible an enhancement in their working relationships. As a result, team building may:[14]

➤ Be one-time or ongoing

➤ Be with the entire team, subteams, or a pair of individuals

➤ Use tools such as the MBTI inventory

➤ Occur when a team forms or at any other point in the team's life

➤ Happen when the group is in conflict or when the group is working well

➤ Be a part of an ongoing culture change effort or occur in isolation.

At any *one* of these six times, I might be called in to provide team-building consultation and coaching.

Most team building occurs with a request from either an individual team member, the team leader, or someone in the organization's human resources department. My team-building approach is detailed in my book, *MBTI Team Building Program: Leader's Resource Guide*. Some but not all of these steps are featured in the chapters of this book. This appendix will give you a flavor of how most team-building interventions go.

When possible, I prefer to do team building with another individual, either one from within the organization or one of my colleagues in type work. Having another person helps ensure that the information gathered in the team-building process is as clear and complete as possible. The other person also serves as a check on my perceptions and evaluations.

Initial Interview

In the first phase of the team-building process, I like to schedule an initial interview with the client and/or the human resources person in the organization. At this session it's important for me and the potential client to determine whether there is a fit for the work that is to be done. I also want to hear the client's objectives and hopes for the team-building process; learn how they heard about me; and judge the appropriateness of a team-building intervention. (Other interventions could be one-on-one conflict resolution, training, or systemwide organizational development planning.) At this initial interview, I can determine whether or not it seems useful to use the MBTI instrument and the concepts of psychological type.

I prefer to hold this meeting at the client's work site because it gives me a chance to read the organizational culture. A book called *The Negotiable Environment*, written by Cecil Williams and two coauthors,[15] offers illustrations and discusses the types of office layout and furniture that STs, SFs, NFs, and NTs prefer. This book has given me insights for my initial impressions of the organization. In the client's environment, I am already looking for clues for psychological type. During this early problem-definition stage I like to obtain as much information as possible about the team or individual's past successes, current needs, and future aspirations.

Contracting

In the contracting phase, I work with the client to develop a written contract that delineates his or her expectations and hopes for the team-building session. I also include my best guess as to costs, facilitation fees, steps in the process, and the use of the MBTI or other instruments.

Formation of Partnership Team

If there is a match between my style, skills, and abilities and the objectives and needs of the client and we agree to go ahead with the team building, the next step is to form a partnership or implementation team with my client and several others in his or her organization. The task of the partnership team is ninefold:[16]

1. To model team building from the very start
2. To be learners in a process designed to train and develop the team and its members
3. To define and fine-tune the team-building objectives and procedures as necessary
4. To assist in the interview process by:
    *   Providing guidance to create a safe environment for the honest exchange of information by all those interviewed
    *   Selecting or creating interview questions that have the greatest potential of yielding the most valuable information
    *   Scheduling interviews, rooms, and so on
5. To serve as a communication conduit to the team builder(s) throughout the process
6. To provide reality checks and context checking as the data emerges
7. To offer guidance and assistance for future training design and to help with its delivery
8. To find a place for an off-site team-building session and provide the necessary resources for the session and to otherwise facilitate a comfortable climate for the team-building process
9. To be sure the team-building process continues once the team builder(s) leave the organization.

There have been numerous times when the partnership team has saved my hide. Because they live and breathe in the organization, they often balance my perceptions, add to my suggestions for subsequent action, and aid in the management of sticky issues that might come along. (Some sticky issues I've experienced have included the uncovering of a religious cult, an office affair, some weapons at the work site, and on a few occasions a racial or ethnic conflict.) Because the people on the partnership team also have a share in the design of the intervention and a sense of the way it will go, they generally are more committed to the process and are able to get others' commitment, too.

Other selection criteria for the partnership team could include asking for volunteers from the client's team who want to experience firsthand a team-building process and learn some skills that can perhaps be used later in their work.

The partnership team is charged with the responsibility of carrying the team building forward and for making sure the action items and the legacy of the actual team-building event continue in the organization.

Interview Questions

The partnership team helps us select interview questions for each team member. Here again the partnership team is able to assist the process in a very cogent way. I have a list of typical interview questions that I offer to this team (which are similar to some of the questions in Appendix B on the coaching process). With that list as a spark to their recall or imagination, the partnership team modifies the questions or comes up some of their own. Usually there are six to eight questions that will be asked of everyone on the team, when the team is small (under eight people).

When the team is very large or there is not enough time to interview six to eight people, we may send out the interview questions to every team member and ask for their written responses. Sometimes I also use a team diagnostic such as one found in my book, *MBTI Team Building Program: Leader's Resource Guide,* or one that is available commercially through human resources publishers.

Interviews and Data Analysis

Once we have determined the interview questions and the individuals who will be interviewed, I schedule approximately an hour to conduct each one. The chapters in this book have many examples of this interview process. During this interviewing step, I can administer the *Myers-Briggs Type Indicator* personality inventory and answer any questions about it.

This is where the mystery of type and team building comes in as I work to find the facts and clues, coming up with "leads" about where the problems might lie. Those of you who pride yourself on being good detectives would most likely enjoy this part of the team-building process. It involves the use of both Sensing and Intuition. This interview process and data analysis is something that I particularly enjoy (weaving together the comments and opinions, the sense data and my own intuitions, into a synthesis about the key issues or problems facing the team).

I also pull together the MBTI data to compare and contrast it to the interview data, looking for type-related clues that can be used in the intervention. When I'm writing the report on interview data, I use my impressions of the environment, the history of the organization, annual reports (if it's a publicly held organization), mission statements, departmental objectives, job descriptions, company newsletters, any product information, and any other material that will help me understand and work with the client.

I prepare a ten- to twenty-page report on my findings, which usually has the following format: an overall summary, a synopsis of each interview question with an overall impression of the findings, and then specific comments made by people (disguised so that anonymity can be maintained) that help to amplify my overall summary.

I am careful not to use words that would identify an individual in particular. For example, if a team member constantly used the phrase "I put my stake in the ground," having that comment in my written report would readily identify that person. At the end of the responses to each interview question, I add several suggestions for the team to consider. Finally, at the conclusion of the report I develop a list of potential action plans, some of which incorporate principles from psychological type data.

One-on-One Consultations

Sometimes during the interview and data gathering stage, it becomes obvious to me that problems may exist between two individuals on the team or with just one of the team members. My contracting arranges for private, known only to me, sessions with such an individual or for conflict mediation and resolution when two individuals are involved. It's usually a judgment call on when, how, and with whom to intervene. (Chapter 5 with Dean and Gwen gives an example of how I often go about this process.)

I believe it's an important professional courtesy to handle issues that involve one person (personality clashes or stylistic differences) where that individual, but not the team, would benefit from some one-on-one coaching. When there are two people involved, then my intervention is usually conflict resolution between them. Conflict resolution can be helped immensely by the use of psychological type and some of the suggestions in this book.

Frequently these one-on-one consultations are brief, since my role is not a therapeutic one. If therapeutic counseling is necessary, I make a referral to a counselor, and if the individual is in agreement that we can share the information, I will help lobby the organization for funds to get that type of help.

Planning Session

Once the interviews have been conducted and, if necessary, the one-on-one consultations are in progress, and the report of the interviews has been compiled, I like to meet again with the client and partnership team to share my findings. In essence, they get a preview of what is going on and work with me to plan the team-building session and strategy.

At this point, we discuss the issues that I have uncovered, plan how much time we will need for the team-building meeting, and decide on items and time frames for the agenda. Here again, the partnership team can play a vital role in the ultimate success of the team-building intervention because they provide extra information as well as an extra evaluation of the process so far.

For example, in one especially contentious governmental agency, the partnership team decided that each person would need to have a copy of my report. They required that team members put their name on the report and return it to me at the end of the session. They wanted this step because in a previous team-building process, another consultant's report was faxed in entirety to the local newspaper. Luckily the local newspaper chose not to publish the information!

The Team-Building Session

The session is planned so that we do the right things in the right sequence in, we hope, an adequate amount of time. This means that we have made a decision about when to work with the MBTI results. Should MBTI results come first in the process or follow the team interview report? Sometimes it's best to start with the results of the interviews because that is first and foremost in people's minds. If we don't do that first, they may not pay as much attention to MBTI data. More frequently, I do the MBTI first because it provides a language and a lens through which the team members can understand the findings on the report and the problems on their team. Sometimes I do individual MBTI interpretations in one-on-one meetings before I do a large-group interpretation so that people can have a chance to think about and confirm their best-fit type and come to the session ready to put this information into practice.

I start the team-building session, after some basic introductions, by asking the client to tell the group why he or she thought the team building was necessary. Additionally, I ask for his or her mission or vision for the team and what he or she hopes to accomplish for the day. I then move on to give a history of the endeavor, which tells chronologically my intervention activities to this point. Then, with the team's help, we establish some norms of conduct for this team-building session. These norms of conduct often include things like:

➤ Speaking for oneself using "I" messages
➤ Critiquing the problem, not the person
➤ Only one person speaking at a time
➤ Impaling no one (it's not the purpose of the session)
➤ Speaking about things from one's own perspective

As we are debriefing both the MBTI and the interview or survey data, I listen for possible action steps, which I note for later use.

Often I subdivide the team and ask each group to select the issue for which they have the most energy. They then form a small, informal team within a team to set some desired implementation plans, dates, and assignments for the team.

Here is a sample agenda for a typical team-building session, which could take up to two days.

A Typical Team-Building Session

1. Personal introductions (name, role, personal update since last meeting)
2. Why we are here (client's presentation on the need for team building)
3. Team-building definitions (if necessary)
   - Terms (what is a team, examples of team characteristics, etc.)
   - Norms of conduct
   - My role in this session
   - Team's role for session
4. History of the endeavor (my presentation with support from partnership team)
   - Listing of meetings, events prior to this to clarify what has occurred so far
   - Agenda for this session
5. Points of clarification, logistics, and "administrivia" for session
6. Basic introductory MBTI[17]
   - History of MBTI
   - Illustration of preference concept
   - Review of MBTI preferences
   - Selecting one's type
   - Return of MBTI results
   - Selected type and reported type clarification
   - Review of scoring and other questions
   - Reading type description
   - Meeting with others of same type
7. Team type exercise[18]
8. Interview or team-building report
9. Use of MBTI data and interview data to solve problems
10. Action implementation planning
11. Closing activity
    - One thing you learned about yourself today
    - One thing you learned that you will apply immediately
    - One thing you learned about the team today
    - One thing you will help the team do differently
12. Evaluation and Wrap-Up

Follow-Up Session

Several weeks to months after the team-building session, I like to hold a follow-up session to determine progress towards goals. Because I am an external consultant and not able to give on-site encouragement and nudging along the way, the implementation is typically left in the hands of the partnership team. From the start, they know that implementation will be a large part of their work.

At the follow-up session, plans are made about the next steps to be taken and who might be the logical person(s) to carry out these steps. Believe it or not, I think my job is to work myself out of a job. I like to leave organizations, teams, and individuals I serve with tools and skills to continue the work and to carry out their own future team-building processes.

The Coaching Process

As I approach each coaching opportunity, an important and deeply held value for me is to support the people and the organizations involved in the process. I see my role as caring for individuals, teams, and organizations as they master the intricacies of "working it out" either alone or with others more successfully and effectively—no small feat!

I need to be clear about the boundaries of my work. I am a *coach* and not a *therapist*. My usual tack is to find what the individual is doing right and enhance that, on the premise that it is better to augment strengths than to try to overcome weaknesses.

Part of the coach's job is to facilitate a greater awareness of the person's expertise about themselves or the work they do. As a coach, I want to present as full a picture as possible and represent accurately any data that I gather. In delivering that data to my client, I take care that it is relevant and fair. I want to offer options for either enhancing or improving upon an existing characteristic or behavior. Also, I need to protect the person's confidentiality and strive to help him or her make necessary changes, and perhaps find time to heal as well.

Finally, in any coaching endeavor I want to develop a partnership with my client. Whatever I ask that individual to do, I ask with his or her well-being in mind. When I find that the situation might compromise my values, for whatever reason, I either decline to take that assignment or discuss the nature of my values conflict with the client or organization in the hope that we can work things out and proceed. Otherwise I refer the intervention to someone else. As a coach, it is important to me that I follow my heart as well as my head and that my work reflect these important guideposts.

If this sounds like a decidedly NF approach to coaching, well, that's because it is! Being an NF, I seek win-win for all involved, enhanced self-esteem for the client, and as many possibilities as we can generate for his or her future development and growth.

The Responsibilities of the Coach

Here are some general principles that I think are essential when I provide professional coaching to another person:

➤ Determine the objective for the coaching process. What does the organization want to achieve; what does the person want to achieve; how do both the client and the organization see the coach's role in meeting this goal; and how will we evaluate change and/or success with the process?

➤ Determine who the client is. Often, individuals are referred by their management or by someone in human resources. It's necessary to be absolutely clear with the referral source, as well as with the person to be coached, what the differing loyalties and responsibilities are. A key point to contract and negotiate involves privacy: What data goes back to the organization and what data resides with the coach and the individual?

➤ Is the person aware of the coach's skills and competencies? Does the person know what coaching implies? Decide if there is buy-in and a relationship of trust between both parties.

➤ Find out if the person to be coached is a victim of selective feedback— if negative feedback has been withheld from him or her. This happens in some organizations when people are reluctant to pass negative information up the ladder, resulting in people at higher levels being uninformed. For managers who have not experienced openness and clarity from others in their work lives, it may be necessary to clearly establish that part of the coaching process may involve relaying information they have not heard before—and may not like hearing! (Also hard at times for Feeling coaches!)

➤ Before starting the process, see if coaching is the best strategy for the individual. Perhaps the person would be better served by getting therapy, attending support group meetings such as Alcoholics Anonymous, or taking a specific training or skills development course.

➤ Establish that you are on the person's side and that this process is one of reciprocity. Listen, and then listen again to what the person is experiencing. While I am on their side and while I do offer my care and support to them, I do expect something back—commitment to the coaching process, to trying out new skills, and to giving me feedback about the merits of the process as we go along.

➤ Learn about the culture or climate of the team or organization where the individual resides. When coaching, be aware of the various ways organizational or team climates operate and affect the person. Also, from a psychological type perspective, how does this person's type interact with the predominant psychological type of the job, team, or organization? Use MBTI concepts to judge the match or mismatch between the person's type and the organization's style.

➤ Finally, appreciate the seriousness of this task. Often the person has a job on the line or relationships in serious disrepair. The person needs to understand the amount of trauma he or she may be causing him or herself or others. At times, you may need to move beyond giving people what they *want* and make sure that they are getting what they *need*.

The Client's Responsibilities

The person to be coached needs to provide input into the coaching process: how our work together will be planned; how it is to proceed; and finally, how both of us will judge its success. He or she has responsibility for the following matters:

➤ Determine the objectives for the process and why skill or behavior changes are necessary.

➤ Ascertain who else has a stake in the outcomes of this coaching relationship besides the individual (boss, teammates, etc.).

➤ Find a sponsor or organizational coach on-site who can help you practice the coaching tips.

➤ Demonstrate commitment by following through with the coaching suggestions and the tasks assigned.

➤ Give direct feedback to the coach about how the coaching process is proceeding toward the targeted goals, needs, and wants.

The Organization's Responsibilities

Finally, the organization has responsibilities for the coaching process. Some of these are:[19]

➤ Provide resources: Make tuition available, if necessary, for off-site courses; arrange for private meeting spaces on-site; and so on.

➤ Decide who is to be involved in the coaching process, what their informational needs are, and what the confidentiality arrangements should be. Aim to have clear communication among all parties.

➤ Determine what constitutes success in the coaching experience and how it will be evaluated.

➤ Assist in finding a mentor within the organization to give help and support to the person being coached.

Questions for Gathering Information for the Coaching Process

I generally use six to eight questions with the person I am coaching. Additionally, I interview as many people who work with that person as possible; for example, the person's boss, co-workers and peers, subordinates, and outside vendors. The two lists of questions that follow are offered separately—questions for the individual to be coached and questions for those with whom he or she interacts.

QUESTIONS YOU MIGHT ASK THE INDIVIDUAL TO BE COACHED	**QUESTIONS YOU MIGHT ASK OF THOSE WITH WHOM THE INDIVIDUAL WORKS**
➤ What do you do well? Describe your interpersonal, leadership or management skills, or key strengths.	➤ What does this individual do well? Describe interpersonal, leadership or management skills, and other key strengths.
➤ What do you do that is less than effective in terms of interpersonal, leadership, or management skills?	➤ What does the individual do that is less than effective in in terms of interpersonal, leadership, or management skills?
➤ What are your greatest needs for development currently? For the future?	➤ What are this person's greatest needs for development currently? For the future?
➤ What skills or talents do you have that are particularly helpful to others?	➤ What skills or talents does this person have that are particularly helpful to others?
➤ What things do you do that get in the way of your having effective relationships with others?	➤ What things does this person do that get in the way of having an effective relationship with others? With you?

➤ If you could wave a magic wand, what would you want to accomplish in this coaching process?

➤ Describe how you solve problems.

➤ Discuss the factors within the organizational or team environment that lessen your effectiveness.

➤ Describe how you handle change.

➤ Tell me about your personal goals and aspirations.

➤ What barriers do you perceive will keep you from achieving your goals and aspirations?

➤ What steps would you be willing to take to remove these barriers?

➤ Tell me your thoughts about conflict. How do you approach resolving conflicts?

➤ What are your views on why we need to work together?

➤ What information would help me be more effective in my coaching with you if I were to know it right now?

➤ If your boss, colleagues, or spouse were to describe you in twenty-five words, what would those words be?

➤ Have I omitted asking you any questions that I should have asked?

➤ If you could wave a magic wand, what do you want this person to accomplish in this coaching process?

➤ Describe how this person solves problems.

➤ Discuss the factors within the organizational or team environment that lessen this individual's effectiveness.

➤ Discuss how this person handles change.

➤ Describe this individual's personal goals and aspirations.

➤ What barriers do you perceive will keep this person from achieving his or her goals and aspirations?

➤ What steps do you think this person would be willing to take to remove these barriers?

➤ How does this individual handle conflict? How do you view him or her when conflict arises?

➤ Why do you think this person needs coaching?

➤ What information would help me be more effective in coaching this person if I were to know it right now?

➤ If you were to describe this person in twenty-five words, what would those words be?

➤ Have I omitted asking you any questions that I should have asked?

The next set of questions deals with psychological type:[20]

MBTI-RELATED QUESTIONS YOU MIGHT ASK THE INDIVIDUAL

➤ As you think about your psychological type preferences, which ones are your assets and which ones offer you the greatest challenges?

➤ How have your personality type preferences influenced your life and career?

➤ Which parts of your psychological type make you feel good? Why?

➤ Which aspects of your psychological type most often cause relationship problems between you and others?

➤ Based on your self-analysis, if someone wants to build a working relationship with you, what fundamental things about your psychological type does that person need to understand?

➤ If you think about your psychological type, which aspects of it are most difficult for you to accept or change?

➤ When you think about the psychological types of your colleagues, teammates, or organization, which ones do you have the most difficulty with, which ones are you drawn toward, and which are the most complementary? Why?

MBTI-RELATED QUESTIONS YOU MIGHT ASK OF THOSE WITH WHOM THE INDIVIDUAL WORKS

➤ As you think about this person's psychological type preferences, which ones are assets and which ones offer the greatest challenges?

➤ How have this person's personality type preferences influenced his or her life and career?

➤ Which aspects of this individual's psychological type make you feel good? Why?

➤ Which parts of this person's psychological type most often cause relationship problems for him or her?

➤ If someone wants to build a working relationship with this person, what are the fundamental things about the person's psychological type he or she needs to understand?

➤ If you think about this individual's psychological type, which aspects of it are the most difficult for you to accept?

➤ When you think about the psychological types of this person's colleagues or teammates, which ones does he or she have the most difficulty with, which is he or she drawn toward, and which ones are most complementary? Why?

➤ In order to be more versatile, which part of your psychological type needs to be strengthened or modified?

➤ When you think about this person becoming more versatile, which part of his or her psychological type needs to be strengthened or modified?

➤ What are the greatest insights you have attained about yourself vis-à-vis psychological type?

➤ In your opinion, what are the greatest insights this person has learned about his or her psychological type?

The Coaching Plan

When I start the coaching process, I like to use the MBTI personality inventory as a vehicle for greater self-awareness and self-acceptance. Here are some steps that I typically take:

1. Before I meet initially with the client, I:
   - Review and record the person's general strengths in relation to their psychological type preferences.
   - Study the typical areas for growth using chapter 9 of this book; prioritize what is most important for this individual's development; and use these areas as a springboard for early discussions.
   - Select from resources such as the MBTI Expanded Analysis Report (EAR); other instruments (such as the *Strong Interest Inventory*™ and the *Fundamental Interpersonal Relations Orientation—Behavior*™ [FIRO-B]); audio or reading resources; biographical data; counseling professionals; college, technical school, community, or in-house educational offerings; role-modeling exercises; videotaping; or "shadowing" someone else in the organization who has mastered a certain skill.
2. In my first meeting, as I discuss the MBTI, I:
   - Have the person choose a best-fit personality type.
   - Share the general strengths and areas of growth for that psychological type with the person.
   - Add to the coaching suggestions from my own knowledge and resources.
   - Develop specific action items with timelines.
3. Practice the necessary skills or behaviors in coaching sessions and then on the job.
4. Report back on skills practice. Determine the next steps for coaching sessions.
5. Evaluate progress toward goals. Decide if and when follow-up should occur.

Additional Resources for the Coaching Process

Here are several suggestions for other resources to use in addition to the standard MBTI instrument:

➤ The *Expanded Analysis Report* (EAR) of the MBTI is particularly helpful for executive development and with individuals who are having trouble clarifying their best-fit type.

➤ The *Strong Interest Inventory* used with the MBTI offers a combination of perspectives when coaching people about their careers.

➤ The "Perception Checklist" can be helpful in gathering information on others' perceptions of the client. It is published in my book *The Strong Interest Inventory Resource: Strategies for Group and Individual Interpretation in Business and Organizational Settings.*[21]

➤ Instruments that use a 360-degree feedback approach or interviews with people can assess how the client manages various interpersonal and functional business interactions.

➤ A discussion of a person's psychological type dynamics (the order of dominance of Sensing, Intuition, Thinking, and Feeling) can help an individual understand whether they are experiencing either tension with or attractions to the various aspects of their type dynamics at work or in life.

➤ Add a values clarification exercise to see what values are most important to the person and how those values influence his or her work or life.

Solving Problems— How to Work It Out

The following problem-solving technique incorporates the strengths of each of the four functions (S, N, T, and F) and can be used to round out your approach to coaching.

1. Use *Sensing* to determine the facts. Define the problem by finding out who, what, when, where, how, and why. Also assess the current situation for specific details. Ask yourself how an unbiased individual would look at the situation. As a final check, ask if these facts can be verified by another person or by an impartial instrument such as a clock.

2. Once you have covered the domain of Sensing, move next to the domain of *Intuition.* Ask yourself specifically, What do all the facts suggest or what do the facts mean? What interpretations can I make from the factual observations? Search for meanings, themes, relationships, and connections with other situations, environments, and so on.

3. After using the perceptive functions of Sensing and Intuition to gain an awareness of not only *what is (S)* but *what could be (N)* found by reading between the lines, then move on to the judging functions of Thinking and Feeling. The *Thinking* task is to objectively evaluate the logical premises suggested by your information. You may want to outline the pros, the cons, and what is interesting about the information. When any alternatives have been generated for action, evaluate those objectives by saying, "If I do this, then what might be the outcomes or consequences?"

4. Once your logical analysis is completed, consider your potential reactions, actions, or interactions by using your *Feeling* function to assess the underlying importance of any conclusions to your values. One way to do this is to ask yourself, What is the impact on my priorities? What is important to me if I take a certain course of action? How might it affect others, the organization, or the community?

Using all four of the functions to communicate with someone might go something like this: "I saw you having lunch with the vice president today [*Sensing*] and I was wondering if you're practicing your networking skills or representing our department to those in higher positions [*Intuition*]. If you are representing us to people in higher positions, then that means there may be more benefits to our department [*Thinking*] and I will be happy because our department has had more top level exposure [*Feeling*]."

Here's a more complicated example of how to use Sensing, Intuition, Thinking, and Feeling to give a difficult communication. I have used the four-function model to coach an individual suspected of having an office romance—yes, it does come up!

Sensing: "Steve, in team interviews, three people mentioned to me that they suspected an office romance between you and Shannon. When I asked for specifics, all three stated that you and Shannon went on three extended business trips this summer when previously you took those types of trips alone. They also noted that Shannon's office was moved closer to your office in September, and finally, that you and Shannon had lunch together alone the past five days."

Intuition: "Three possible interpretations come up. The first one is that you are having an *affair* with Shannon. This was the interpretation made by the three people on your team. The second one is that all of the facts in the case are coincidental and their summation is greater than the actual situation. The third one is that you are *coaching* Shannon on some new assignment."

Thinking: "If the *affair* interpretation is correct, then the current situation needs adjustments because there could conceivably be ethical and legal ramifications for both you and Shannon. If all of the facts in this case are *coincidental*, then a word to the wise is sufficient. Clear the air and watch out for the implications people are making from the amount of time you are spending with Shannon. If you are *coaching* her, then clarify with the team that your relationship is a coaching one."

Feeling: "I know that you value fairness in the workplace. The trips, office move, and lunches seem to compromise that value of fairness and equal access, as well as being a potential source of embarrassment to both you and Shannon."

Using this process can lend logic and empathy to these types of situations, giving you a method to avoid tripping over the difficulties of confronting someone with unpleasant news. I suppose you might wonder about the outcome in the above case. In fact, there was no affair. Shannon wanted to transfer to the New York office. To help her accomplish this goal, Steve arranged for her to join him on a project for the New York office that involved several weekend trips. Her office was moved closer to his to help them both manage the New York project. Also, the lunches had served as coaching sessions for Shannon. She had received an offer from New York and was trying to negotiate moving expenses and better salary treatment. Finally, Steve was surprised that a relatively innocuous and coincidental string of events could be so misinterpreted. He was both embarrassed and upset and felt he needed to clear the air with people in his office.

Steve called a team meeting and used the same model—the facts in the case, the interpretations, the logical outcomes, and the importance of his values—to communicate with his team. While an office romance seemed plausible, there were no flames, just smoke. Steve explained fully his role with Shannon. He and Shannon endured some kidding at the end of the session, but the air was clear.

Notes

1. For more information about this "functions lens" for viewing team dynamics, see Sandra Krebs Hirsh, *MBTI Team Building Program: Leaders Resource Guide*, Palo Alto, CA: Consulting Psychologists Press, 1992.
2. Adapted from Hirsh, *MBTI Team Building Program: Leader's Resource Guide*, p. 104. Copyright © 1992 by Consulting Psychologists Press. Adapted by permission.
3. Ibid., p. 106.
4. I am indebted to Barbara A. Tuckner of Barbara Tuckner Consulting, St. Paul, MN, for her help in formulating the coaching strategies, "When You're One or Few Amongst the Many."
5. Adapted from Hirsh, *MBTI Team Building Program: Leader's Resource Guide,* Reproducible Master 50. Copyright © 1992 by Consulting Psychologists Press. Adapted by permission.
6. Ibid., Reproducible Master 49.
7. Some of these suggestions build on those provided by Catherine Fitzgerald in *Developing Leaders: Research and Applications in Psychological Type and Leadership Development,* Palo Alto, CA: Davies-Black Publishing, 1997.
8. Ibid.
9. See Hirsh, *MBTI Team Building Program: Leader's Resource Guide,* pp. 63–67.
10. I am indebted to Susan Scanlon's article "Why Teamwork Can Be So Interesting" in the Spring 1985 *Type Reporter,* pp. 1–2.
11. Paul Hershey and Kenneth Blanchard's situational leadership model compares and contrasts leaders' experience with their followers' readiness to complete tasks, resulting in four leadership styles: Delegating, Participating, Telling, and Selling. See Hershey and Blanchard, *The Situational Leader,* New York: Warner Books, 1984, p. 160.
12. Adapted from Naomi Quenk, *Beside Ourselves,* Palo Alto, CA: Davies-Black Publishing, 1993. Copyright © 1993 by Davies-Black Publishing. Adapted by permission.

13. Adapted from Sandra Krebs Hirsh, *Using the Myers-Briggs Type Indicator in Organizations* (2d ed.), Palo Alto, CA: Consulting Psychologists Press, 1991. Copyright © 1991 by Consulting Psychologists Press. Adapted by permission.

14. This definition was formulated with Sandra L. Davis, president of MDA Consulting, Minneapolis, MN.

15. C. Williams, D. Armstrong, and C. Malcolm, *The Negotiable Environment*, Ann Arbor, MI: Facility Management Institute, 1985.

16. I am indebted to Barbara A. Tuckner, and John C. Buchanan, of Buchanan and Associates, Minneapolis, MN, for their assistance in outlining this process.

17. See Hirsh, *Using the Myers-Briggs Type Indicator in Organizations*.

18. See Hirsh, *MBTI Team Building Program: Leader's Resource Guide*.

19. I am indebted to the coaching expertise of John C. Buchanan of Buchanan and Associates, Minneapolis, MN.

20. I am indebted to Douglas Peters of Douglas Peters Associates, Minneapolis, MN, for the formulation of many of these MBTI-related coaching questions.

21. Sandra Krebs Hirsh, *Strong Interest Inventory Resource: Strategies for Group and Individual Interpretation in Business and Organizational Settings.* Palo Alto, CA: Consulting Psychologists Press, 1995.

Index

About the Authors

Sandra Krebs Hirsh is a management consultant, providing career management and organizational development consultation. She holds graduate degrees in American Studies and Industrial Relations. She is the coauthor of *LifeTypes*, *LifeKeys*, and *Introduction to Type in Organizations*, which has sold over one million copies. She also authored *Using the MBTI in Organizations, MBTI Team Building Program*, and *Strong Interest Inventory Resource: Strategies for Group and Individual Interpretations in Business and Organizational Settings*. She is much in demand worldwide for her expertise in human resources and organizational development.

Jane A. G. Kise is a freelance writer and management consultant in the fields of strategic planning and team building. She holds an MBA from the University of Minnesota. She is the principle author of *LifeKeys: Who You Are, Why You're Here, What You Do Best*.